HALF IN LOVE

ALSO BY LINDA GRAY SEXTON

NONFICTION

Anne Sexton: A Self-Portrait in Letters

Between Two Worlds: Young Women in Crisis

Searching for Mercy Street: My Journey Back to My Mother, Anne Sexton

FICTION

Rituals

Mirror Images

Points of Light

Private Acts

HALF IN LOVE
{surviving the legacy of suicide}

A MEMOIR

LINDA GRAY SEXTON

COUNTERPOINT · BERKELEY

Library of Congress Cataloging-in-Publication Data is available.

978-1-58243-718-7

Jacket design by Candice Woo
Interior design by Neuwirth & Associates, Inc.
Printed in the United States of America

COUNTERPOINT
1919 Fifth Street
Berkeley, CA 94710
www.counterpointpress.com

Distributed by Publishers Group West

10 9 8 7 6 5 4 3 2 1

To Brad,

for remaining resolute

Darkling I listen; and for many a time
I have been half in love with easeful Death,
Called him soft names in many a mused rhyme,
To take him into the air my quiet breath;
Now more than ever it seems rich to die,
To cease upon the midnight with no pain.

—JOHN KEATS
"ODE TO A NIGHTINGALE"

CONTENTS

PREFACE

SOMETIMES, EVEN MY bones resonate with the melodies of my childhood.

Ebullience and depression; love and warmth; the frightening separations and the joyous, if fragile, reunions. This is how I come to remember, simply because the old rhythms will always reverberate, always remain.

Long ago, I graphed the fevers of my mother's innumerable attempts at suicide. In 1974, when I was twenty-one and a college senior, my mother committed suicide after having tried many, many times. In 1994, when I was forty, I published a memoir, *Searching for Mercy Street: My Journey Back to My Mother, Anne Sexton*, about our complex relationship.

In 1997, as I turned forty-five—the same age my mother had been when she died—my world fractured in ways I could never, ever, have foreseen. I found myself drawn into my own vortex of depression, desperate for relief from the intense interior pain that obliterated nearly every waking moment. I tried once, twice, three times, to kill myself—even though I was a daughter, a sister, a wife and, most importantly, a mother.

Before my mother's death, she appointed me literary executor of all her posthumously published work, as well as the guardian of the enormous archive that required a home in a university library. *Searching for Mercy Street* dealt with my maturing as a woman and as a mother, as well as the acceptance of my sorrow that my mother had found parenting my sister and me to be so onerous. The book was my attempt to reach out to her, after her death, despite her many problems. With the arrival of my two sons, I discovered a fresh understanding of, and compassion for, how difficult being a parent truly is, even when it is not complicated by mental illness. In all these ways, I came to know my mother, this time as an adult.

Searching for Mercy Street was only a prelude. That book focused on coming to terms with my mother's life, while I had yet to learn how to come to terms with my mother's death. I needed to confront and disentangle myself from the strong tentacles her suicide had attached to my life. I needed to confront my own struggle with depression, bipolar illness, and our family's history of successful suicides. This struggle reflects the emotional, and perhaps biological, legacy that was passed on from my mother to me. It illustrates how I came to make decisions as a fifty-year-old woman, for myself and my family, away from the magnetism of my mother and her powerful sphere of influence. What a shock to discover myself following the same terrible path she had walked, despite all my determination that this should and would not happen. Not only for myself, but for my children.

While I knew first-hand that depression can leave entire families helpless, it stunned me to learn that, in the United States alone, someone kills himself every seventeen minutes. I realized that I was not alone in the tractor beam of the disease. I thought about the many others there were, trapped alone under the bell jars of their depression and suicidal urges—and their families, prisoners as well. I hope this book speaks for them all.

With the help of a family that strove to forgive and accept, with the benefit of excellent psychotherapy and the best of modern medications, I was able to break the cycle of self-destruction upon which I had been raised. One day, it occurred to me that I had outlived my mother, and so had stopped the familial battle with suicide. I had lived to see my sons surpass the age I was when my mother took her own life. I had not abandoned my children as I had been abandoned. I was a mother who lived, despite it all. At last, I had moved into my own pioneer territory.

{the story}

Do not go gentle into that good night.
Rage, rage against the dying of the light.

—DYLAN THOMAS

{a terrible act}

IN DECEMBER OF 1997, I fell into a pit of loneliness and
sorrow and couldn't climb out. I couldn't talk with those I loved
about my grief or my despair, so afraid that by speaking about
such things, I would make them even more real. I worried,
unconsciously, that even if I described the pain wrapped around
my heart, I would not be heard. I worried, consciously, that
others—no matter how close—would perceive me to be preoccupied with myself in unattractive ways. Who could really
understand how I felt and refrain from making negative judg-
ments about it all?

I had feared the approach of my forty-fifth birthday for years;
my mother had killed herself the month before her own birthday
on that forty-fifth year of her life. Now here I was—just six
months away from my own—on a slippery road in the rain, a road
slick with curves and no guard rail. No longer could I imagine, or
believe, that I would outlive my mother by besting the number
of years she, and now I, experienced as so achingly turbulent.

I had been hiding my depression fairly well—following each
day's routines—but still it gnawed away in my gut like a wolf in

a trap, and at last it gathered itself for the attack. At my younger son's bar mitzvah in October, I had gotten drunk in public, but no one seemed to notice anything strange, perhaps because I had been keeping my drinking private. Alcohol helped keep me quiet, sedated, and isolated.

That particular night in December, my husband, Jim, had already phoned me from his hotel room on the East Coast, where he was traveling for business. I reassured him that all was well, and then went into the kitchen to pour another martini, which was really just gin, straight up and crowded by a raft of olives. As I came back to the bedroom from the kitchen, I stopped at the oil portraits of my mother and her mother that hung in my back hall; originally they had been mounted on facing walls in a front room in my grandmother's house, where no one could avoid them.

For the first time in my life, I envied my mother for the solution she had found in order to quell the pain of her depression. For the first time in my life, my emotions pushed aside all concern for the family who would remain if I joined my mother— even though I, too, had once been part of such a family so abandoned. I knew well the agony of that rejection.

My thoughts of suicide did not mean that I didn't care about these very important people in my life: it was more as if the pain that accompanied my depression had moved onto a new plain, and, in my confusion, it seemed to require a new and different sort of release.

As I stood in front of the portraits, I toasted my mother for the job she had done. "You really knew how to do it," I told her with admiration. "You got it right." And in that moment—when all I knew warped and slid out of time, out of sync with all I had previously believed—I saw her action as courageous. How had she managed it? Having done extensive reading on the subject— though I had not let myself wonder why I was doing such reading—I now knew how hard it was to kill oneself. Pills easily vomited, hanging gone awry, monoxide poisoning interrupted at the last minute.

From my own experience as the daughter of a suicide, I knew, intimately, how many people—especially family and friends—thought of this quintessential act of self-destruction as a self-indulgent, self-involved, selfish choice—or even a temper tantrum that took no one else into consideration. But now I saw the reality of it: interior pain, urgent, could indeed pressure you to take your own life. What once I had tried so hard to avoid and push away with such determination for over forty years, suddenly seemed natural, and I ached to surrender to it. All those years of denying I had missed her toppled in an instant, and now, here, was the truth: despite the years of relishing my independence from my mother, I now wanted to be by her side once again.

The portrait shone in the half-light of the narrow hallway: my mother's black hair, the sad blue eyes that belied her thick red lipsticked smile, the depression that leaked from her gaze and pulled at me, strong as a lighthouse beam. She had made her first suicide attempt shortly before her mother, my grandmother, Gaga, asked her to sit for this painting. Looking up at her portrait compelled me to recognize exactly what I had inherited: the lust to sit in the driver's seat of death. It was surely significant that she, the celebrated poet, Anne Sexton, had often told me, "Never be a writer, Linda," but not once in her foreshortened life had she ever said, "Never be a suicide."

I HAD NOTHING planned that night. Suicide simply came up from behind and took me in a bear hug.

I ran a tub and got in, slowly, perhaps still somewhat reluctantly, balancing my martini on the rim. A sharp paring knife lay beside it. Next to the knife stood two small brown bottles:

Valium and Dalmane, prescribed for some other difficulty, some other time. Their labels were perilously out of date.

"You need those because you've got no courage," sneered an inner voice, mocking me. "No courage at all."

I ignored the voice and concentrated on the way the water ran clear and hot against my belly and between my legs. All my tools assembled, I closed my eyes and drifted. For the first time in weeks, all at once, I felt peaceful.

Jim would not return from his trip until the following afternoon. Nathaniel, my older son, and Gabe, my younger, were asleep, their beds distant in another part of our silent California ranch. Because they knew all about their grandmother's suicide, I had accordingly made, from time to time, promises about my life. Regret nevertheless did not stop me.

The dog sat on the tub mat and watched me with still brown eyes.

I sipped my drink, ate the olives, swallowed some pills, put my wedding band in the soap dish. My toes curled as I waved them under the gush of hot water from the chrome tap. The dog whined, a mosquito against the white background.

I had given the children, thirteen and fourteen now, a special childlike goodnight. I told them that I would see them at breakfast, just as I always did, and then I tucked them into bed. Tucked in—what a lovely way to say goodbye: tight woolen corners and smooth sheets, melodies built around the promise of sweet dreams. Even as I lay in the tub, I did not consider what would happen if—when—they were the ones to discover me.

Nathaniel, I promise you that I will never . . . .

The thought of violating his trust was horrific and untenable. Why couldn't I feel, deeply, what a betrayal it would be? Why, this time, did my love for my children not help me to push away the desire to die and to push away the desperation that had dogged me all my life, as it had so many times before? This time I was numb. This time I was dumb. The urgency pressed in upon me and flushed every family face, every family voice, from my mind.

I was ready, at last, to cheat on love.

Ready to renege on assurances that now felt as if they had been too easily given to everyone—children, husband, sister, father, friends. Immersed in communing with my mother, I became a small child that night, a vulnerable daughter. She seemed right then to hover in the room, guiding me. I knew that when I was finished, she would be waiting to fold me into her arms, and I would go home with her one more time. I was going to turn the tables; once this act was complete, I could never be abandoned again, neither by my husband's absences, nor my children's growing independence, nor my sister's emotional distance, nor my father's inevitable death, nor the retreat of friends.

I looked for the right place to start: the room circled slowly, then faster and faster, as if I were riding a wild carousel. A few veins looked promising. My index finger palpated, looking for the best candidate. I studied the thoroughfares of my wrist carefully. Excitement shimmered inside me. Was this simply a desire to escape pain, or a biological imperative, or a role model I could not resist, or simply the voice in my head goading me on? Perhaps every one of them.

I picked up the knife.

I did not ask why.

I wondered only at what angle to draw the blade.

I was ready to make music with the keyboard of my wrist.

The first cut was quick but firm. It hurt and for a minute I held my breath, but the cut was not deep enough or long enough. The thin line began to sting. Though I had lowered the knife vertically, trying to slice with the grain and follow the thick vine of veins and arteries that twined toward my heart, my hand had rotated so that instead the cut ran from side to side, across the tendons that guarded my wrist.

I looked for another spot and tried again. This time the blade entered me with a rasping sound, as if it had struck bone. A thick bubble of blood parted the fleshy edges of the cut; they were as voluptuous as the cream and pink lips of a conch shell. I lifted my wrist to my tongue.

Salt and iron, that taste of childhood, when sucking on the hurt to make it better really worked.

"Make a wound to match the wound," encouraged the voice in my head.

As I sliced, once more and then again and again, the pain of my body rose to meet the pain inside of me. Thrilled by the unexpected sense of relief, I tried the inside of my elbow, where the blood bubbled, rich blue, near the surface. And then my ankles, where pulses throbbed in sweet relief against the bone. Each cut stunned me with a little climax. Only the jugular went untouched, too difficult to see without a mirror. All of it was made so much the better by remembering that my mother had never once cut herself. This was my territory.

"Mommy, promise you would never do what Grandma Anne did," Gabe had once pled.

"I promise, Gabe. Never."

Boys, I promise you I will never . . . .

And then, chin on chest, I slept at last, water lapping at my lips.

RED. ALL AROUND me was red. I was lying in the cold red.

Under the dark surface of the water, my body was invisible. I tried to sit up and failed; I rolled sideways on one hip instead, my hand scrabbling against the floor tiles for the phone I thought I had put there.

Frightened, I woke a friend. She used her second phone line to call the police secretly while continuing to soothe me. I didn't notice the long moments in which I couldn't hear her voice. It seemed I wanted to be saved after all.

But then I heard the marching. Their heels striking the hardwood, their boots shining blackest black, they came to me in a roll of thunder. I shrunk down under the blanket of the water, shivering, screaming that I would never forgive my friend as I dropped the phone clumsily onto the floor. I closed my eyes, crossed my arms across my breasts. But they pounded on the bathroom door and in an instant defeated the lock. Armed with holsters and guns and nightsticks, they hauled me by the armpits from my red pool. I struggled vaguely against being saved, as useless as a fat white fish. They loaded me onto the gurney and strapped me down.

It was only then, being rushed on my back down the hall, that I thought clearly of my children and allowed horror to flood through me. At last. Too late.

I slurred a futile shout into a world of cotton, trying to stop my slip out into the cold, star-needled night without them: as if I could take my sons with me, as if Nathaniel could crouch beside me in the ambulance and hold my hand, as if Gabe could tell me he loved me, even though the lights blared and the sirens flashed, even though the world had gone upside down and underwater. As if I could take back my terrible act, as if I could tighten the slack lips that could not kiss, mend the broken arms that could not hold, repair the promises cracked as old mirrors—all this from a mother who, as her own mother before her, had lost her grip on love.

{sinking into sleep}

The real motives which impel a man to take his own life . . .
belong to the internal world, devious, contradictory, labyrinthine,
and mostly out of sight.

— A. ALVAREZ
"THE SAVAGE GOD"

{voices}

MY MOTHER KILLED herself in her bright red Mercury Cougar, in the closed garage of our house in an affluent Boston suburb, that autumn of 1974, three months following my twenty-first birthday. In late July, she and I toasted with champagne. In September, I began my senior year at Harvard College. In early October, I picked out a coffin.

The morning after her suicide, my sister, Joy, and I opened our mother's closet. Joy had just returned home for the funeral from her private school in Maine, where she was a high school senior. We looked for and found our mother's full-length red polyester dress, with the slits up the sides and a low neckline. As a very popular, Pulitzer Prize-winning member of the "confessional" school of poetry—which had formed in the late 1950s and early '60s—my mother had found her own voice within the nurturing atmosphere of the tight circle of poets that included Robert Lowell and Sylvia Plath. This dress was usually worn for her SRO "readings" on the poetry circuit, but suddenly its purpose had changed: it was this dramatic dress, bought to suit her dramatic style, that was the most quintessentially Anne Sexton, and so Joy pulled it off the hanger to be our mother's burial clothing. I rummaged through drawers for underwear—and took the gold bangle bracelets that she had left on her bedside table for myself.

It seemed as if she was merely going on a trip planned well in advance, rather than to the crematorium, but we gathered up the stand of three palest green Hartman bags stored in our dusty attic. I do not remember now exactly what the clothes were, but only to what purpose we put them. Taking out just the best of the lot—perhaps a few silk blouses or wool trousers or a warm winter coat—we gave most to my mother's best friend, but kept these few things for ourselves; all the rest we then packed up into those suitcases and sent on to a charity. Yet, I didn't want to give any of those clothes away, not even the ones with moth holes and milk spots, although keeping them would have served nothing. I still wanted to hold them against my body the way a child clings to her favorite blanket with its familiar smell.

OUR MOTHER'S ROWDY laughter still hung in the kitchen and in her writing room, as did the painful memories that emanated from the sort of relentless depression that began for us both when we were each very young. She set the stage for a drama that swung on the bold elevations and declines of her mood, and of her suicide attempts—it was a series of roles that she would begin to play for me over and over, beginning when I was about three years old. Later, starting to breach the boundaries of parental discretion in her attempt to bond with me, she spilled many of her secrets: the ways the voices she heard whispered in the leaves outside her bedroom window could be heard if you were quiet; the affairs with other men; the kinds of sexual behavior she most enjoyed.

She had also told me of that voice she heard in her head, an urgent and smart-ass voice, and soon I, too, heard a voice of my own, louder as I grew older, a voice I had been trained to hear. My intense emotional identification with her had become extreme. Never once did I feel surprised that she would share such private confessions with someone as young as I.

My inner voice was one that never shut up. It urged me into depression, into considering what might happen to me if I could not stop listening, and it battered at the walls of my self-confidence. One day when I was an adolescent, I got purposely drunk, and then tried, in a halfhearted, ineffectual manner, to slit my wrists. Once again I was following my mother's example: it seemed that my life would always imitate hers. My mother found me a psychiatrist, a blond woman who coolly chain-smoked behind her desk and inquired about my dreams. Now my mother and I were both in therapy.

As I worked with Dr. Bauman once a week through my four years of high school, she came to a new determination regarding my emotionally charged moods that were dominated by angry meltdowns and teary episodes; I had moved beyond the normal expressions of a hormonally challenged adolescent girl, and was beginning to experience a deepening sense of sadness that would plague me on and off during those years and others to come.

My mother's mental illness and suicide attempts had separated us, quite literally, time and again when I was a little girl, and so, when I was very young, I became highly invested in staying close to her: I made her bed, I listened to her read her favorite poetry aloud, I imitated her in gesture and expression so that we became like Siamese twins—if she needed me, not even insanity could separate us.

Later, when she took me with her on her "reading trips," I organized tickets and meals, and we held hands as we strolled through the streets of various towns. But there was a price to pay for such camaraderie: once, only one hour before a scheduled performance at a Virginia college, she refused to get up from the bathtub and get dressed. I was the one left to convince her to dry off, and later, inebriation made it necessary for me to drag her back to our cheap motel, her head lolling on my shoulder. I was always the one "fixing" things.

There were no more trips to live with relatives when she grew ill and couldn't care for me, because now I took care of her. With my love, I would keep her safe: every afternoon, she waited eagerly for the orange school bus to drop me at the corner. She found it was nearly impossible to write for an entire day at white heat. By the time the grandfather clock in the hall chimed three, she was ready for a break and thus she gave me the gift of her unwavering attention as we sat at the kitchen table and traded stories of our days. How I loved it!

Dr. Bauman continued to focus on getting me to break away from my mother psychologically, but with little success, and by my middle adolescence my mother and I had become best friends. We would allow nothing to interrupt that. Dr. Bauman termed our relationship a "destructive symbiosis," but my mother refused to give me my freedom, which I didn't want in any case. The summer I turned seventeen, I was allowed to stay home from the camp I had attended for the previous five years, to be at my mother's side. This was probably the last unadulterated time we would spend without the impetus of my drive to independence. The voice in my head was becoming more entrenched and I began to be dragged downward emotionally. I spent my entire time composing melancholy verses laden with the imagery of death, highly derivative of my mother's and Sylvia Plath's work, rather than establishing a voice of my own. One lyric in particular repeated: I was down the rabbit hole of darkness—unable to climb out.

It was just another way in which my life had begun to resemble hers. In the background, Dr. Bauman's insistent voice, counseling that separation from my mother was vitally important, began to nag at me; and on those occasions when I inevitably hated my mother as teenagers often do, I found our relationship beginning to feel a little claustrophobic.

TWO WEEKS AFTER her memorial service, I made a tour of our home, room by room. Joy and I had lived in that same house for most of our lives. Now my mother had left it to us in her will. Right after her suicide, it was easy to see how it was marked with the disorder of her life, even less organized since her divorce from my father two years previously, when she decided that she had had enough of his perceived disinterest in her work and lack of empathy for her depression—as well as his violent temper. This separation did not turn out well: in eighteen months, she considered seducing him back in order to calm the frantic nature of her life and to keep her safe from the voices and demons that corroded her fragile balance, but he refused. Away at college, I no longer kept the vigil that prevented her from her own self-destructive urges. By moving out of the house, I had established a move toward the independence that Dr. Bauman had tried to help me find back in the earlier years of my adolescence.

That day, I walked first into her writing room, which remained disciplined by the order of her secretary's filing system—correspondence scrupulously maintained, financial books fine-tuned for the tax man. But I could see beneath the surface of that calm ocean a creative chaos rolled: shelves stuffed with books; file cabinets overflowing with letters and poetry manuscripts; the small inspirational clippings from newspapers and books that she had Scotch-taped above her desk, now yellowing with age; the curve of her desk chair, its springs permanently bent into a C shape from the way she repeatedly tipped herself backwards to rest her feet up on the bookshelf.

So much of her remained. On her desk, the ashtrays overflowed and left a musty smell in the air. In the master bedroom, the dirty clothes were flung over, but not into, the hamper. In the kitchen, the coffee cups stood in the sink with brown skins on their surface, and her chair at the rectangular table was pushed back, as if she had just left the spot where we had shared so many difficult and yet wonderful talks when I was living at home. My last stop was the garage, where she had finally succeeded in leaving us, her car, even then, still parked in its usual space.

Though I could not see them, I knew that there were many boxes of correspondence and poetry drafts shoved up into the dusty attic. These artifacts of her artistry were also part of my inheritance—especially because she had named me the literary executor of her estate on my twenty-first birthday. And so, once again, I was tied to her side, actively in thrall to the negative themes of her depression, anxiety, and suicide, as well as to the positive ones—a celebration of life, religion, and faith—and, last but not least, love of family, friend, and stranger. I could not see at the time that I had stepped into a dangerous undertow.

The appointment as literary executor entailed supervising the publication of her posthumous volumes of poetry, as well as cataloguing the enormous amount of material she had generated between the late 1950s and her suicide. Only after I had mapped out the scope of it all would I be able to start the search for a permanent home to house her archive at a reputable university's library. When she had begun writing, she had experienced success nearly immediately; prestigious literary magazines like the *New Yorker* and the *Hudson Review* quickly accepted her efforts, as well as other, smaller publications. Houghton Mifflin Company published her first collection of poetry, *To Bedlam and Partway Back*, in 1960. She went on to write nine volumes and established an enormous following of dedicated fans.

Now here it was, all of it ours—from the poems to the house.

Never had I wanted it less. Never had I felt it to be more mine. Unlike the rest of my numb and shocked family, I was relieved that the roller coaster of her life—and therefore of ours—had stopped. I was both ashamed and grateful that the anger I had felt at her many attempts to die would at last wither away. And yet I knew, in the deepest part of my soul, that I would never stop missing her, that the grief would never really end, that I would always experience her presence in my life.

As the months after her suicide passed, I relied more and more on my college friends, especially one classmate, Jim Fisk, who lived in my dormitory. The relationship had begun in friendship during our sophomore year and then evolved into love and support during those first turbulent months following my mother's death, providing me with protection from the worst emotional storms.

On the one hand, I felt embarrassment that she had finally done what she'd been writing about for all those years—it was so undeniably predictable—and on the other, I felt a twisted sort of pride—it took true guts to pull it off and not be rescued. And there was no doubt in my mind that she had intended not to be rescued.

As she had acknowledged in the poem "Suicide Note," published in *Live or Die*, the book for which she won the Pulitzer Prize: "At this time let me somehow bequeath all the leftovers to my daughters and their daughters." Whether she intended it, the "leftovers" implied all the emotional and written garbage she left behind; her particular voice embodied by worksheet after worksheet, the pages filled with black correction marks, revisions that would discard some of her precious words, as well as any kind of satisfied and happy life.

There were calls from colleges and venues where she had booked speaking engagements, all wondering what would happen now. Some "gigs" (as she had come to call them) had to be cancelled, their deposits returned, but many places invited me to come instead, as a stand-in, interested in me because I was her daughter as well as her literary executor. I read her poetry from podiums as if it were mine, or, at least, as if I were some sort of expert on the subject. I accepted the praise I earned for my "bravery" in confronting her death and carrying on her traditions and her work. And, after graduation, I studied poetry at the Radcliffe Institute as had she—but not in the kind of fellowship she had won, only in workshops for which I had to pay a fee. Nevertheless, I was dreaming that the legacy of words had been passed down. It was a time in which to keep busy with someone else's successful writing, I thought, until my own began to command some respect. I kept working but I submitted none of the poems anywhere. I knew my writing wasn't nearly good enough yet. Still derivative, still with no voice of my own, except for the intermittent one in my head.

At home there was the comfort of Jim, who held me, often, until I stopped crying. We started living together in June of 1975, right after he and I graduated. Sometime during that summer, Joy and I had invited my father to move back into the house that he and my mother had bought in the sixties—the house my mother had won in the divorce and then willed to Joy and me—so that he could leave behind his claustrophobic apartment. Soon thereafter, over his protests, I began commuting back and forth between the house and Jim's small studio apartment. He opposed the idea that Jim and I were living together, if only for a few days a week. It felt to me as if everything was working out as smoothly as possible in such a difficult situation. We were all back in the same place once again.

But five years after we all moved into the big house together, Joy and I decided to sell it. At last, we wanted to put some distance between ourselves and the past, to become young adults with our own apartments. In moving on with our separate lives, we had to push my father out of the home he so loved, and force him to go live in his second wife's house (he had remarried in 1977), which she had been renting for a nice sum. Despite his anger at being uprooted, he was instrumental in helping me clean out the house for sale. Though Joy had promised to help, she didn't turn up at all on those weekends, perhaps because saying goodbye to so many family belongings was too painful for her to confront, once again emphasizing the different ways in which we dealt with death. And so it was Daddy and me, working silently side by side, taking rugs and old furniture to the dump, cleaning mother's bookshelves of all the volumes that seemed old or unimportant, selling off the extra beds and linens. We both cried quietly, in different rooms of the house. Suddenly it seemed that the present was just too much. I was overwhelmingly grateful I was not alone.

When it was time for me to place my mother's archive, now chronicled by the extensive written catalog of her correspondence, manuscript material, and memorabilia on which I had labored for over a year, I relied on someone else: it was Jim who made the financial deal with the University of Texas at Austin for her archive. Box after box had to be packed up—seventy of them—and then lugged down to the post office in the back seat of the Volkswagen three or so at a time. Jim worked with me, side by side, and this cemented our devotion to each other even further: I could depend on him completely. Once again, I was not alone.

{my mother's legacies}

UNCONSCIOUSLY, MY MOTHER had bequeathed to me two entirely unique legacies, and they were inextricably and mysteriously entwined: the compulsion to create with words, as well as the compulsion to stare down into the abyss of suicide. Both compulsions have been with me for as long as I can remember.

She had left me a legacy of the "word" and because I had written and loved poetry from the time I was quite young, because I had shared her love of this as well, she regarded me as a serious reader and critic from the time I was an early teen. It was not totally surprising that she chose me as her literary executor. Originally she had asked her best friend, Maxine Kumin—undoubtedly a better, more experienced choice—but another close friend and advisor on the faculty at Yale had cautioned that a daughter might be better so as to avoid conflicts with others within the family. Intuiting the family's raw feelings about touchy or intimate material, one of us might be able to make more sensitive choices.

When my mother asked me without warning if I would serve as her literary executor, I consented, simultaneously thrilled and dismayed at the impending responsibility, just as I had once been simultaneously thrilled and dismayed at her confessions when I was a teenager. This appointment served, once again, to draw me into her professional world, just as I had once been drawn into the process of revising her poetry.

At the time, she was in the midst of drawing up her will and giving away small mementos from her writing life. Still, not one of us—neither family, nor friends—allowed ourselves to see where she was headed. I was proud to have been selected as the one to edit, publish, and ultimately carry on her written legacy: in some way I already knew that this would finally stitch me to her as tightly as a second skin. I would keep her alive in the hearts and minds of many avid readers, making certain that her poetry continued to be popular and her name famous, and the most important result of all: I would not have to give her up.

I HAD TO deal with many other people and emotions beyond my own. First and most important to me was my father: despite their divorce, he now sobbed that my mother had been his one true love, and it was his fault that she had died, because when she had approached him about reconciliation just before her death, he had made the proud gesture of refusing. There were her fans, now needy and bereft. And then all of her closest friends, most of whom felt some kind of overwhelming guilt at the distance they had put between her, her illness, and themselves in the later years of her life. Everyone had something strong to say, or advise, or demand, certain that they should have input into what happened next to the poetry and to the literary estate, right down to book jackets and foreign rights. The fracas made accomplishing anything difficult.

In my mother's history, the commonplace and the special jumbled together in one frustrating, magical heap. I believed that if only I could parse it all out I might at last understand her, and, thus—more importantly—understand myself. Even after my separation from her during my college years, even after her death, we were tied together, inextricably, like thick and ropy vines, and I believed that what was true for her was also true for me. When I had pleaded, in eighth grade, for my first bra, she put her hand down my shirt and weighed my breast, cupping it in her palm as if it were her own. At that point, the lack of privacy moved on to a new level: she owned my maturing body as well as my maturing mind. Earlier she had written a poem about it, "Little Girl, My Stringbean, My Lovely Woman."

I did not protest at her invasive touch. There was no one to say "stop" when she came to my bed early in the mornings, intrusive before I was awake, intent on "cuddling," her body loathsome as she curled around me in such an inappropriate way. Once again, she did not protect me from her own self-destructive urges. My desire to keep her safe was a burden that I believed I had to bear because I loved her so. The thought that she might leave again permanently, or withdraw from the intimacy our minds shared at this point in time, still terrified me. Though my life, for many years, had already been dominated by the legacy of her suicide, right after her death I still couldn't see, understand, or admit to it.

LIKE SO MANY other suicides, my mother left no note of explanation as to why she poisoned herself with carbon monoxide, and like so many of the family members of successful suicides, I wanted to know, fervently, why she had done it—even though her life had been pockmarked with the attempts necessary for a final successful production, even though her trademark poetry demonstrated time and again, in one metaphor after another, the pain that drove her toward death. This time around, however, the language of the image, the legacy of the word, wasn't enough for me. I needed to hear an answer both logical and concrete: from the coroner, I longed to hear that she was dying of an incurable cancer, the same cancer that had killed her own mother; from the police, I fantasized I would hear suspicions of murder. However, it seemed no one else in the family worried about such ideas. I felt alone with them, bent under the burden of what any, or all, of it meant. The weight of my wish that she had not died as a result of her own devices was a heavy one.

More important than the legacy of suicide—still unformed in my mind—was this distraction of how and why she died. These questions were of paramount importance to me—and both my father and Joy protected their privacy with vague answers when I brought up the subject of suicide itself. My father, who had asked to see the casket opened before her cremation, did cry abjectly. "I wish I hadn't seen her like that," he sobbed. "I wish I could remember her just as she was, my Princess Anne."

Of course, in the end, all I could glean about her death was the obvious: her hand holding the vodka martini, turning the key, tuning in the radio as she waited for the fumes to reach her. There was no other conclusion that could be drawn about the cause of her death. And so I wondered how long it had taken to die. Had she choked, coughing on the fumes? Or was it just like a deep gentle sleep? These questions I didn't ask of anyone, because they seemed in poor taste; an adult would surely already know the answers and so I subsided, forced into the sophisticated role that I perceived I must uphold—my curiosity unquenched. I was already being sucked into the whirlwind of wondering how a person went about killing herself successfully.

Still, I naively believed I could simply reject, out of hand, any kind of destructive legacy that would result from suicide; I didn't believe such an inheritance would be given to me. I reassured myself that it wasn't like inheriting your aunt's big nose or your father's tendency to run to fat—it wasn't inevitable. And so, I focused my fascination with her on the successful writing arena of her life, rather than on the tragic event of her death. And this did indeed work for a while.

Looking back, I can see now that my intense "need to know" emanated from my belief—ever stronger with the passing years—that whatever happened in her life would undoubtedly happen in mine. I wanted to know what my future held, and yet I dreaded knowing. Inexorably, the legacy approached, like thunder in the ever-shortening distance.

AFTER MY MOTHER'S death, I began to fold myself down into the rich fabric provided by the details of her life, and when I matured into my late thirties, still entranced by her, I first began to admit to myself, on some conscious level, that a legacy of suicide both existed and flourished in the growing muck of my life. It became hard to see beyond the murk. In the thrall of the strong and desperate love we had shared, I began to ask myself where she ended and I began. She herself had made no attempt to sever the ties that bound us, cheek to cheek, in the dance of depression and death. The need to have me constantly by her side overrode the good-mother instincts she had, and thus, perhaps on some level, she did want me to be just like her—at the same time that, dominated by ambivalence, she did not want any of these things to impact my life.

Sometime after the publication of her biography, in 1991, I also began to realize that the suicidal tendency wasn't confined to her alone. My mother's family was peppered with mental illness, alcoholism, and the desire to take one's own life. In the late fifties, her father spent many mornings in our family's kitchen, talking of his own suicidal feelings and sharing hers, just prior to the stroke that killed him. His aunt had slowly succumbed to a complete emotional breakdown for which she was hospitalized until her death. After my mother died, her oldest sister and her father's sister both killed themselves, handing the legacy down and on to another generation in their own families. I wondered about my cousins. Did they feel this same push, this intense desire to look out over the edge? And, if so, was that impulse simply a response to the way suicide expressed itself genetically, a bad balance of chemicals in the body? Or was it the influence of living with someone who was mentally ill? Or was it both? Inevitably, a new worry arose: What would happen to my future children? How would they be touched?

My mother's family had grown angrier and angrier each time she made a suicide attempt, and needed both emotional and financial support. The Harveys came from a long line of ancestors, those who arrived on the Mayflower and became part of the prestigious citizens of Plymouth. One had even gone on, later, to become the governor of Maine; my mother was extremely proud of her heritage, especially of her grand-father, who had been a "literary" man, editor-in-chief of the *Lewiston Evening Journal*, a prominent newspaper in Maine, for many years.

But in those early years of her illness, her incapacitation was anathema to her proud parents and her two siblings, who could only see the damage her mental disease brought down on the family's good name. They did not understand why she couldn't simply "keep a stiff upper lip." As my mother "flaunted" repeated disclosures of the family's secrets in a variety of maga-zines and journals, she brought shame to them all, they felt, by making everyone's personal life public. It seemed to them that she was ignoring her family's upscale social heritage, and thus her parents saw no reason to fund her illness with their wealth, wealth that was growing, in any case, more and more precarious due to her father's profligate lifestyle. Psychiatrists and private hospitals were expensive, and so her in-laws began to take over some of the bills.

My father's father—whom we called Poppy—had, at the beginning of his marriage, used his wife's considerable wealth to invest in a stock market doomed to fail, and when it indeed began to plummet, he squandered the rest of it on a series of ill-fated margin calls. Later, he would undertake a series of disastrous business ventures. Accordingly, there was precious little money to go around. My grandmother, Nana, had been brought up in a family that was socially secure, with maids and cooks—but now she learned how to darn socks and turn collars, making every penny count. She resented my mother's illness most of all, draining as it did her remaining funds, and she didn't really care about my mother's troubles. She had enough of her own.

IN JUNE OF 1975, when my father moved back into the family house, it seemed at first that we had reconstituted our family, even without its missing member. Initially, we were all happy to be living together again, but soon a variety of struggles began. Despite the fact that we had begun to establish ourselves as young adults, my father still treated us as children. After a while, Joy and I began to resent his interferences and chafe under his criticisms. Each of us wanted to have our own place, but neither of us had the money. Joy had postponed college and was taking a little time off before finding a job. We were stuck living with Daddy.

Although I had just graduated from college, I buried myself in work, beginning to edit the volume of my mother's abundant correspondence, *Anne Sexton: A Self-Portrait in Letters*, and in my mind, her life thus began to seem, little by little, to belong to me; slowly, Joy and I began to fight a silent battle, one that was rooted in the extreme stubbornness of both our natures, usually repressed, but here brought to the fore by our difficult situation. Joy resented each decision I made about my mother's estate because I had made it; and over time, experiencing such negative reactions when I did consult her, I began to refuse to include her at all and plowed ahead on my own uncertain but determined path. I relied heavily on my mother's editor at Houghton Mifflin, and her initial biographer, as well. And so, the harder I worked, the angrier Joy became; and the angrier she became, the more self-righteous I grew. Round and round the two of us went.

It seemed we were not wading through my mother's estate, but swimming through her emotions and her life; I felt that in Joy's heart there must be a key question that went unspoken—in fact, I wondered if perhaps she had not even consciously recognized it at that time, or maybe ever: why had my mother chosen me to be her literary executor? Surely the choice echoed back through all those years when she and I had holed up in her writing room to "talk poetry," back to all the years when the study door had been shut, metaphorically, or when mother and I sat at the kitchen table, conversing intimately, bound together in this precious time robbed from both my father and my sister. Why were Joy and I not assigned to the task together?

Our mother's choice and all its alternatives must have stung my sister's pride, and I empathized with the obvious wound. It made it difficult for Joy not to resent me, even when, later, there was nothing overt to resent in my electing to pursue work in a field that resembled our mother's. Publication did not seem, in Joy's eyes, to validate me as a writer.

Yet, no one understood me in quite the way she did. She was a part of my past, a testament to all those early experiences, the sounds, the colors, and the shapes. Hadn't we visited our mother in the mental hospitals together? Hadn't we held hands through it all? When we were kids, we had a tacit agreement: if one of us would be okay, then the other would be too. Joy was the one person who definitely understood how I felt about everything. She might not agree, but she would understand. Even when we were angry with the other, we quickly forgave.

After my mother died, the strong tie between Joy and me should have been at its tightest: with our mother's suicide, we both shared an enormous, devastating loss. I felt I could comfort Joy as I always had before, believing that she still looked up to me for advice and encouragement. It didn't seem strange, this time, to turn to her for understanding.

"I miss Mom so much," I whispered one afternoon, the June after her suicide. We sat on the bed in Joy's room, me on the edge, she against the headboard, her legs drawn up to her chest. Still squeezed by grief, I wanted to remember and to reminisce with my compatriot from childhood. Grief shared, it seemed to me, would be more manageable.

"I don't want to talk about it!"

The sudden shrillness of her tone startled me. Speechless, I said nothing.

"My memories are all I have left and I won't let you steal them!"

I drew back, startled. "Steal them? I'm not 'stealing' anything."

"A minute ago you came in here and announced you're taking her desk to do your writing, without ever considering that I might want it!"

I was nonplussed.

Still, I knew then that I had made a terrible mistake by giving her no choice about it, by simply deciding to take it as my own. My mother's desk was of battered brown wood with scratches in its leather top (one a deep carving Joy herself had made with a pair of scissors when she was little, an act that became a humorous family anecdote) and numerous cigarette burns (my mother often forgot her lit cigarettes until they burned down and fell from the ashtray onto the desktop). It was a desk that emanated history, a desk from which many moving and masterful poems had been created. It was the essence of our mother and, as such, it was natural we both would want to have it.

I looked down at the blanket on Joy's bed and then back at her, where she hugged a pillow tightly to her chest, as if to defend herself.

"I need more space than my old desk," I said. "But if you believe you really should have it, then we should talk about it. Why don't you think about it some more?"

She never brought up the issue of the desk again, and I never pursued it, taking advantage of her silence. After a short time passed, I used the lack of further discussion simply to commandeer the desk; perhaps, on some level, I was retaliating for her refusal to discuss our mother's suicide—a refusal, back then, that to me felt cruel. And so, I worked at the desk, typing away on my mother's old electric Smith Corona.

Tension escalated daily: nothing passed without some kind of argument. In addition to everything else, it soon became apparent that Joy was also angry at my involvement with the volume of letters I was working on, a veritable biography regarding our mother's life; I thought it might help her if she became part of the process of publication, as well. She had a strong talent and interest in photography, having spent the summer before my mother's death in a private tutorial with a well-known local photographer. I suggested she be the one to choose the photographs that would comprise an important part of the book.

She never fulfilled the opportunity, however, procrastinating until my editor and I regretfully did it ourselves to stay on deadline. Perhaps this was one more way of distancing herself from our mother's death and her own resentment at my determined involvement in it.

Joy spent her first year after graduation studying photography at the Museum School in Boston, but over the following summer she decided to apply to the very prestigious Rhode Island School of Design. Although she was admitted, she decided not to enroll, because in order to study photography she would be required to take certain arts courses in which she had no interest. It turned out to be a good decision for her, as instead, in 1976, she went to work. Quickly she began to cherish the self-reliance and newfound freedom a paying job afforded her. She was even able to move out from under my father's domination and rented her own apartment in the city. First she worked in an insurance company as an assistant bookkeeper, and then switched to the billing and membership departments of the Massachusetts Teachers Association.

But by 1980, she decided she was ready to return to school, and after some career counseling, she entered Simmons College in Boston, intent on receiving a Bachelor of Science in nursing. Not only did she pay her own way by using some part of her inheritance from our mother, but—despite her earlier performance in high school—she excelled at difficult courses like chemistry and physics, fields she would never have dared explore earlier in her life. She did her rotations through Boston's Beth Israel Hospital on the medical and surgical units, and, upon graduation, decided to pursue a career in the field of community nursing or home care.

Slowly, inexorably, the silence stretched between us. There was no retreat. With each passing year, as we walked our separate ways, the ground beneath our feet grew stony and hard. I could not say how she felt or predict what she would do next.

Grieving for our mother appeared to be a different process for Joy than it was for me. For Joy, it seemed, it was private, experienced on her own, or at least, not with me. Perhaps she grieved with friends, letting loose her feelings and anguish in a place she felt safe. For me, Joy's distance was very painful because I expected to be able to connect with her in the way we had as children. But we had matured. Much had changed. I had many questions to which I might never know the answers. And yet, during those years of mutual estrangement, there was some occasional common ground: at Christmas, she and I decorated the tree together and hung our mother's favorite ornament, a small gold papier-mâché typewriter, in a carefully selected place of prominence.

AS THE YEARS piled up, the situation between Joy and me worsened. We could not communicate or connect with each other and I was at a loss as to how to improve it. She was unable, or unwilling, to talk about all the subtleties of my mother's death. I felt I couldn't ask about many things that I didn't know or understand—all those details I wouldn't ask anyone else because they would sound prurient. Joy and I knew intimately the backdrops that silhouetted every one of my mother's attempts at suicide, silhouettes that might make sense of what had at last happened— when so many other times our mother had failed at leaving this world. Right after her death, my queries were endless.

Does dying by carbon monoxide hurt?

Did she choke, trying to get air, trying to take another breath?

Had she scrabbled at the door handle, wanting to get out at the last minute?

Have you ever read a book about suicide?

Do you know how many people kill themselves every hour?

Are you starting to have trouble picturing her face unless you're looking at a photograph of her?

What were you doing when they came to tell you she was dead?

She called my dorm room that afternoon and I didn't call back. Did she try to call you?

Did you try to call back?

Did you cry then?
Can you cry now?
How did you say goodbye?
Were you sad?
Were you angry?
Do you think it's our fault?

{up and down}

WHEN I WAS young, perhaps eight years old, my mother had
again come back home from the hospital and she brought me a
present—a round wicker basket woven in Occupational Therapy. I watched her in amazement, moving through the house as
though nothing had happened, even though such a short time
ago we'd seen her in that place with its big locked doors and all
its nurses in snowy, angelic white. Had that stay really changed
her? I wondered. Was this the last time she would have to be
hospitalized? Would she keep to her promise not to try to kill
herself again? Or would she break it as easily as a pencil point
can snap under pressure?

On her second day back, I was anxious to rush home from
school, especially because it appeared that New England was in for
a blizzard and my father, traveling in upstate New York, wouldn't
be home until late. We all clamored to be let out of school early,
but when the noontime bell didn't sound, I fell silent. By the time
we were dismissed at the usual three o'clock, the snow was already
deep enough to cave in over the tops of our red plastic boots and
chap the backs of our knees sore; our frozen mittens were streaked

with snail trails from running noses. Joy had gathered together a small band of her friends and everyone now complained about the cold. As I rushed home, I worried about my mother the whole way while everyone chattered in her loudest voice to cover up my silence. The public report of my mother's condition through the neighborhood was humiliating—everyone knew where and how our mother had passed her hours the week before.

On such a snowy day, the light emanating from our small brick house beckoned to us as we walked through the drifts. Once there and ensconced, with no trouble from my mother, we'd all feel safe and cozy; one by one all the girls would call their mothers to tell them they'd be home before five. This seemed to me the true meaning of neighborhood—when you could walk home safely in the middle of a blizzard because there was always someone to accompany you just a few houses down, where everyone lived in a cozy, three-bedroom, cookie-cutter place on a similarly tiny piece of real estate.

When we got up the steps of the breezeway, we used the edge of the last stair step to peel off our stiff boots that fastened with one inadequate button, and we wrung out our hems, which had dragged beside us, soggy and cold. My navy blue snow jacket was wet, so I hung it on a hook in the breezeway. In the morning it would be really cold, with the fake fur in little frozen icicles along the cuffs and hood. I didn't want to leave my good warm jacket outside, but my mother didn't want it defrosting and making puddles indoors.

I went through the door, holding my breath. So much would depend on the first look she gave us. This day, we were in luck. She paid no attention to us except for a distracted hello because she was studying, with intensity, countertops loaded with ingredients. It seemed surprising that she would be doing something so mundane when yesterday she'd gone straight to bed in the afternoon and we were only allowed to come in and kiss her after dinner. Now here she was, knee-deep in mixing bowls, absorbed in a new kind of theatrics.

Joy and her friends dipped their hands into the cookie jar silently and then quickly crept past me and up the stairs to Joy's small bedroom. I sunk into a chair, hoping my mother's mood was good, watching the muscles in her slender arms as she beat whatever was in the bowl. When she had just returned from the hospital, I was always in search of feeling safe: I never brought friends home when I couldn't be sure of my mother's behavior, though Joy always did, using them as a shield. I longed to spend time with her alone. To know that she was feeling better.

On snowbound afternoons, sometimes she and I might write a poem, or, more likely, memorize one she chose by another poet, like Edna St. Vincent Millay or Emily Dickinson, both of whom she had revered during her own adolescence. Happily, I memorized anything she loved.

The snow drove its way up the screen, the wind ranted and howled, and sometimes the electricity went out. If he were home by then, Daddy would light a fire in the fireplace, or if he were still on the road, snow pelting a headlamps of his Buick, then my mother lit it, filling half the house with smoke, and opening windows and doors to the freezing air until she got the draft drawing properly.

At some point, descriptions of such small details would come to be included in the pages of my first attempts at writing short stories and poetry. Those eerie afternoons were made special because of the grainy gray half-light that allowed all the sharp edges of reality to slip away. What difference did it make what time dinner was? What difference did it make if the girls stayed past five? Though chalking some of this up to the wild swings of the creative urge, I also began to sense that my mother's unstable mood contributed to a sort of permissive, free-wheeling attitude, one which could be extremely pleasurable in its unexpected freedoms and slippery boundaries. In those hours that we sat together at the kitchen table, all that mattered was the sound of the words, slipping easily between us, becoming part of the happiness I felt at having her home again.

That particular day, as I sat growing ever more glum with her continued silence and my own swelling vision of an inevitable violin practice to come, I realized she still had on her hat. She probably had gone somewhere in the car, even though she was under strict orders not to be driving because they had upped her sedatives again. In those years, drugs for the mentally afflicted were limited, and the prospect of prescribing accurately for a patient as disturbed as my mother was a crap shoot.

There was a sack of sugar spilling its contents onto the counter and I deduced she was making sweets of some sort. As I watched, she began to unwrap five sticks of butter, a mountain of yellow fat that rested on the cutting board beside her, waiting to be creamed. I sighed in an exaggerated whisper and settled back in my chair nervously, still hoping for a sign that she would include me. This wasn't very different than what I had done as a small child—waiting and hoping for the attention I so craved.

Suddenly, she began to sing happily in her loudest voice—flat as usual, because she couldn't hold a tune. First she sang "Somewhere over the Rainbow" and then "Summertime." She sounded hoarse, but if she were singing it must mean she was happy and coming out of her depression. She stirred the red mixing bowl and then beat something in the green bowl, and then put them all into the yellow. These nesting bowls each had a different color keyed to its size—yellowy beige for eight cups, green for six, red and blue for two cups each. Those colors made it easier not to make a mistake about what you were combining with what.

Then she stopped and frowned and dragged a chair over to the upper cabinets and began to hurl down a variety of objects.

"Get your coat," she said over her shoulder. "And you'll have to put your boots back on."

I said nothing, mystified about what was going on in her mind.

"Ginger snaps—and I don't have any ginger! I can't believe I went to the market—you know how I hate that market! I hate the way they look at me! Thank God your father goes on Saturdays!"

Still talking, with one arm rummaging in the cabinet and the other arm bringing to her nose a rain of items she maybe thought too old, or something she never used, she put back only a favored few, ready for the next haphazard closet cleaning. She was infinitely distractible. If the cabinet needed cleaning, she did it immediately, whether or not she was in the middle of baking cookies.

"Probably hat and mittens you can do without. Get a move on!"

Now worried about how "up" she was, I went to the breezeway, slipped into my freezing coat and wet boots.

She came to the door. "Go across the street to Mrs. Scott's and ask her for some ginger." She wiped her face with a floury hand. "How could I forget the most important ingredient? What a dumb bunny!"

She smiled and I was reminded that we were like characters in a play: yesterday she had been in a mental hospital—today she was home baking.

Her voice suddenly seemed shrill to me and I noticed then that she had on too much lipstick. And it was crooked. A sudden tension gripped my body: I would do anything to keep her mood stable. "Sure," I said. "Sure, I'll go. Right now." I wanted it all to be fine, I wanted her to be fine. My ambition to make it so was relentless.

And so I entered the eye of a different storm, shivering in my cold wet coat. Mrs. Scott had to dig around at the back of her cabinet for the ginger. It was Canada Dry—just like the kind we drank at home. As I negotiated my way back through the wind and snow, very cold now, I was still happy that when I came into the warmth of the kitchen I would have fulfilled my mission, and that I would undoubtedly please my mother.

On the way, I stumbled upon one of our new kittens, born two months before to our cat, Rosy. Her legs outstretched in death, with a thick rime of bloody ice covering her teeth, the kitty was pressed into the snow bank. Otherwise, she looked perfectly normal—until I picked her up and for the first time felt death in my arms, solid, square, frozen.

Rosy was a good and well-loved cat, even though she had allowed her entire litter of kittens to starve nearly to death, an act my mother and father had tried to counteract by hand-feeding them with a doll's plastic baby bottle. Only this one had survived. As soon as the ground thawed, we buried the kitten in the backyard under a Popsicle stick cross. Joy and I loved that last little kitty, one of our first pets ever to die.

EVEN AS A very young child, I had been waiting for my mother to die. I'd been conscious of the idea of death early on—reinforced that day when I found the kitten buried in the snow bank. No amount of explanation from Mommy or Daddy about the "spirit," about how "the soul lived on in your heart," made me feel any better. Neither of my parents were religious and I didn't believe them. This kitten was dead; the others from this litter were dead: they would never nestle in my lap or purr again. By the time I was turning nine, I realized that if my mother succeeded in killing herself, she would disappear from our lives in just the same way.

Over the years of my childhood, we lost two cats, eight kittens, and five Dalmatians. When three of my grandparents—both my mother's parents and my father's father—died when I was six and seven, I saw death from natural causes stride among humans for the first time. It was no different than the deaths of the animals, except that the pain was bigger, the loss greater. No more cuddling with Gaga after my bath in the early evening, wrapped in a big Turkish towel, watching the sun sink red over the horizon. No more playing on my grandfather's knee. No more rides in Poppy's turquoise Corvette. These brushes with Death convinced me that He waited around nearly every corner in our brick colonial in our small Boston suburb. It seemed like a game we played—tag, maybe: who would be tapped on the shoulder next by Death? Nearly always it was my mother, though for a long time she outran him.

Death didn't ride on a black horse, but instead walked in my Daddy's hip-deep fishing waders, the bones of his face chiseled visible, his muscles rounded stronger than any man's. I always pictured his features sharp as a fox's; he had cunning dark eyes and a hat with a snap-brim. I believed in him utterly, just the way I believed in Santa, the Tooth Fairy, and the Easter Bunny. I had seen power in his handiwork. Close up, the air around him smelled like the not-so-long-ago odor of my sister's potty pail.

When my mother took an overdose, Death came into the room and stood at the head of her bed. When my father, or my Nana, or her best friend, took her to the hospital, Death waited on the threshold and watched for his opportunity. Sometimes Death lived at our house, slithering between the big bottles of her sleeping pills and tranquilizers, twining around the packs of cigarettes and bottles of booze. Death was the itinerant sales-man, always knocking on our green front door. My mother never failed to let him in.

And then there were the times that Death traveled through her hands down into me: when she screamed at me that it was my fault that my sister was being taken away to live at my grand-mother's, that I was the one who had made her "sick." Or worse, the times she would go into a trance and wake to find herself choking me in my crib to stop my crying.

Perhaps in self-protection, perhaps simply in weariness, by the time I had reached late adolescence, I no longer took her attempts to die seriously, nor did I feel compassion when she grew depressed enough to try. In fact, part of me simply wished she would succumb. There could be no peace with her engaging in such dramatic convulsions, and each attempt hurt us all: the big rejection, a slap in the face. We took it personally because no one better educated in the torturous twists and turns of those half in love with death bothered to explain it to us in any other way.

Obviously, we thought, we must have failed once again, and we were angry—both with her and with ourselves—for that failure. I don't think it occurred to any of us that our mother was in pain, and that such pain could drive her to desperation. We knew nothing about support groups; there was no counseling available for a furious, emotionally needy family. The psychiatrist, who tried to make us see that her illness was "not her fault," gradually became an enemy as he instructed us that anger would only defeat her treatment, and left it at that. But to us, her suicide attempts seemed just bids for pity and sympathy: it was better to think she was merely being self-indulgent than to understand she wanted to leave us all for good, or that she was in excruciating turmoil.

Family members discussed none of this. As a child, I heard no name given to her illness, no reassurance that she would return from her visits to some mysterious place and, once again, scoop me up into her welcoming arms.

My father, weighted down with caring for a sick wife and trying to earn enough money to keep us all afloat, never spoke of her illness, and both Nana and his sister, Joan, were also sworn to secrecy. The feelings of resentment about how her sickness had taken control of the family did nothing to improve the already disintegrating sense of normalcy. In later years, even Joy and I stifled our real feelings. On the outside we were smooth and polite—but inside we were seething with rage.

Most children don't worry about their parent's death the way I did. This, too, was part of the legacy she left: to worry, to want to protect, to wonder how I'd survive if she succeeded in killing herself. In most families, children think only of their parents' deaths if there is a serious physical illness or hospitalization, or if someone else close to the family dies. When I thought of my father dying, for instance, I felt like a butterfly touching down gingerly on a very thorny rose, and then taking off again as quickly as possible. I didn't need or want to dwell on the thought of his death. With my mother it was different: the possibility of her death lived in every breath I took. If she wasn't making an attempt, then she was acting crazy or talking about her crazy thoughts, or reading an explicit poem aloud.

I LEARNED OF my mother's suicide in the office of a close family friend who was also a doctor in Health Services at my college. Away at Harvard, I was only a half hour from home. It was after the clinic had closed for the day, sometime past five o'clock, only a few hours since she had been discovered dead in her car.

In the semi-darkness of Dr. Loring's office, the lamp from his desk cast a jaundiced light against the taut skin of his face. He looked frightened. I knew what he was going to say before he said it. I was filled then with a curious sort of calm, a calm that I would shortly name as relief. It was all over. I was relieved that I wouldn't have to wait any longer for that inevitable phone call. I was relieved that I wouldn't have to bear any longer the crazy episodes and demanding phone calls. At last, there would be peace.

He gave me privacy in which to make phone calls, and as I sat at his big desk, I believe I cried, but only a little. Mostly I needed Nana, and I began phoning around to find her. I wanted her the way a child wants her mother. Eventually, I discovered that she was at the family home, sitting alone in the writing room beside my mother's body and waiting for the coroner to arrive. She had been called by the young couple who lived in as help and support for my solitary mother; it was they who carried her in from the garage and laid her on the couch; then they had summoned Nana, even though she was technically not part of my mother's life anymore, due to my parents' divorce.

Later, after supper, Nana helped me sort through my mother's red phone book, and I began to call her closest friends. Even so, I did not realize that I was about to take charge of my mother's remaining life and death. If I had ever been a young girl to begin with, I would certainly never be a young girl again.

BUT ON THAT wintry afternoon when I was seven or eight, when the snow dumped down in drifts like confectioner's sugar, and my mother readied her endless bowls of batter for the cookies, we carefully laid out the kitten in a shoebox and then put her on the back steps of the breezeway. When she realized that I had not brought back powdered ginger but ginger ale instead, she started to laugh. "You told her it was for cookies? She ought to know better!" And in an instant she had scooped up her coat and swept off into the darkness.

Despite the warmth of the house, I was still shivering; I watched her through a wintry window that had become a perfect surface for scratching ice pictures, tic-tac-toes, and secret names, easily erased in a second with a wet thumb. With her black hair and black coat, my mother seemed to glide on the tops of the white snow banks under the light streaming from the streetlamps. She disappeared quickly. After a moment, she returned in the scope of my faithful watch, the sweet smoke of her breath and the crescent of her face under her hat the only parts of her visible.

"Look!" She burst into the light and heat of the kitchen. Her whole being shone with a frantic energy. "When I told her I was baking as many pans as I could, she was shocked! She had two extra so she lent them to me. Let's see now." She began multiplying in the air with her dough-dusty fingers and I just hoped it was right—had she successfully readjusted the recipe for five times the normal amount? This kind of baking was the real Anne: all about instinct and nothing about measuring cups.

Just as she interlaced fragile words of poetry among the sweet and spicy, so did she weave stories into the very texture of our lives. A story here, an image there: she built her tales out of daily occurrences, and her suicide attempts and her mental illness were ordinary events to which she gave no less weight than the tale of a daughter's maturation, or an elegy for her parents, or a villanelle cooked up in Robert Lowell's class. These were often the topics that her poetry introduced to the reading public; one has only to read her letters from the late 1950s to see the somewhat humorous, flippant way she described her visits at the "summer hotel" and realize what a saleswoman she was, glamourizing her illness, and thus giving it, and herself, a chic cachet. In 1969, some of her best poems, contained in the Pulitzer Prize–winning *Live or Die*, were titled "Wanting to Die," "Suicide Note," and "Live."

As a child I had watched the way she made her illness into a career. The love and the attention her disease brought to her were plain to see. Once depression became subject matter, she began to write about it more and more openly in her poetry. It even won her praise and respect and to me that somehow felt unfair. The aspect of public acclamation confused me. Though I hated her insanity, she was coining this shameful aspect of the illness and eventually she would be able to support herself financially upon it. Sadly, I realized that I wanted to be able to rise up someday and spin the straw of my own misery into gold, just the way my mother did. Sadly, I also realized I wanted none of it.

WHETHER I WAS two or four, six or ten, whether it was January or July, my mother's mental illness forced her to leave me behind over and over again. At the very beginning of her illness, before Joy was born and then again when she was an infant, I, too, was sent to stay with my paternal grandmother, Nana, who was like a fairy godmother. Over the years, there were dolls and toys, and we were coddled and fed the special foods we liked. There was no rampage to make pan after pan of cookies that would inevitably get stale before they were eaten, or to be sent out into the darkness in search of a forgotten ingredient. At Nana's we were treated like the children we were, and then some.

After Joy's birth, however, when Nana fell ill with Ménière's disease—a disease of the inner ear that destroys an individual's balance and produces a stagger—I, as the older child, was first sent out to my mother's mother, Gaga, and then to other relatives in less fortunate circumstances. After Nana's condition was diagnosed, she fell under the only known cure at the time: the severing of the main nerve of the ear. That operation rendered her totally deaf on one side and did not rectify her slight stagger. It was all she could do to take care of newborn Joy. I longed for the times I would sometimes get to go to visit Nana in her snug ranch house surrounded by hemlocks that soughed in the night wind. For nearly two years, Joy was the one chosen to live with her. For months at a time, I was packed up and sent off, hating Joy for having usurped my place there.

Going to Gaga's was as far from Nana's as a two-year-old could get. Simply by being there, I was reliving my mother's childhood in her parents' home, though it was not until I was an adult that I perceived such similarities. Gaga was a beautiful woman who dressed in stylish silk dresses, wool suits, and a mink coat, who sat up ramrod straight at the dinner table and snapped her index finger against my mother's wrist whenever little Anne slumped. With rigor, Gaga gave my mother repeated enemas and vaginal examinations that trespassed far beyond the boundaries of a prepubescent girl's privacy. Despite these bizarrely intrusive behaviors, Gaga nevertheless put on a rigidly full face for the role she was expected to fulfill as a society matron, supervising a full-time cook, two maids, and a house with four garages. Her example was always before my mother as a torment. She could never fulfill her mother's requirements.

Gaga's requirements for her young granddaughter were no less high. I was expected to be quiet, to speak when spoken to, and, mostly, never to cry—no matter how much I missed my mother and father. Later, when Gaga's deteriorating health made it impossible for her to care for a two-year-old (even when that care required only supervision of the nanny), I was sent to my mother's elder sister, Alison. After that, whenever my mother felt unable to cope with the disturbing aspects of her life, she would park me at Alison's while she went to the hospital for a short stay. Being with Alison and Henry meant trying to shoehorn my way into a family that already had four children and little income because my uncle was a drunk. It seemed my mother's depressions were almost always topped off by a needy child—me—dragging around on the hem of her skirt.

NANA'S SURGERY CHANGED her life forever: once a beautiful, elegant woman who led parties and bridge clubs, she now became somewhat reclusive; tending mainly to her grown son's family, she created a whole new world within it for herself. Long gone were the days when she was noted in the Boston society pages as motoring to Washington to stay with the President and Mrs. Roosevelt at the White House. (My father was ensconced in Lincoln's bedroom, where he set the curtains on fire while playing with matches.)

Increasingly deaf as her other ear became impaired as well,

Nana now wanted the safety of home, where she didn't have to make a fool of herself by answering a question strangely. Little by little, her limitations in the hearing world eroded her desire to participate in the noisy business of daily life. In our home the uproar was equivalent, albeit blessedly silent. And, as my mother's illness grew protracted and, especially after the death of my grandfather in a car accident, my grandmother was looking for a place to settle.

In the cracked and shattered shards of our small family, Nana found her greatest role. My mother believed herself incapable of raising a family and keeping a house, and so she took a step back, then two, then three. Living nearby, Nana moved forward into our family with grace, as my mother retreated; the choreography of Nana's dance was based on the transfer of power between her and my mother. Although my father and mother should have been the head of our little band of four, they weren't. Instead, Nana went mano a mano with something more powerful than even she was—Anne's illness. And in the end, the illness always won.

My mother often said that Nana preferred sick people to healthy ones because illness gave her the opportunity to define a new role for herself in any situation. Whether or not this was true, my grandmother rescued my mother again and again from chores she did not want to perform (sewing, cooking, driving us to the doctor, dentist, and after-school activities) and the roles my mother did not want to play (a housewife and devoted mother). How we loved Nana for being the traditional mother we did not have.

As my mother would recount in the tapes and transcriptions she had made under therapy with her first psychiatrist, she slapped me, pushed me away, and once threw me against a wall. She also shook and choked me as I lay in my crib, probably still crying. Later in life I was told by Nana that I was the difficult child, while Joy was sociable, easy to take care of. The intense form of postpartum depression from which my mother suffered, neither named nor diagnosed, could have ended in infanticide; luckily, the family intervened before a disaster could occur.

Because I have no direct memories of these encounters, I had to read them, in her own words, in her journals, which she had entrusted to me before her death and instructed me to read, so that I could find them an appropriate home. How I wished she had destroyed the journals; to have to confront those events in the indelible ink of her pen felt like a terrible betrayal, a hurt that could never be healed. Yet I asked myself to forgive her even this, because I loved her and because I knew her sickness drove her to actions that she never would have allowed herself had she been sane.

In those early years, which child did she crave? As she would write in "The Double Image" in 1958, it was Joy, the vulnerable child, "the butterfly girl with jelly bean cheeks." All these were good reasons to move me away from her. Only after reading through her transcripts did I realize how often she had been out of the hospital for weeks, months, getting her hair and nails done, going to her poetry class, how so many days passed before she came to get me from one of my stays at my Aunt Alison's house.

I huddled in the wind of these repeated abandonments. I hated her sickness when I was too young to understand it. Only with time did I come to empathize with her, spinning in the whirl-wind plague of her illness.

{freefall}

WHEN YOU GROW up with a mother whose life is in continual freefall, motherhood itself seems a treacherous jungle gym with slippery bars, tricky drops, and deceptively large spaces, a structure that only the surefooted should attempt to navigate. My father, frequently away, had little impact on our young lives because he was overwhelmed by the strong voices of Nana and Gaga, who told him what to do about my mother's situation.

As we grew older, both Joy and I were sent to day camp during the summer to get us out and away from my mother, who appeared incapable of taking care of us on a daily basis. At camp, I learned all kinds of privileged activities: how to swim, how to sail, how to ride a horse, how to hold a bow and arrow, how to braid brightly colored gimp into lanyards and bracelets. Despite their reservations about spending any more money on relieving my mother's needs, all four parents nevertheless pooled their funds to send us each year, until my father's salary increased and my parents were able to swing it themselves.

It made me anxious, however, to be away from my mother for an entire day. As the hours passed, I would look at the round face of my Timex and count up the minutes until I could go home, my heart clenching with anxiety and making it difficult to breathe. Part of me wanted to stay in the neighborhood all day every day, playing hopscotch, riding my bike, eating tuna fish sandwiches with potato chips on top for lunch. I wanted to be the guardian of her world and keep her away from her own destructive hand—and yet I was ambivalent about the responsibility this required.

I found a rusty and discarded pair of roller skates, the kind that strap onto your shoes and tighten with a key. When my father was around to take over caring for my mother, on Saturdays or Sundays after church, I would race out of the house and screw my skates on tightly around my red Keds. I used those skates nonstop as a way of transporting myself out from under my obligation to her. Up and down the cement sidewalks I went, losing myself in the one-two rhythm of my wheels.

My sister simply removed herself from the scene as much as possible: she became a social butterfly at summer camp, in the neighborhood, and at school. By the time she was a teenager, she had more friends than she could keep track of. In the afternoons, the phone rang and rang and she developed the habit of refusing to answer so that someone, usually me, would take messages for her. She was very pretty, with a lovely, buxom Raquel Welch–type figure, just as my mother was striking, with her dark hair and blue green eyes, her leggy, sexy style. I was trapped between two beauties. In our high school years, Joy would be invited to both my junior and senior proms while I went babysitting or sat at home watching television. My jealousy was keen. My silly cat's-eye glasses and flat chest won me no points with the opposite sex.

There were so many boys for Joy, and so few for me. She once smuggled her steady over the garage roof into her bedroom, just down the hall from our parents' room. I couldn't believe her audacity but I both envied and admired it.

Joy, it seemed, got away with everything, while I was too terrified that any kind of trouble would upset the family's fragile balance; Joy was adolescent with a list of "joyful" antics that matched those of our mother. Certainly, our house was never dull, and I was never surprised when my sister was grounded or, as a small child, spanked. None of this stopped her: she went her merry way while I stayed on the prescribed path for the most part, never looking to one side or the other, doing whatever was expected of me. I rarely got in trouble: boring old Linda.

LIKE CLOCKWORK EVERY evening, right about five o'clock, my father would arrive home and say "sun's over the yardarm," and hang his suit jacket over the back of the blond, wooden Eames chair in my mother's study. Then he repaired to the kitchen to get dinner started as he pulled bottles out of the liquor cabinet. Booze was a pillar that seemed, at that time, to prop up our family: there were nights when they drank heavily, and later, over the dinner table, graced us with exuberant affection and my father's dry sense of humor.

He mixed their drinks in exactly the same spot on the counter, using his favorite paring knife for details like lemon peel, and the silver ice bucket, even though we rarely had company. My father mixed martinis as intensely as if he were conducting a symphony: a little lemon rubbed on the rim of the glass; vermouth poured over the ice in the professional-looking stainless steel shaker, then drained into the sink; gin added; the final drink poured into the glasses with a tiny strainer holding back the ice.

My father taught me everything he knew about mixing the perfect drink sometime before I was twelve, and on those nights he was away from home, traveling across the Northeast as a broker of raw grades of various types of wool, I loved to play barkeep and take charge of my mother's needs. There was something comforting about being able to offer her something so tangible, something that relaxed her and gave her pleasure. She wouldn't try suicide on my watch, I thought with satisfaction. I did not know then that there was a technical name—codependence—for the guilt-ridden process of coddling and care-taking the alcoholic.

My mother's tastes were kaleidoscopic and so her preferences came on like fashion fads: during my early childhood, there were extra-dry gin martinis, straight up, with olives, in the classical V-shaped glass, while Bloody Marys were served strong in a lowball; after a trip to Italy, she insisted on a Negroni jubilee; my early adolescence was the era of Wild Turkey, Jack Daniels, and after-dinner stingers—a nasty brew of crème de menthe and brandy, preferably over crushed ice, with a tiny silver straw for sipping; when I left for college, she had shifted to vodka straight and pure on the rocks; after their divorce, she added a screwdriver or two in lieu of breakfast.

In the name of responsible drinking, my parents introduced my sister and me to alcohol at the family dinner table. In anticipation of the legal drinking age of my eighteenth birthday, a carefully poured, discreet glass of wine or champagne at family occasions, was gradually replaced by the right to accompany my parents in their evening ritual of cocktail hour on occasional weekend nights, despite my grandmother's indignant disapproval. Nana seemed to be the only one afraid of alcohol, in response to the family penchant for abusing it.

Nevertheless, at the Sexton's every night, a lengthy cocktail hour was de rigueur, a time during which they sometimes shut themselves into my mother's writing room and just plain "drank"—sometimes a chaste two-lowball limit, but more often than not a hefty diet of three. My mother set the pace, and he matched it. No one mentioned—or perhaps even, at that point, knew—that alcohol was a depressant and that adding it to the heavy load of medication she already took daily was undoubtedly a tragedy in the making. The two of them stole glasses or individual-serving martini pitchers or shot glasses from bars and restaurants the way some people steal soap or towels from hotels; they brought home their booty with glee and used it like a trophy.

But soon my parents began to have violent arguments. Or, what we called "arguments," even though they often escalated into "fights." These fights frightened us to our cores.

Because they had starting their drinking ritual at five o'clock, by seven they were both a little drunk, uninhibited, and my mother often said things she didn't mean—vituperative, nasty, barbed things, as my father strode around the room, trying to keep his temper, clenching and unclenching his fists. Many nights they forgot to close the door, and if it were a night when they had gone over their limit of two drinks, the conclusion to the argument was nearly inevitable. These were the nights when dinner would be tense and delayed. At such mealtimes there would be none of the happy entertainment they had offered in earlier years, joking around and teasing each other.

Their competing voices would rise up the staircase and through the floor of my bedroom on the second story, exactly over my mother's writing room. Initially, Joy would come in where I was sitting at my desk doing homework; together we tried to ignore the escalating noise beneath us. After a short while, I would begin to prowl around my room, feeling restless and anxious. Then, drawn like bugs to a streetlamp, Joy and I would silently move to a vantage point on the staircase to watch like spies through the balusters, our faces pressed against the wooden bars. From our perch we could just see our parents. We always listened intently. Nothing was as important, and, really, we couldn't help ourselves. Despite the escalating shouts that pierced our hearts, we stood by in case our mother needed us, as if we were guardians in place to save her. At that point, we sometimes interfered if we were convinced that he might really hurt her.

Our mother would tilt back in her desk chair, putting her feet up on the bookcase provocatively, a position that always infuriated my father because of the dent her shoes were scuffing into the pretty wood. A sense of foreboding choked off my breathing. At that juncture, to some extent, both of them were in danger, because there was always the chance that my mother might call the authorities and he might wind up at the police station. And if the fight lasted long enough, the outcome was inevitable. He would give in to the urge and punch her in the face.

At this point, Joy and I would launch ourselves like twin rockets down the stairs to separate them, to pull him off and take him into a separate corner (not an easy task), to comfort her and to calm the situation. Once or twice my mother screamed at me to call the police and, shaking with fear, I did.

Joy and I played the role of watchdog: this, it seems now, was a good part of the glue that bound us together. How many times after our parents fought did we both worry that she might take out the bottle of pills once again?

By the time the police car arrived, the anger had gone like dirty water sucked down the drain, and my father was both calm and solicitous. Silence over what had occurred once again descended. No one spoke of it—it was just crammed away until the next eruption. We didn't talk about the violence any more than we talked about her mental illness. It went without saying that he would stay, that she wouldn't press charges, and that this would happen again, regardless of good behavior. She needed him because he made her secure in the knowledge that he would never leave her no matter what she did: he would nurture her through her depressions, comfort and steady her through her manic surges.

We made a secret of those verbal and physical furies. We said nothing, when, after he had punched her, he knelt in contrition and applied cold compresses, as if he had had no part in the act. We said nothing when she kissed the top of his head in forgiveness. A hurricane had swept through and when it moved on out, he simply went to bundle up the branches and rake the leaves. We covered his act with silence and thus became complicit, giving sanction to both of them to do it one more time. Another sort of legacy had been established.

THE OTHER FAMILIES in our neighborhood looked nothing like my own family. My father did not run the family, nor did my mother. It was my mother's illness that had seized control. My adulation of her was not tempered by the fact that she was mentally ill. We never used the word "crazy"—though when the ambulance arrived in the driveway to take her away, the neighborhood children whispered that Mrs. Sexton was nuts again. At eight I still did not understand the word "nuts"; one afternoon when she had just returned from the hospital I stopped her on the staircase, where she stood with a book under her arm.

"What does nuts mean?" I asked, averting my eyes from her face. I felt safe enough, at last, to ask the big question. "On the playground today Nancy said you'll probably eat rat poison someday and die."

She sank down on the step and drew me over beside her, her face flattened with sorrow—later I would understand that her sorrow was meant not for herself, but for me. "Nuts is what some people call it," she answered. "I'm sorry she was being so mean."

As we sat there I felt embarrassed, not knowing what to say. This was one of the only childhood memories where I can remember talking about her mental illness so frankly.

"But can you catch it? Like when Joy got sick last summer?"

"No. You can't. It's just tiredness in your mind. You rest and then in a while you feel better."

This was all the information I would, as a child, ever receive regarding her illness: Nana, my father, my mother's parents—none of them enlightened Joy and me about what hurricanes plagued my mother and repeatedly took her from us. It was only on the playground that I had at last heard the word that described what was happening to this woman I needed and loved so desperately.

AS WE GREW older, we were still both taken care of by Nana, nearly all the time, though we never went to live with her again. Over our kitchen sink, she shampooed our hair; at bedtime she gave endless backrubs; and she sewed creative and beautiful clothes for both us and our Barbies. She spoiled us mercilessly. When at her house for an overnight, she even let us eat Beech-Nut baby food from a small jar. Macaroni and Bacon and Plums with Tapioca were our favorites. My mother was aghast. She forbade the practice but Nana just swore us to secrecy. Joy remembered that sometimes, when my mother or father arrived to pick us up after a weekend visit, Nana would shut out all the lights and lock the door—buying us one more night at her house as my parents, bewildered that we were not home, would turn and drive away. Looking back on that time, I understand now that Nana was returning part of our childhood to us, even while she was driving my mother speechless with what she thought of as interference and meddling.

As children, we were enticed, in general, to forget about where my mother was or what was happening to her. Things didn't change much as we grew older. That curious gray silence still wrapped itself around the house, forbidding questions. I wanted my mother back but the adults indicated nothing, not a single word, their demeanor such that if we did not talk about our mother then she really couldn't be missing, or sick. I learned not to introduce discussion of the cocoon of depression that settled around me, gauze-like, whenever she was gone, an emotional state that made it hard to think or feel. I told no one about my anxiety, or my pounding heart, my shaking hands—my fear. I was still too young to know words like "depression" or "anxiety" to convey the sensations coursing through me. Mostly it all felt like a stomachache. And for that complaint Nana gave me a dose of Pepto and a stern unspoken message: play with your dolls, be as good as your dolls, live a simple life like your dolls—far away from the early death that your mother seeks again and again.

Despite Nana and Daddy's unspoken disapproval, I nevertheless did adore and emulate my mother, as increasingly the years passed and then flowed into a fast-moving current. As time went on, I intuitively began to understand where she went when she left us: an institution. I could see, not surprisingly, what a boldly beautiful, charismatic woman she was, despite her illness—or perhaps because of that part of what was yet unrecognized as her manic depressive state—moods which made her wildly, giddily happy, at least for a time. She was eager to have fun, eager to write poems side by side with me, eager to discuss books like *Madame Bovary*. She made me feel loved. After having been rejected when I was younger, this was the strongest magic of all: I was no longer an ugly outcast, but a precious, deeply prized best friend.

Secretly I began to wish—despite Nana's warnings—that even if it meant taking on the roller coaster of moods that swooped and plunged, my life could be something like my mother's. It became impossible to dissect her illness from her personality so cleanly, and after a while I didn't even want to. My own moods were already beginning to move hand in hand with my mother's. If she was unhappy, how could I be happy? If she became suicidal in her twenties, would the overpowering attachment I felt with her then become a spider's web of disastrous expectation? Would my life follow hers, even to the point of calamity?

By the time I had reached the end of middle school, I idolized my mother and all she did. Every day I wanted to wear our blue cotton mother-daughter dresses with the buttons like candy hearts. I wanted to curl my hair just the way my mother did hers. I studied my eyes in the mirror to see if they had become the same changeable sea-green blue as hers. If I were good enough, if I were interesting enough, she would never again abandon me.

She decided that I should sign up for violin lessons with the music program at school, rather than the piano I would have preferred, because the violin was her favorite instrument. Once again, I was happy to comply: I could do something this fragile mother wanted, and thereby make her happy. I spent at least an hour every afternoon scraping my chalky bow across the strings, surely showing no talent at all. But that didn't matter. Violin lessons were one of the few after-school activities to which she drove me—rather than asking Nana to do it—and the time in the car, before and after lessons, abounded with girl talk.

During these years, I sneaked her thick red lipsticks and her spiky high heels, then her hard pink hair rollers and Aqua Net. I donned her falsies and her silky nylon stockings on days she was out of the house, and then I would pose in front of the windows as if I were on a stage, one of her Salem menthols in hand. Later, I would commit to memory many of her poems and often I struggled through books beyond my ability (like Kafka's *Metamorphosis* or Kurt Vonnegut's *Slaughterhouse-Five* or Erik Erikson's *Young Man Luther*) just to give her pleasure, as her friends nodded in admiration.

When I was beginning to write my own poetry seriously, and to set it as lyrics to what I was composing on my guitar, she hailed it as promising. I had a crush on my mother the way most prepubescent girls develop a crush on a female movie star or a camp counselor. To me, my mother seemed perfect—even if, clearly, she was not "normal." Who wanted the boring "normal" anyway, I told myself, ignoring my ambivalent, inner voice, which pointed out that I was lying to myself yet again. I still wanted the mother of the apron, who was modeled on Nana, yet simultaneously I wanted the successful career woman my mother was fast becoming. The identification between us at this time strengthened even further.

It was impossible to forget the free gesture with which she threw back her head when amused; I loved the deep whisky gravel of her voice. I loved the way her enormous hazel blue eyes wept copious tears or widened with little girl amazement. Everything about her was arrestingly intense, and I loved that.

"Normal," on the other hand, was nearly everywhere I looked in my neighborhood of the early 1960s: the women on our block who sold pies at church socials and brought cupcakes to school for their children's birthdays; the women who wore housedresses and aprons instead of sleek pantsuits; the women who belonged to weekly bridge groups, or ran the PTA; the women who squirreled away "pin money" for the ice cream truck that clanged down the street on summer nights instead of earning some kind of income from the steadily increasing flow of checks from poetry journals.

"Normal" were the women who bore in silence the obtuseness of their husbands rather than provoking full-scale war by arguing. It appeared, from the outside looking in, that in the homes of my friends, family peace reigned, controlled by the authority of the father. Little by little, I craved this sort of normalcy less and less, and desired, more and more, to be like my flamboyant mother, so different from these traditional homebodies.

So my mother was crazy and unconventional, and our life was a continual string of surprises. It meant you never knew, when you woke up in the morning, whether she was going to be "up" or "down." "Up" meant setting the new hi-fi to earsplitting levels and dancing through the house in her towel after a shower, or putting on classical music and pirouetting steps she'd learned sometime, somewhere—possibly as far back as the childhood she claimed had been so traumatic.

"Up" meant getting sauced enough on martinis to charm all the men at a neighborhood cocktail party, or to lie with me on her back in the yard, new spring grass pressing damply under our shoulders, looking for shapes in the clouds of a new April sky: there, she would point, an iron, a bunny, a turtle, a bicycle. Were there more downs than ups? It certainly seemed so, but it is also true that the downs affected us more deeply than the ups and thus were remembered with greater clarity and pain. The ups were part of the legacy, but they were the forgotten part.

Interestingly enough, her psychiatrists treated only her depression, right from the start—never thinking, apparently, of what was then called manic-depression—until the late sixties, when she was in her early forties. Mind-numbing drugs like Thorazine muted the constant emotional pain but, because she was so sedated, took away her ability to write.

Finances pressed on my parents intensely; they were living on a shoestring, with no money for any kind of "luxuries," or for full-time babysitters or nannies. In lieu of love, my mother's mother, on a practical note, paid for a cleaning lady to come two days a week and Nana pitched in until her presence became intrusive. In addition to washing dishes and bringing over meals, she also drove us to the activities that were in accordance with whatever she thought "young ladies" should be educated in: dancing school, the orthodontist she perceived we needed, and the skating lessons which would bring both balance and grace. My mother remained sick and, so it appeared, ungrateful. Her mental illness obviously wasn't, as they had first hoped and believed, going to slip away quickly. It became more entrenched every day.

"She was still living in her own childhood," observed the voice, providing me for once with insight instead of an insult.

Again, my sister and I were partnered: we didn't look for someone to blame—we were obviously the guilty ones and all we knew was the reality that she couldn't fulfill her role as our mother without a great deal of help from others. The engines of her mental illness revved to drown out everything else with a full-throated roar. The family went into a huddle, increasingly taking shifts with the childcare, shuttling my mother to her innumerable psychiatrist appointments and the hospital. One of the main ideas that arose during this period was that until she had had the babies to care for she had been fine, using a Mixmaster and selling cosmetics, for a while, door-to-door. And then she had even conquered the strict demands of a writing career, though no one gave her much credit for that. Even worse, no one seemed to remember the difficulties of her adolescence, the wild mood swings that often brought her depression back again. The family still ruled her depression and desperation—all that often led to suicide attempts—as mere temper tantrums.

I do not remember talking much about my mother, or even how life had been at Nana's or Alison's—those places I had been dumped in my early years. I remember only that I was scared I would never be allowed to return home. And so I learned my mission: keep my eyes straight ahead, be obedient, compliant, willing, and frozen in place unless someone asked if I wanted something.

MY MOTHER HAD taught me, by example, how hard it was to be a mother. When I was thirteen, I began to babysit for twenty-five cents an hour, pocket money with which to buy records and penny candy. I shortly discovered, however, that when the parents for whom I was babysitting went out the door, trusting me to be alone with their children, I became undone with anxiety. My heart thudded offbeat, my breath grew ever shorter.

Nevertheless, children appeared to like me as I suggested games of hangman and Monopoly, and the phone rang with job offers nearly every weekend. Because I had no dates in high school, I often accepted, but also sometimes avoided taking the Saturday night offers because of the unsettling way being with children made me feel. I just wasn't comfortable with them, especially the young ones who defied me constantly. Still, I assumed that someday I would have a family of my own, even though I imagined it to be as different as possible from the one in which I had grown up.

As I grew older, the legacy shadowed me, still invisible, and my fantasy of family refined itself. I would always be slender and blond; I would wear flattering, tightly fit jeans rather than baggy pantsuits; I would be flexible and ready for a new plan and extra guests at any moment; I would be renowned as an excellent cook; I would be emotionally open without being out of control; I would drink martinis, but never get drunk; I would have a career but my children would come first; I would neither leave them nor send them away.

I'd thought I could pick the sort of mother I would be, as simply as I might pluck events or holidays from a river of experience. I'd thought I could consciously choose the foundation on which I would build the style of my mothering. I'd thought that decisiveness and self-control were the ways we shaped our futures; if those futures were handed down from generation to generation, then to succeed at changing them was still within reach with the application of a little bit of effort. It didn't occur to me then that there was some secret code in both learned behavior and genetic, biological expression that was embedded within us. I could not see that these two factors might actually govern what I did, and what kind of mother I would be, regardless of how I strove to aim at a particular vision of myself in this role. I began to discover, slowly, that it was not a question of pure willpower.

DEPRESSION IS A country with no borders. In my mid-thirties, just after my children were born, I found myself to be a citizen there. Having suffered a postpartum depression, as had my mother, I could not look back and see the safe ground where my life and I once were, where the lives of other people continued to move; my depression changed from the low-grade chronic variety I'd experienced for the majority of my life, starting from when I was fourteen, into what is termed the "clinical" form of the disease. I had vanished into the twilight zone.

Initially, in this more acute form of depression, my days were spent in total bewilderment. I didn't understand what was happening to me, what the black despair that descended over me really meant. In my dreams, I existed on the barren surface of some dry desert, where I scuttled like a shiny-shelled beetle in search of protection from the hard sun. Every pore of my body ached and blossomed into a visceral pain that, in an unexpected way, was not merely psychological, but physical as well. These feelings were not comprehensible to my remaining family. How could pain in your mind turn into pain in your body? From where, exactly, did it emanate? I could not explain how sick I felt, while inside my gut gnawed the wolf, trying to find his way out. My stomach hurt all the time, and I began to suffer from severe migraines and mysterious anxiety, as well as repeated episodes that felt remarkably like the flu.

Looking for relief, I drank more and used the medication prescribed for the migraines that now plagued me increasingly, in ways for which it had not been intended. One night I dreamt again of the desert, of a smooth oval opening that I crawled into to escape the scorching heat. I lay there panting and then began the long descent through the small round hole at its center. Down and down I went, squeezed by the walls, so desperate to end the ache in my mind and body that I pushed onward despite my intense claustrophobia. Anything would be better than enduring the world in which I existed, alone, under that giant burning sun. The bottom opened onto a metallic conveyor belt that operated in the near-total blackness of a tunnel. Drugged with dread, I got on and marched in a doomed effort to outpace it. It was no longer just a nighttime dream; it was now a daytime nightmare.

I was in a void where painkillers and booze and my psychoactive medications did not exist because they did not help. Perhaps this was what my mother's undermedicated episodes had felt like. Slowly, I began to realize that though there was no clock down there, a lot of time passed. Interestingly, my mother, whose works bore witness to all the sorrows of the soul, had never truly described her disturbed motivations and thoughts to me *in detail*, despite her tales about simple depression, told to me with a bit of a flare. I had no basis for comparison—was it possible that she had suffered distress such as this? I knew only that I was destined to get on that walkway and put one foot after the last, my mind hurtling forward at ferocious speed, my breath coming faster and faster in a doomed attempt to outrun a machine that could never be outrun.

There was no exit. I leaned on the railing and wept. Every day that silent march, even when I was awake. On the outside I was often doing perfectly normal things, but inside I was in the dark, foot after foot on the rubber platform as I made breakfast for the kids, shopped for groceries, cooked supper, went to sleep. On the outside I wore a smiling mask so no one could know where I really was: sunk so far down in my head that only the whites of my eyes were showing.

And it was in this way that an obsessive daisy chain of thoughts began to circle in my mind around one word: suicide.

{stories about the nut house}

MY MOTHER'S STORIES about the "nut house"—her words, not mine—frightened me when I was growing up. Images of old women with wild white hair pacing back and forth in long white nightgowns, uttering strings of blank white words, took root in my imagination. Insanity had no color: it was white and hollow, cold and unearthly. Barred windows filtered white moonlight. Every door was locked and nurses stood guard, with great steel rings of keys clanking from their waists. Here there were padded rooms for violent inmates, and seclusion rooms with tubs that had canvas covers against which patients drummed their feet until they were numb.

Where had I drawn all this grist for my concept of a mental hospital?

Some of it was firsthand, seen when I visited my mother. As for the rest, I accumulated these pictures from books like *The Bell Jar*, *Sybil*, *Valley of the Dolls*, and *I Never Promised You a Rose Garden*—and, especially, Ken Kesey's much talked about *One Flew Over the Cuckoo's Nest*, as well as movies like *The Snake Pit*.

The most important source was my mother herself. Her

dramatic nature lent itself to both the starring and directing roles, and she cast the outlines of her own experiences in vibrant color as she handed them down with far greater enthusiasm than she did her recipe for pineapple upside-down cake. One day when I was sixteen, she had just returned home from hospitalization after another attempt to take her life; I was getting just a little exasperated with her at the same time I was beginning—just beginning—to declare my own independence. Though I regularly experienced my own depression at this time, it did not approach the levels to which she could sink when depression trapped her again, barely breathing under a bell jar, where there was no oxygen. The same day she had been hospitalized, I went on a date with the only boyfriend I ever had in high school. When she learned I had gone out and had not been curled up at home in terror for what she had once again just barely avoided, she was enraged. A few days later, we sat at the kitchen table and stirred sugar and milk into our cups of tea. As close as we still were, I felt trapped by discussing her hospital stay, but I didn't know how to escape.

"Oh, Linda," she said, inhaling deeply as she lit another cigarette. "It was awful." Poke, poke with the cigarette, as she waved her hand around to punctuate her sentences. The smoke drifted up over us. "They call it a suicide watch—some nurse sitting beside you constantly, like a guard in a prison. And they tied my hands like a crucifixion." Still with the cigarette between her fingers, she held her hands up above her head and crossed them at the wrists.

"I kept begging for a ciggie." A tear slid down her cheek. "But that bitch wouldn't untie me for even one second. 'It's your punishment,' she kept saying. 'You're only getting what you deserve.'"

I had grown accustomed to the many facets of my mother's attempts to end her life, and at this point, like so many who face a parent's suicide attempt, I felt only annoyance that I had to comfort her again when my gut was clenched with anger about another set of histrionics. Perhaps, secretly, teenage Linda did agree with the nasty nurse that Anne deserved her discomfort and humiliation. How ashamed I was of that heartless emotion, and so I buried it as fast as I would a dead skunk. The odor lingered, however. That day I chose to hide the unacceptable by comforting my mother with a sudden wholehearted sympathy. As I grew older, I would begin to feel guilty about my anger at her depressions and her suicide attempts, as yet another psychiatrist counseled the entire family to be supportive. "Don't be hard on her," he instructed us. We sagged under the weight of hearing this exhortation once again.

Not unlike other families, mine still, after all that time, did not understand the intensity of the pain my mother suffered from her depression. What I would ask for myself later, I could not find in myself then; and so, when it happened to me, I stifled the urge to confess. Her medication, mainly Thorazine, was plainly ill-suited for her need to create the poetry that kept her with one foot on the ground. She hated the Thorazine and made many attempts to find another drug.

Once off the drug, she could see more definitively what it had cost her: she had been too "wooly" to do anything except vegetate. At that time, however, there really wasn't too much else to offer. Thorazine was the miracle drug of the decade. It was not until the last year of her life that she threw out her many jugs of pills and went cold turkey, with vodka smoothing the transition. From then on, she was able to work with a clearer head, but her alcohol intake began to suck her down into an inward spiral. The doctors then tried lithium—wondering, absurdly, for the very first time if she could possibly be a manic-depressive—but it did not improve her stability as alcohol inhibits the drug's efficacy.

I relied on that story of her imprisonment at the hands of a nasty nurse, relied on that picture of her and my reaction to it, for nearly thirty-six years, until my own depression began to exceed the boundaries I had known before. At that age, I began to examine it; suddenly it didn't stand up to the wind of my scrutiny. Memory turned like a slimy fish in my hands at this idea of abuse in a mental hospital. I suspected myself of a hardened heart at the same time I suspected her of exaggeration. However, perhaps it didn't matter whether my mother really had her arms bound up into the air, because she still wove a tale worthy of Scheherazade. Perhaps the nurse had been kind rather than cruel: my mother still made me believe what she had said. Some tone she used helped me to see the scene that way, and she impressed me with the drama—a certain kind of perverted glamour—despite my claustrophobia at being trapped inside her insane world once again. With that manipulation, I was able to turn angrily on the abusive nurse as well. What a relief that was, so much better than feeling angry at my mother herself. Once again, she had used a story to win some sort of attention from me, and with this particular one she had added yet another layer to the mystique of suicide, a mystique that I had begun to believe would at some point, inevitably, touch down in my life as well.

{marriage and motherhood}

IN ADOLESCENCE, I fantasized that I would break the family chain of suicide and madness, the bad spell cast over motherhood.

One afternoon, my mother lay on her bed, with a good friend in the chair beside her. She was propped up on pillows, chain-smoking and crushing the butts into the black china ashtray at her elbow.

The conversation had moved on to Betty Friedan's *The Feminine Mystique*, a new, controversial bible for all "liberated women" of the sixties. Both my mother and her friend considered themselves to be feminists—as did I by the time I entered college. I read Simone de Beauvoir, Germaine Greer, Doris Lessing, Susan Brownmiller, and *Our Bodies, Ourselves* by the Boston Women's Health Book Collective. I attended meetings of an offshoot of the Collective, where feminists gathered weekly to discuss the changing role of women in our new society of the late sixties.

That day on my mother's bed, the discussion wheeled around onto how to escape from simply being a housewife to how to manage children and a career at the same time.

After a time, I laughed sarcastically. "There's only one way for Joy and me to be mothers."

My mother turned to me with interest.

"Not to be mothers at all," I went on flippantly. "Because we're all cursed. And until all the Sexton women die out, the curse will never end."

With my nasty comment, I had let my mother know what I thought of the job she had done. None of us could be mothers because it was inevitable that we would be *bad* mothers—just as she had been. I ignored the meaning behind my own words: we would have to *die*.

Of course my words that day were just an overblown adolescent exaggeration, but because it reflected on the sort of mother she had been, I could see quite plainly the pain on her face. I tucked my smug reaction away, where it wasn't perceptible, realizing that her look pleased me. I had reached that point in adolescence where I was strenuously rejecting my mother, at the same time I was still running toward her. I hated what I had come to see as her psychological intrusions—yet I still modeled myself after her, often without even realizing it. My old unconscious goals of being just like her remained intact at the same time I was making faces at her behind her back. My friends would giggle: we all hated our parents, our mothers in particular. I was still in therapy with Dr. Bauman, who encouraged the distance I was building between my mother and myself, no matter how superficial or tenuous.

The most obvious way to break the chain of cursed Sexton women was to be different than my parents, and the nearer I got to being out of my teens, the more I desired this. My parents had been so young when they eloped at nineteen: perhaps their immaturity made my mother's "motherhood" more difficult than it might have been. If my father's abandonment of college in their first year together created certain restrictions and financial hardship early on, I would marry the exact opposite of his example: a professional man, preferably one with a graduate degree. In my mind these dos and don'ts were to be followed point to point, the way an insecure driver traces the lines on a road map so as to arrive, on time, at a guaranteed location—that kind of control brought me a sensation of peace.

In my mid-twenties, despite all I had learned from watching my mother struggle to be my parent, despite the fact that depression had followed me just as it had followed her, I was nevertheless determined to try my hand at mothering. In the first year of my marriage, it didn't occur to me (or I wouldn't let myself think of it) that having children might be too stressful for a young woman who had never really had a functioning mother herself. The idea of the legacy was nowhere in evidence—neither understood nor felt; I was still many years away from recognizing that such a thing even existed, and so I felt secure and at peace for the first time in all my twenty-five years.

After my mother's death, after marriage and the dimming of my depression for a time when I was in my twenties, the solution to my dilemma about motherhood seemed obvious: I would get pregnant and have my children later than my parents had. Ultimately I did not adhere to this resolution, and began trying to conceive a few months after I married, choosing the fast track to parenthood because my gynecologist warned me that I had endometriosis, a condition that could hamper fertility. I didn't want to wait until it was too late.

AFTER MY MOTHER'S death, I graduated from college and left behind the safety of classes and books and instead clung to the safe companionship of Jim. In the months prior to commencement, my peers asked me what I would be doing afterwards, and it was an uncomfortable question for which I had no answer. I was anxiety ridden: the future had always been bounded by age-related expectations (high school, four years of college, the lure of graduate school), but now it was up to me to find something particular that I wanted to do, perhaps even something I had never done before. For the first three years of college, the future had been safely ahead of me, way past graduation, and therefore, like a fuzzy haze, it was easy to avoid considering it. As the end of senior year pressed near, I lived from day to day, trying not to get overwhelmed by the situation. Though I had terminated with Dr. Bauman a year earlier, I now thought about calling her to talk over my feelings of inadequacy and my sorrow at my mother's death, but decided against it: what good would discussing it do?

A degree in English and American Language and Literature cum laude was not in the least bit marketable in the mid-seventies, when most of my classmates were applying to medical or business or law schools for postgraduate degrees. I, however, had chosen to major in a field that was safe—though its requirements were rigorous—but still familiar territory because I was wondering if I could write poetry for a living. Of course, during high school, I considered myself lucky to have so much attention paid to me by my mother and Maxine Kumin—who would also go on to win a Pulitzer Prize for her collections of verse—and I didn't want to squander all the time they spent helping me to create a Springback binder thick with poems.

Concentrating in English felt safe, and my decision to persevere with it had seemed a sensible course. I had been able to take creative writing workshops, and was encouraged by my instructors. I wanted to be as risk-free as possible, and writing seemed an act of joy and fulfillment. It was even, possibly, lucrative enough to sustain me: I had only to look at my mother's example to know how successful such a career might be. By the time of her death, she had been making a living at it for many years, pulling in about $50,000 a year, which was a reasonable sum back in 1974, especially in the world of poetry.

I was unspeakably thrilled that the question of "what comes next" was answered when, one day in the spring, Houghton Mifflin asked me to edit the volume of my mother's correspondence. Jim, especially, was happy and relieved: the problem of a job for me had been resolved. He had been worrying, silently, that I would not be able to find work. He was perhaps even more concerned that I would not be able to throw off the effects of my mother's death, which appeared to persist in the form of a depression that intermittently roared up again. Warm and nurturing in a time of great difficulty, he was a friend as well as a lover.

It was a gift, this offer made by the publisher. I don't know what I might have done without it. Ever since I was a young child, looking into the future had felt forbidden. It had been enough to hold my breath every day, hoping that my mother would not have another breakdown. There is an actual psychiatric term for being unable to see beyond a day at a time as you are maturing; in medical circles it is known as a "foreshortened" or "shortchanged" future. Later in life, my hope for my mother and me as mothers would shift: sometimes I just wanted her to live to be old—a grandmother to my children.

AT TWENTY-FIVE, JIM and I married. We took our vows in Harvard's Memorial Church, just as he was about to begin his final year at Harvard Medical School. As I went up the aisle on my father's arm, joy overtook me. The ring slid easily onto my finger and Jim literally lifted me off my feet when he kissed me in front of the congregation. Despite the dismal rainy day, our reception for one hundred was a true celebration under the yellow and white striped tent in our backyard, with music we had recorded and food we chose. Even the untraditional chocolate wedding cake was a success. My father said that such a soggy day bore the signs of fertility, and everyone laughed. I was more supremely happy than I had ever been at any time in my life.

After I threw my bouquet, we took off in our chariot, a battered Volkswagen Rabbit; I felt a thrill of excitement for the life I was about to embark upon, partnered with a kind and ambitious man. I was nearly ready, I thought, to start a family in the not too distant future. And, most importantly, I believed I was not mentally ill, as my mother had been at the time of her marriage, and that I would never be so. Depression seemed in the distant past, even though it had been acute only two or three years before. As time passed, Jim and I became more and more tightly bonded; I thought his support could forever heal my feelings over my mother's loss.

Over the ensuing four years, working as a med student in the rapidly changing environment of medical practice in the eighties, Jim came to a new conclusion: he knew, with certainty, that he didn't want to practice medicine. He declined to take an internship and his parents were furious with this "fickle" switch in career; but right after his graduation, he was accepted in the Harvard Business School class of 1982, intent on a career in medically related business. I began work on my first novel, *Rituals*, which would eventually be published by Doubleday. It was autobiographical fiction that portrayed a college senior who initially sinks under, but then eventually conquers, the emotional challenges she faces when her mother dies suddenly. I had found a niche: confessional fiction instead of confessional poetry. For this book, I received a tiny advance and began to work with a skilled editor, finding fulfillment and a preoccupation with work.

Married, I took days one hour at a time, without looking very far ahead in planning for my future. I had a faithful husband; I had the beginnings of a successful career, albeit as a novelist rather than as a poet. I couldn't have imagined that there would come a day when all these plans would spin off into oblivion. I couldn't imagine a day when the depressions of my former years might return.

AT THE TIME of my marriage, I discovered a woman whom I would begin to call "my other mother," just as she called me "her third daughter." Rachael was stable and loving, fifty-some-odd years when we first met—close in age to what my own mother would have been had she not committed suicide. Rachael's loyalty to her family was unstinting: two daughters, six grandchildren, a mother and father held close throughout the years, and an extended family of in-laws. It was an intense family typical of religious Jews who liked to commune together—and she offered Jim and me the chance to join it.

If my own mother had been unable to grant me an adult friendship, Rachael's unconditional love was truly a sustaining force in my young married life. What I could not get in support from Jim's increasingly critical mother (who took me to task for everything from my hairstyle to the furniture arrangement in my home), I would always find in Rachael. As I began to seek balance in my new role as a wife, I gradually began to lean on Rachael for all the love I craved from an older woman, and she enabled me to repel the allure of self-destruction for many years. The positive example she provided drove back the out-of-control impulses my mother had taught me—even if only for a time.

Rachael came into my life when Jim and I began to date, just after my twenty-first birthday—right after my mother had died, when I was vulnerable and looking for a substitute for what I had lost. Later, right before our wedding, I converted to Judaism, the religion in which Jim had been raised, and Rachael and I then had an unbreakable bond. She was thrilled and curious about every aspect of the conversion ceremony. She had been raised in a

Conservative Jewish family and naturally she observed all the laws of that branch of Judaism, keeping the laws of Kashrut: two sets of silverware, one set of china for meat and another for milk, no cream in your coffee at dinner after a roast. In the early years of my marriage, we grew to know each other as well as a mother and an adult daughter would: she was the one who procured the champagne and the smoked salmon for our wedding, the one who would eventually take me shopping for maternity clothes, the one who babysat for Nathaniel when I had a dentist appointment, the one who invited us to a Friday night dinner.

Though I did not keep kosher, Rachael and I traded recipes, and on the High Holy Days that we were apart, I sent her, via FedEx, two of my famous homemade challahs. Today, her handwritten recipes are scattered through my card file, and are some of the items I treasure most in the world, with her name printed at the top, her writing in purple ink. She was the one who taught me how to make matzo ball soup, pot roast, potato latkes and applesauce, rosemary chicken, cranberry chutney, and my father-in-law's favorite bittersweet chocolate cake.

Religious rituals had become increasingly important to me: having grown up with few such holidays and celebrations other than Christmas, the stability and spirituality of the Jewish observances seemed more and more beautiful. I believed, fervently, that they were the insurance that would cement and unite our family, and thus render us safe from strife or separation or madness. At the other extreme was Jim's mother, who would have died of shame before she kept kosher. She was mortified when, during a publicity shoot for *Rituals*, *People* magazine photographed me braiding the yellow egg dough for my challah. "Couldn't it just have been regular white bread," she asked irritably.

She had remarked before my conversion: "Why do you want to leave the privileged majority to become one of the persecuted minority?" and I was nonplussed. I had no answer for her hatred of the rituals upon which she herself had been raised. My father-in-law, who had grown up as an Orthodox Jew, reacted jubilantly when he learned I was to convert, and my own father at least tried to keep his dislike of my conversion in some sort of remote check, and to be supportive.

If my mother had been alive during my conversion to Judaism, I felt certain that she would have applauded my decision to find a spirituality of my own. At the very end of her life, she had discovered "God" (whom she felt might be a woman), and had written some of her most mystical and personal poetry. *The Awful Rowing toward God* was completed just before her death. Reading it, years later, I understood without reservation exactly what she had meant by "awful rowing." This was one aspect of her legacy that I had been able to embrace.

A FEW MONTHS after Jim and I were married, we eagerly began trying to get pregnant—but motherhood eluded me, as if God or fate thought it were a good joke that a woman like me, one without a mother herself to guide the way, could dare to try and be a mother. I miscarried three times, and with each loss, Jim and I grew more devastated. A deep furrow creased the smooth skin around his mouth.

Each of the babies I lost brought death and depression back into my life, each time bloody and terrifying as I crouched over the toilet, supremely alone because the hemorrhages often occurred when Jim was out of the apartment. Thinking desperately of alternatives, we devised the idea of using another woman's womb, fertilized with our egg and sperm. But our specialists informed us, sadly, that there was no such procedure. We were about ten years away from being able to participate in the new solutions in fertility and conception: neither IVF nor GIFT, nor surrogacy options, existed at that time.

These miscarriages were accompanied by a silent and lonely grief. There were no funerals, no headstones, no periods of public mourning. No sympathy cards, no flowers to mark the passing of those lives that had already felt very real to us. My mother-in-law told me to think of the miscarriages as if I had just lost my appendix; my father-in-law told me that I'd have a lot of fun trying to conceive again; Nana, once again wrapped in silence, didn't mention what had happened to me, even though she had miscarried herself before my father's birth. Interestingly enough, it was my father whose empathy carried me through this time: he called frequently and seemed strong enough to bear the brunt of my grief. Despite Rachael's support, I once again wished for the solace my own mother might have provided.

When I couldn't retain my pregnancies, we became convinced that we were unable to be parents, unless we adopted. As the final specialist put it, "I don't give odds—but if I were willing, in this case I'd say it's about a million to one that you will ever bear a pregnancy to term."

In addition to registering with several adoption agencies, we also interviewed attorneys who specialized in private placements. The odds of finding a healthy, newborn, baby with a good prenatal history were astronomically low, and at one point we even considered an illegal "black market" adoption. After rejecting this as too risky, we crossed our fingers and began to wait, hoping fervently that eventually an infant would become available and that we would meet the agencies', and the prospective mother's, exacting standards.

In June of 1982, just as Jim finished at business school, we moved to Manhattan so that he could start a job in a prestigious investment banking firm. Away from my family and friends, I grew sad, feeling empty and alone, with Rachael as my only mainstay. The second bedroom, which had been meant to be a nursery, was turned into my writing room. We gave up penciling in the chart that mapped ovulation, gave up taking my basal temperature every morning before coffee, gave up the mild fertility drugs I had used for every other pregnancy. In those days there were neither kits to tell you when and if you had ovulated, nor sticks to hold under the stream of your urine to tell you if you had at last succeeded in conceiving.

And then, suddenly, I was pregnant once again. This fourth time was entirely accidental and both Jim and I were wary and weary. We had been so devastated by the former losses that we didn't know if we could survive the wound of another one.

I followed the obstetrician's orders, and went to bed for the remainder of the entire pregnancy (eight months). Slowly, as I grew rounder and clumsier, time was freighted with the markers of each month passing: now the baby had fingers and toes that it sucked; now it turned freely in its warm house and kicked me hard while I was trying to sleep. Frightened and living with the constant reminders of what had gone before, I hated going to the bathroom, holding my breath as I wiped myself, afraid I would see the telltale signs of blood on the toilet paper.

I tried to work from bed, already in the midst of my second novel, typing with the computer's keyboard balanced on a tray. During this time of enforced rest and intense worry, I also tried to tie my days down to something firm and concrete; I constructed an elaborate map—my own personal Doctor Spock version—of a child's well-being, and I was determined to follow it. I'd read all the popular books, like those written by Berry Brazelton and Penelope Leach. I studied the material put out by the somewhat radical La Leche League, so that I would know what to do when breastfeeding. I interviewed a pediatrician in my new city to make sure he was a doctor who agreed with my philosophies. And, of course, I followed the development of my baby. We had an ultrasound and saw the heartbeat for the second time.

MY FIRST SON seemed resolutely clung to our mother-son umbilical bond. It took thirty-six hours of Lamaze-directed labor with no pain relief, and then three hours of agonizing pushing, before this wizened baby made his appearance. Jim was transformed from boy to man as he sat with the small blue-blanketed package, so tiny that it fit along the length of his arm from elbow to wrist. I was finally an ecstatic mother.

When we joyously returned home from the hospital, I nevertheless grew frightened. I had once cared for an infant, but only for a few hours of babysitting at a time. Now I had a baby of my own and I was determined to succeed in being the kind of mother my own hadn't managed to be. I had read that if your mother had suffered a postpartum depression, your odds were far greater of having the same experience—but I was resolved not to grow depressed. I was determined, in this regard, not to be like her in any way. Yet, despite my compulsion to hold this baby and love him till he couldn't be loved anymore, I slumped into being afraid to be alone with him.

I was overwhelmed by the constant breast feeding every two hours, more frequent than the four-hour schedule formula would have provided me, as formula lasts twice as long in the infant's stomach. Breast feeding wasn't the easy, natural experience I had thought it would be: it was hard making sure he had had enough at each individual feeding, and then trying to pump some extra milk that could be refrigerated so that I might have a few hours out of the house once I dared to leave him with a babysitter. I had four breast infections before I finally gave it up and switched to formula. There were many days when, exhausted, I put him to bed earlier than his already early bedtime. Our pediatrician diagnosed "colic" when Nathaniel's crankiness persisted all through his early months and exhausted me by six o'clock in the evening. The routine was grueling: he wouldn't stop crying, even though he had been fed and changed and rocked. Despite my initial delight; a postpartum depression did overwhelm me, even though I had dismissed the possibility of such a problem when I was so wildly happy to be pregnant at last. I had thought our "miracle baby" would protect me.

"What a fool," the voice observed darkly. "Your mother had this sort of depression, why wouldn't you?"

On the nights Nathaniel wouldn't cease wailing, I took my father's advice: I would lock myself in the bathroom with a glass of wine, turn on the shower, and wait twenty minutes. Usually when I emerged, red-faced and hot and steamy, his shrill and enraged scream would have stopped. But the sinking feeling inside me did not. I found myself challenged by my long-awaited motherhood, adrift without my own mother to show me the way—even if this was a fantasy she undoubtedly wouldn't have been able to fulfill.

Rachael accepted me with all my fears and limitations, and helped, over time, to make me feel like a good wife and mother. The anxiety over being a mother was entrenched but I just kept pushing it back. Jim and I, fearing that we would have similar difficulties in conceiving and carrying another pregnancy to term, began working on having our second child shortly after Nathaniel's first birthday. I did not allow myself to wonder how much bed rest I would need this time around, as at this point a major part of my life was devoted to chasing Nathaniel through the apartment, or taking him to the playground for dates with other toddlers his own age. When he was in the middle of the year that led to the "terrible twos," I got pregnant again. For this, my fifth pregnancy, the doctor ruled that I was safe to lead a normal life, on two feet, with no special drugs or bed rest. With my ambivalence over motherhood somewhat abated, I danced my way through the pregnancy of Gabe while awaiting the surprises he would bring to our family of three. Unlike my previous labor, Gabe's delivery was smooth and uncomplicated. He was only twenty months behind his stubborn, strong-minded, older brother, and at nine-and-a-half pounds, he was huge.

He arrived on October fourth of 1984, the tenth anniversary of my mother's death. I had been two weeks overdue with this second pregnancy, and when he was born at last, I reflected with Jim that I had somehow held on to Gabe with my body and mind and refused to let my labor—that hormone-controlled event—start until that particular day dawned. Where one life had been extinguished, another life now began.

Once again, Rachael and her husband were by our sides with laughter and celebration. She adored both of my children with all her heart, never finding fault with them the way my demanding in-laws did; consequently, Nathaniel and Gabe were equally fond of her, especially in their early years, when their grandparents seemed incapable of playing with them, or being a part of their lives, except for coming to visit and then doing nothing but harp on the way Jim and I were handling our parenthood.

As time passed, Jim's mother became more and more virulently opposed to the Jewish rituals and education we chose to observe, especially those that involved our children. Nothing we did with Gabe and Nathaniel fit with her concept of parenting. Why didn't we have a full-time infant nurse, and then a British nanny? Why didn't Nathaniel, at two years old, know how to shake hands and greet an adult? Shaken by her continuing criticism, I relied increasingly on Rachael during this time of uncertainty about my mothering skills and instincts. She coached me about how to put my children on a variety of schedules according to their ages: when they should nap, be fed, be outdoors in the sandbox. When Nathaniel was born, she'd cooked up a beautiful and abundant spread and set the table with silver and linen for his bris, to which we had invited a small group of family and friends. Jim's mother refused to attend, but turned up late in the day, drunk from the hours she had spent waiting in a bar for our celebration to end.

By the time of Gabe's birth, I had recovered the buoyancy I had felt on marrying and on seeing my children's faces for the first time. I daydreamed about having another baby—or two. Despite my previous postpartum depression, no such mood overtook me again. It seemed I had broken the spell of my mother's grip at last.

BUT AS NATHANIEL grew into the throes of his second year as a toddler, full of bright-eyed questions, my fears reasserted themselves. He was inquisitive, intelligent, and easily frustrated when he didn't get his way, or discovered something he couldn't quite yet manage. Gabe was more like a lazy trout, floating downstream, mellowed out in life's current. I loved both my children and their merry faces, but I didn't know quite what to do with them for all those hours of the day. As they grew older and more demanding, my heart began to squeeze with uncertainty every time either of them cried. I felt less effective as a mother of toddlers than of infants. In a perfect contradiction, I loved the smell of their fair and curly hair, the soft baby odor that was always there whenever I drew breath, and at the same time I felt angry when one refused his afternoon nap and thus kept me from my own. Still, I didn't break down and try to commit suicide, or even go into the hospital for a rest, but it was at this time that I began to alternate, with a deep ambivalence, between the claustrophobia at being shut in with them, and the continuing passion over being a mother at last.

As I watched the children grow past every milestone—turning over, sitting up, crawling, walking, talking—all of them felt like astounding events. I called Nathaniel my "miracle boy," simply because he had come despite the dire warnings, foiling the predictions of the medical world. Gabe smiled his way month to month of his first year, a genuinely "easy" baby. A question lingered at the back of my mind, however. Could I possibly raise both of these children unscathed through the many years of childhood?

I wanted to go back to work, for just a few hours a day, partly because I was eager to start my new novel, but also as a way of taking a break from Nathaniel's unceasing two-year-old's demands, and from the inevitable stress of a new baby, no matter how adorable. Motherhood became infinitely more difficult once I went back to work for even a few hours a day. By the time Gabe was eighteen months old, Nathaniel had begun to push him over from behind, pull his hair, and tear up his crayoned pictures, even while he demonstrated his love by feeding his younger brother Cheerios one by one, helping him master sticky masses of Play-Doh, and showing him how to scoop leaves with their small matching rakes into big piles and then jump in. He was the consummate older brother. The days scooted by, each faster than the last, each taxing in one way or another. Subtly, I was developing brittle feelings of inadequacy that reminded me of my mother, and I had to fight hard to stay my temper, my sometimes vicious voice, and, worst of all, my hand. I gave up the dream of having more children.

We moved out of our small Manhattan apartment to a wealthy suburb for the express reason of hiring a nanny who would help with the childcare and the housework and enable me to write part of each day. When our eighteen-year-old blond Mormon from Salt Lake City arrived, she fulfilled nearly all our expectations: my fears lessened and the boys seemed to settle down somewhat. I was quite confident that I could now balance being a mother and a writer simultaneously.

WHAT I COULDN'T know then was that for me, the race to motherhood was just beginning. I didn't have the first idea about how to raise a child: when to say yes or no, whether to spank or just scold, how to keep my cool in the grocery store when the "I want" scream began to escalate in the checkout line, how not to lose my temper one hundred times a day when I had a toddler who was exhibiting both a sunny nature and an impatient one. I discovered I didn't have that most important thing of all: a good role model. I didn't know what being a good mother required. I didn't feel with my heart or memory or instincts the contours and edges of a good mother's shape and bones. I had only a cloudy intellectualized image based on what I had seen in other peoples' homes as I was growing up.

To my shock, many of the dos and don'ts to which I had pledged to adhere simply didn't seem to work when it came down to the day-to-day grind of caring for small, ever-changing children. Despite my best intentions, I was inconsistent. Sometimes I loved too much and made poor decisions, or sometimes I bent the rules and weakened important boundaries. Sometimes I forgot basic safety, like leaving the antihistamine in the over-the-sink cabinet where five-year-old Nathaniel found it and managed to defeat its childproof cap. My mother had handed me a recipe for motherhood in which the butter and sugar and flour didn't add up to a cake batter that would rise. Perhaps her mother had done the same thing.

As time passed, this legacy of poor mothering skills set in motion further crises that tapped into the mire of depression my mother had left me. As Jim began traveling for his job, leaving the majority of the parenting to me, I had to go it solo. I spent a lot of time feeling overwhelmed and alone, especially when Jim was absent for three or four days a week; slowly, I started to feel like a single mother, and threatened him, half-heartedly, that if he didn't at least start coming home to celebrate the Jewish holidays, I would begin taking the children to church.

My feelings of isolation progressed: soon I awoke every morning at five o'clock, sweating and with my heart pounding with extreme anxiety, unable to breathe. The nameless fear made mothering increasingly difficult and the work on my third novel nearly impossible. Each morning I found I dreaded the children waking more and more. I started up with a psychoanalyst, and three times a week I went to see him, in a pattern that mirrored my mother's experience. For the first time, I lay on the couch, just as my mother had. It was during this period that I began taking my first medication for my "psychological" illnesses, the anti-anxiety drug Xanax.

Jim and I began to argue about how much he had really been away and I started keeping a calendar as a way of proving to him the truth of his absences. Our relationship began, gradually, to falter. It seemed that whenever we were together, we couldn't help but bicker and fight about the lack of time he was spending with the family. Unlike my parents, however, we never got physical during those heated episodes. Still, our separations were wearing me down.

A year later, he switched careers and employers again, into another aspect of the financial world. He didn't seem to be worried about the uncertainty of these shifts or how they would look on his résumé, and I felt I had to trust his instincts. Nevertheless, for the first time, I allowed myself to wonder how long he would stay with this new job. I hated it because it, too, required nearly full-time attention.

And yet, he still made the time to give me a great deal of help with my career, just as he had at the beginning of our relationship, when I was so preoccupied with my mother's. From one year to the next, regardless of the rigorous demands of his own career, he made the time to edit my books, helping to "clean them up" before I sent them on to my agent; he held my hand through publication parties and readings, and made sure fans didn't make mincemeat of me after public events; he oversaw negotiations for my book contracts; he made some of the deals for my mother's posthumous publications; and he helped us maneuver through the tricky waters of privacy as my mother's biographer wrote her very revelatory and controversial book. He had taken us through so many legal situations that I had come to see him as our family's psychological "consigliere," even though he had no formal training in the law. He was able to draft a contract on a moment's notice, and knew how to agitate and negotiate well enough that he almost always got what he wanted. Jim was stalwart, a guardian, and I counted on him in all these ways and more. I always would.

As Jim moved further into the depths of his career, I grew more and more desperate, less able to handle Nathaniel's demands. Nearly all my psychiatric sessions centered on my perceived problems as a mother who was failing so abysmally at ministering to my "difficult" child. My therapist berated me for my lack of nurturing instincts: "*Nathaniel* is not a difficult child!" he bellowed at me during one tearful session, after I confessed to spanking Nathaniel following the discovery that he had torn every page from all the books in his room, including the rows of illustrated classics we had so lovingly collected for him and Gabe. "*You* are a difficult mother!" he exclaimed angrily. I believed every word he said, swamped in self-loathing. It did not occur to me that his badgering me was inappropriate—it just seemed like some sort of "tough love."

I wanted to lie down and sleep all day. But as the mother of a toddler and an infant, I couldn't choose sleep. I was beginning a slide down into the rabbit hole inside my mind, and for some reason I couldn't understand, I wasn't able to hang on in the way I had at the beginning. But I didn't tell my friends, not even Rachael, of my darkening mood. I believed that as long as I was a mother, I was obligated to stay stable.

A metaphor occurred to me that illustrated how I really felt: I was a soldier in a war zone, and I had to stay awake at my post.

The enemy, however, was no person. Instead it was depression, and, like a seductress, it stole up on me—just as sleep inevitably would, quietly pulling down the gray shades of my eyelids and making them as heavy as if they were weighted with the wet dirt of the grave. Increasingly, my world went into slow-motion and I spun out of myself, out of my head and heart, my face averted so no one would know the shame of what was happening to me and how I was giving in. I was trying so hard—but, little by little, I was starting to fail.

{california}

IN 1989, JUST before our tenth anniversary, Jim's desire to travel less took us to California, despite my intense fears of leaving family and friends on the East Coast. A lucrative position had become available the year before. For that first year, he traveled back and forth, loving this new job that used both his medical and business acumen, but felt exhausted from a schedule that dumped him home late Friday night and then required him to fly back on Monday morning. Our days together had shrunk to two and a half each week. And so there was a powerful lure to moving near the company—once we relocated, the new job would not require him to travel at all.

Still, I didn't want to leave everyone and everything we knew in a move clear across the country. I did not want to go to a place where tennis courts and luxury convertibles were de rigueur, to a place where my best friends from college did not live, a place where Rachael was not snugged up in her apartment.

And, almost nearly as important, having written trial scripts for several years for the "soaps," I had at last received an offer to take over as head writer on *The Guiding Light*, with a salary of close to one million dollars. Unfortunately, the opportunity was contingent upon my remaining in New York: the city with its bright and sleek towers was the optimal place to be for any kind of an author. But Jim, intent on beginning his new position, and I, wanting to concentrate on my fiction, pushed aside both the offer and my concerns about leaving the literary mecca of Manhattan.

WE SETTLED THE family in a place that was an easy commute for Jim, a suburb that was the wealthiest in the country, a spot that exceeded expensive enclaves like Hollywood, with its glamorous movie stars, or Palm Beach, with its thousands of millionaire retirees. Computer geeks and techno nerds dominated this area in Northern California, often growing rich overnight when their small start-up companies (which generally paid staff in part by giving them stock options) went public. People whose wealth was created in such a way littered the landscape there in the 1990s, and as more and more money was generated from those stock options and the burgeoning "tech" market, the surrounding residential areas grew astronomically more expensive.

It became apparent to us as soon as we left New York that the past few years of our marriage had been dominated by Jim's work. With his new job allowing family dinners for the four of us every night of the week, and real vacations, we both felt our new standard of living would be a fresh test of the marriage.

When I moved to California, I talked to Rachael less because the time difference always interfered. We did not grow apart, however, we just made do in other ways. Calling her once a month, I discovered we could just pick up where we had left off. Trying to deal with humor about the very intense migraines from which we both suffered, she sent me a small sculpture of a woman reclining in pain, holding her head with her hands. She had a twin on her bureau, and I put mine on my dresser, too. Often I picked it up, rubbing it like a potent amulet, and looking at the inscription she had written on the bottom: "Oh! Our aching heads!"

The gamble of the move succeeded. Jim was, indeed, home every night for suppers and homework and bedtimes, and all the support made me realize just how difficult it had been to feel like a single parent. Nathaniel had begun first grade, Gabe kindergarten. For the first time, Jim was now my partner in discipline, singing lullabies, buying Christmas and birthday presents, and initiating a rough and tumble across the front lawn on weekends. Nearly every night, as the sun began to lower itself, he taught the boys how to throw a baseball. I loved the sound of the satisfying pock of the ball as it smacked into the glove.

BECAUSE THE RELOCATION had worked out so beautifully, my depression and anxiety abated. This was the happiest time of my life, filled with family and intimacy and celebration. I luxuriated in the warmth of the California sun and the love of my children and husband. I showered my family with home-cooked meals that quickly became favorites requested again and again. I stopped needing recipes and began to rely on what my mother had liked to call "mother wit."

In addition to running a household and writing a new book—another novel, *Private Acts*—there were still occasional bouts of depression, though usually not lasting longer than a few days. Over the ensuing five years, I was eager and able to take on all sorts of "extracurricular work," both in my children's classrooms where I worked as a volunteer tutor several times a week, and on the boards of several charities.

Twice a month, with five other women from my temple, I wrapped myself in a mammoth white apron at a soup kitchen in the basement of a Lutheran church: first we assembled and then we cooked—huge boxes of spaghetti, industrial-sized cans of beans, enormous vats of macaroni and cheese. This nurturing of strangers was very different from the tension-filled dinner tables of my childhood, where my father rapped Joy on the head if she didn't eat fast enough and where my mother choked on every morsel of meat she put into her mouth. I also managed a "Meals on Wheels" program for AIDS patients through our synagogue, taking meals to the homebound, and frequently invited the boys' friends to impromptu suppers when their own parents were too caught up in their careers to return home in time for dinner. I had become the aproned mother, but one who baked her batches under control.

My expanding world brought me even more happiness, a surge of quiet joy. Inevitably, I reveled in the knowledge that I was at last moving beyond one of the examples my mother had set: she had never been well enough for, or perhaps interested enough, in volunteer work. Family dinners were closed affairs, when no one was ever invited on the spur of the moment to the table. Now, the new people I met often did not know of my mother, or of the fact that I was her daughter. I cloaked myself in satisfying secrecy and struck out on my own, as I immersed myself in guiding both my children and my writing. I felt I had my relationship with my mother in hand at last, and the legacy was pushed to the background. And, for a while, it stayed there, untouched.

IN 1994, WITH the publication of my first memoir, *Searching for Mercy Street*, I hoped my family would accept the insights I offered about our early lives and about my mother. I dreamed that perhaps this book would bring my father and Joy and me closer, just as my work at being a better mother than my own was bringing me closer to my boys. This was a wish not to be fulfilled.

The time for Joy to read the galleys of the book arrived. After a few days, she called to tell me how she felt that she had made "a narrow escape." Those words stayed with me, like certain phrases you cannot help but remember from the Bible or Shakespeare. "There are so many places you fell through the ice, where I just stepped right around," she said, as if none of the book had touched her in any way: it felt to me like she was wearing her white cotton gloves to church, as we had as little girls. "I didn't know how to help you." Did her voice have a tinge of smugness—or was I only imagining it, being too sensitive. Was my need so great that nothing would have been enough? I kept trying to control my emotions, which were running high and near the surface as we talked.

"It could have been me," she went on. "I'm so sorry for you. Sometimes I think we come from different families."

Her exile to Nana's house, from a newborn to a toddler, had its upside, for, as we both conceded, Nana's was definitely the better place to be.

And so, it hadn't been Joy who was left to withstand the assault of my mother's emotional and physical intimacies and intrusions, from my birth to my departure for college. Yes, I decided, Joy was right: in so many ways we had come from two different families.

Suddenly I was very glad that we were talking on the phone, so she couldn't see my eyes in the fading light. My sensibilities did not extend to comprehend how anyone could watch someone else's extreme difficulties with equanimity and then say, "It could have been me," with gratitude in her voice. To say that, in such a painful and complex situation, to someone as close as your sister, after everything we had gone through together. To say, "I'm so sorry *for you*."

But really, what did I want from her so desperately? Perhaps it was simply that I did not want to be pitied, I wanted to be understood. From the sister of my youth, I wanted the comfort of: "This must be terrible for you—I love you so much, Linda—what can I do?"

All the smaller steps away from each other, all the little difficulties we had been having for a decade or two, were just warm-ups for the giant leap we would shortly make, creating a terrible silence that would extend between us for the next thirteen years. It marked our first major separation, in a way that would never be erased. We might have been able to work it out, we might have been able to forgive each other, if one of us had overcome the silence and challenged it with truth. We might have found peace with each other if we had been brave enough to discuss and perhaps even to argue, to confront all the other breaches, to pull apart our own failings and understand what had gone so terribly wrong. If only we had been able to look at all our mother had left and how we felt about it. But we didn't. Or, perhaps, we couldn't.

Even though I was forty at this point, and the mother of teen-agers, I still needed Joy because Joy held many of the keys to my past. As did my father. Living so far from my family now, I was jealous of the time the two of them spent together and that jealousy made worse the estrangement between us. Joy seemed to have the undivided attention of my father, who was now my only parent.

Yet, later in the year, she came to California to visit me. Together we had a wonderful time picking out photos for *Searching for Mercy Street*, remembering times spent as little girls. Our work, hand in hand with all the snapshots of our childhood, rescued them from a final fading in the attic. Unlike those years when I was working on *Anne Sexton: A Self-Portrait in Letters*, when she had withdrawn from helping out by refusing to contribute her ideas and thoughts about the photographic record of the book, she now eagerly participated and generously orchestrated this photo gallery.

In those afternoons of rooting through the cardboard boxes full of our mother's mementos, we remembered all our secret childhood intimacies: Christmas's doll house and Easter's eggs, or in the bathtub naked, or running through the Slip 'n Slide; on a summer camp pony, at the beach with bucket and shovel, on Poppy's lap one per knee, or with my mother, taffeta-stiff skirts, on the way to a wedding. Always smiling shyly for the camera, the comfort at being together shining out as a beacon right over the absolutely inevitable red-eye.

However, after she left, I began to have little downward slips in my mood, and my internist prescribed Prozac—which also promised to treat my migraine headaches—but only if I sought out a psychiatrist who would monitor the drug's influence on me. New articles were just beginning to be published in the medical journals that linked Prozac and other SSRIs to sudden suicides, though only in a very few cases. This idea was pushed aside, into the background of all the extremely positive praise the drug was rapidly garnering.

And so I looked for and found a therapist, for "talk therapy" and for supervision over my adjustment to the Prozac. Dr. Benjamin Berns was a gentle, wise, nurturing soul. He was short, bald, and incredibly energetic for a man in his early seventies. He helped me to stay on the happy and balanced path that my life had now taken, and supported me through some more intense plunges into my past. For once, I felt strong enough to challenge my past, even those memories that were painful, and at this time I began to reconcile myself to the idea that I might be intermittently in therapy for the rest of my life. Being in treatment was an education of the intellect and the soul that always proved productive for me, even when I was not in the midst of a crisis.

The Prozac did improve my mood initially. It was, I told friends, like driving with the parking brake off, for the first time in my life.

IT WAS AFTERNOON, late March of 1995, and Nathaniel, just twelve years old, had been crying for over an hour. I was starting to feel frightened. The scene reminded me of all the times during my own childhood when I had tried to comfort my mother and could not.

The sorrow rolled out of him in waves, and I blinked back the tears that came in reflex. In this way was my motherhood declared: I would be strong for him; I would not let my past get in the way of his present. We had grown very close as he moved into adolescence: an empathetic child, he often sensed my moods in ways beyond his years.

He kept crying, and I began to wonder if he needed to go to the pediatrician for a sedative. On top of Nathaniel's distress, I didn't want the usually sunny Gabe to become anxious or frightened by his brother's dark upset, and so I had shut the door to the room.

"I just feel so bad inside, Mommy," Nathaniel said. "All my teachers hate me."

"Why would they hate you?" I smoothed his hair back from his forehead and when I kissed him there was the taste of sweat on his skin.

"I'm a big disappointment." That year, for seventh grade, we had switched Nathaniel from a public to a private school with high standards and a low student-to-teacher ratio. The private middle school forbade parent participation in the classroom or at home, and maturing students were expected to do their work solo. The time had arrived for him to begin handling his school performance on his own. Attempting to be a good mother, I had backed off.

But this particular afternoon at dismissal time, his teacher took me aside and explained that he had fifteen math homework assignments outstanding and fourteen more in English. "He hasn't turned in anything for the past two weeks," she said, when I reacted with surprise and dismay. "Didn't you know he was falling behind?"

"You told us in September that seventh grade was supposed to be their first independent year. Let them fail and take the consequences. No monitoring of homework or binders."

"That's for the average seventh grader. Nathaniel's very bright but he's drowning."

Surely somewhere I must have failed as a mother, to have a son whose difficulties had occurred so rapidly without my intuiting it.

"Every morning I wake up and wish I weren't here," he said tearfully. "Wish I didn't have to go back to school ever again."

I tensed.

To me, the phrase "wish I weren't here" meant more than it might to another mother: to me, it could never be an empty or idle threat, even though Nathaniel was a markedly dramatic child, who might only be using the theatrical sound of the phrase to communicate his distress. I was about to chastise him for this drama when another thought occurred.

"Linda," said the bitter voice inside. "Why don't you listen to what he is saying? Why do you think of yourself first?"

Suddenly I knew I shouldn't be on the wrong end of this situation—it wasn't me crying, it was my son. I held him even tighter. Though I didn't want to ask him a lot of intimate questions, I knew from experience what could happen, however unlikely, if I didn't. I clutched him to me and rocked him as if I could still protect him with my body.

I had to be a good enough mother to see him through this crisis, despite the fact that the worst of it might never come to pass. A few days later, I called a friend who was a doctor and got a recommendation for someone who specialized in adolescents and their troubles.

A week later, Nathaniel was sitting in that office. Jim and Gabe and I came in for subsequent sessions to help draw a full and detailed family picture. I began to keep a vigil about attention deficit disorder, such a common difficulty in teens, and also about depression in adolescents, hoping to educate myself, worrying about both of my children.

I was as obsessive about reading material as I had been about watching those grisly films on mental illness back when I was an adolescent. I was shocked to learn that suicide is one of the leading causes of death among teenagers. My innate fears about the legacy had a basis in scientific truth. At his school, two students had made a suicide pact, only thwarted at the last minute by accident. The newspapers said that young adults commonly turn depression into anger, masking their true troubled feelings, and then they lash out to relieve the pressure. I began to worry even more.

As I had done when I was trying to get pregnant, I went to the library and focused on the newest studies, especially those done on twins who were raised apart. The biological concordance between bipolar patients (or those with other affective disorders) and parents (or siblings) was eighty percent. This suggested that several different mental diseases were highly heritable, and that suicide, too, could run through families, insinuating itself into the fabric of shared lives like a pulled thread. My reading only emphasized what I feared, even if that fear might eventually be resolved into something less dark, or even totally untrue.

I had so many questions. An article in a local newspaper indicated just how imperative it was to ask difficult questions that no one wants to face in oneself, but especially in our children.

"Do you feel depressed?" I imagined asking him that day when I lay holding him on the bed.

"Anxious?"

"Are you having trouble sleeping?"

"Would you ever try to hurt yourself?"

"How?"

But I didn't ask. I stayed silent and kept my worrying to myself.

The doctor pleased us by being very cautious about labeling Nathaniel's problems prematurely or prescribing medication too freely or quickly. But it was obviously time for therapy.

Driving back and forth to his sessions each week, we had the opportunity to talk about serious personal subjects, and this relieved me. My worry about my son, calmed for a time with the new therapeutic protocol, percolated just below the surface of my mind. I stood guard against it.

I wondered and worried about Gabe, as well. He had earned the name "Joy Boy" from his school teachers and appeared to be the happy-go-lucky one in his relationship with his darker, more easily injured, older brother—but who could really tell? He and Nathaniel were tightly bound to each other, best friends who refused to be shaken by such problems.

WHEN MY MOTHER had her first nervous breakdown and made that initial suicide attempt, she was labeled an "hysteric." This old-fashioned term stuck with her over the years as her psychiatrists focused, one by one, on the depressive side of her personality. Today, she might well have been given a diagnosis of some form of bipolar illness, and been treated with the wide variety of mood stabilizers and antidepressants now available. I often thought, bitterly, that had she been born twenty years later, she might still be alive today. Her premature death was not surprising: I now discovered that twenty-five percent of all untreated manic depressives succeed at taking their own lives.

A year after my concerns over Nathaniel began, the migraines I had suffered since I was a teenager began to take a sharp turn for the worse; it seemed nearly every day that I had a headache, and, in addition, every month, one of the "monster" headaches so terrifying in their ferocity: I would vomit repeatedly and need to hide in the dark of my bedroom, for one or two or even five days. The pain was increasing as the months passed, and I began to supplement my Fiorinal—a barbiturate—with Tylenol #3—codeine. At first I resisted so much strong medication, remembering my mother's addiction to various pills. But eventually, worn down by the pain, I relinquished my objections.

A few years later, having decided that perhaps I didn't have to suffer any longer, I sought out the help of a new physician, Norman Greid, who was double boarded in both psychiatry and neurology. Slowly, he began treating my affective illness as well as the "monster" headaches. We moved from discussions of my migraines to explorations of my moods. Very short, full-bearded, and mustached, he dressed nattily, often sporting leather-plaited suspenders over his starched shirts, his small feet caressed by shoes of Italian leather. Ultimately, Norman did not cure me of my headaches or my bipolar disorder, but over the course of the two years I saw him, he lightened my pocketbook by tens of thousands of dollars. Nevertheless he did provide me with a very valuable piece of information.

Instead of my former diagnosis of dysthmia, Norman entered Bipolar II on my chart, a document that all too quickly became as thick as a dictionary. I began a "cocktail" of new, different, more heavy-duty psychiatric drugs. All of them were calculated to keep my moods running smoothly; the list of medications had expanded quickly and I officially became what I thought of as a "drug baby."

When Greid gave me my new diagnosis, I was horrified, and yet relieved. At last I knew that the turmoil of terrifying thoughts I had begun to experience with a new frequency was a disease with a name and medications designed to ameliorate it. In a different decade, I probably would have been diagnosed solely with depression, with nothing but "talk therapy" prescribed, as had my mother.

Not understanding much about bipolar disorder in either forms I or II, I delved into a thick tome, newly published and hailed by the medical establishment to be the current bible on bipolar disorder. I read it, relieved when I learned that Bipolar II is a second division of the disorder, a milder version that is characterized by similar distinct conditions. This was the way I began to discover what was actually wrong with me, after long years of diagnoses of simple unipolar depression.

Greid confirmed what I was learning first-hand: that there were rapid cycles between moods—prolonged depression on the one end and occasional nervous agitation on the other, symptoms that could last only a day or so, or months. I was discovering that only once in a while did mania occur, and when it did it was painfully agitated, rather than euphoric. Aspects of my personality that I had simply accepted, such as my speech and thought—either rapid-fire or, on the other hand, molasses-slow—were also part of the disorder. Bipolar II differs from Bipolar I in its total lack of psychosis, and the depressed end of the mood swing can be even more severe than the one experienced in traditional "manic depression." And then, worst of all for me, was one of the most important aspects of the disease: a family history of the same symptoms.

In the late nineties, I began to experience much of this for the first time—quick swings from despondence to a sudden agitation, marked by pacing or banging my head against the wall. In desperation, I hid this even from Jim, worried he might react with extreme alarm. When I admitted it to Greid, he prescribed a course of Risperdal (Risperidone) that I could take ad lib when I needed it, and this new antipsychotic calmed me down so that I could go to bed and sleep off the moods, something like passing out when drunk. He explained to me that my drinking, sometimes out of control, might well be an attempt to self-medicate, rather than a true case of alcoholism.

I hated the persistent stigma of mental illness and the hovering specter of suicide: it alienated me from my friends and kept me from confiding too much about the way I was feeling. Greid told me how lucky I was: only one in three people get treatment, mostly because they are afraid to reach out. I, at least, had sought help, perhaps because I had the example of my mother and her endless trail of psychiatrists. The medical community considers mood disorders to be medical conditions—just like stroke, or diabetes, or cardiac disease. Ninety percent of those who take their own lives suffer from a mental illness such as bipolar disorder or depression.

In most world cultures suicide is taboo—perceived as a sin and an affront to God, a cold rebuke to one's family, the ultimate in callous ingratitude. Long ago, suicides were buried at the crossroads as a way of scattering and dispersing their spirits, rather than allowing them the blessing of a proper ceremony on hallowed church grounds. Today, we live in a time where suicide is still often disdained as an act of cowardice or a lack of moral fortitude.

OVER THE NEXT few years, it seemed imperative to educate my adolescent children about the legacy they might face later in their lives with regard to drugs and alcohol and mental illness: I wanted them to understand the familial tendencies toward psychiatric problems, the generations of alcoholism and drug abuse, as well as to warn them that even, at times, I had difficulty avoiding all this myself. I worried, however, that opening up my own frightening truths to them might backfire. As teens, they might well see themselves to be invincible and invulnerable. Perhaps they would believe that where I had failed somewhat, they would go on to conquer totally.

There was nothing definitive, nothing that dictated strictly that either of my children must, inexorably, inherit any of these legacies—even though in my mother's family alone there were three suicides within two generations, deaths that were undoubtedly enabled by the greasy slide of alcohol. And in Jim's family, too, there were also suicides: his maternal grandmother, who took an overdose of sleeping medication while in the bathtub, slipping down under the water to her death; and his mother's cousin, who shot himself in the head when Jim and I were in our twenties.

When the children became teenagers, Jim and I began to argue—how much should we enlighten them about their family's dark history? It separated us in a new way, one that we had not before experienced. He did not want to shadow their futures with dire predictions that might never come to pass. For me, however, the truth was something grittier and more basic; at the same time it was more elusive and painful. I felt an urgent need to educate my children, and to do so at an early enough moment to make it possible for them to avoid these proclivities. Slowly I began to realize that Jim did not want to tell them not only because he worried about revealing so much about our families, but also because he was ashamed of me and the way the legacy from my mother had already manifest itself in our lives. This made sense, I decided, in light of the fact that he always pulled away from me, a little bit, whenever I had had too much to drink, or was anxious, or depressed. Or perhaps, I wondered, such intense feelings simply might have frightened him beyond bearing.

All through my pregnancies, and Nathaniel and Gabe's early infancies, one particular fantasy was so intense I could have reached out and touched it: I would be the mother with the cookies and the wise words and the generous heart; the sane mother upon whom my children could always depend; the mother who stayed alive. No jugs of pills, no trips to the hospital while unconscious. Nothing dramatic. I would lead my life on the plain pine planks of an ordinary proscenium. As time went on, it crushed me to discover, with resounding force, that my own requirements had created an image in my imagination that I would never be able to sustain.

BY THE SUMMER of 1997, my emotional stability began to disintegrate. Depression began to rule, and it felt as if it were due to the loss of the contented vision Jim and I had shared of our future: after the rejection of my fifth novel, Jim's position within the company, which had begun with such promise, began to slip. Our hopes for ourselves as individuals and for our family as well, now eroded under the uncertainty of a new and threatening present. The creation of my newest novel had consumed all of the years during and following the successful publication of the memoir, and I couldn't conceive of what to do next. Stunned, I spent my working hours flipping aimlessly through the rejected manuscript, while Jim was once again working harder and harder, later and later, hours stolen from all the evenings we once shared after the children were in bed. By ten o'clock the house was quiet, except for the clack-clattering of Jim's fingers on the keyboard of his computer in the bedroom. From my perch on the bed, where I usually sat to read or watch television, I began to adjust to seeing only his back. We bought a set of earphones so that I could watch television movies without interrupting his concentration. Many nights I fell asleep alone.

At work, Jim disagreed increasingly with his boss—the CEO of the company. He gradually outgrew his position there, and he and his boss decided it was time for him to move on, despite eight years of fruitful work and easy camaraderie. He began to look for a new position, not an easy task when you are forty-four with a senior résumé, and eventually he found one, but his future still felt uncertain. Tension shimmered in the house, worry clouded both our faces. He was scared. I was scared. We never talked about it. In fact, we talked less and less, and argued more and more. Two years later, he founded a company of his own.

I was in the midst of a precipitous and vicious dive downward, but I kept pushing it to the back of my mind. I didn't want to burden Jim with my negative mood when he was in the midst of creating a brand-new career for himself. Despite his anxiety about me—especially regarding the amount of narcotic medication I was taking for my migraines—he seemed to accept my mood, and we just didn't talk about it. Perhaps he saw that I was headed south and buried himself in his work, accepting my denials that I was depressed instead of challenging me as he always had in the past. In the meanwhile, a few publishers rejected another novel for which I had written a quick outline and a few chapters. My agent and I decided to let it die. My writing career appeared to be stalled and I began to worry whether I would ever publish a book again. The hold of depression tightened so that I woke every morning with anxiety dominating my body. Though I tried to harden myself against these blows to my career, my sadness deepened, down and down, into a state more profoundly miserable than anything I had ever known. Terrifyingly, I once again had no vision of the future. In despair, I relied increasingly on Ben Berns and Norman Greid, my therapists. Still, the concept of inherited suicide remained undiscussed, simply shoved back into the darkness, where, like a fungus, it put out roots and began to spread.

OCTOBER AND NOVEMBER came: complete with the anniversaries of my mother's death and birthday, dates that seemed especially cruel that year. As always, I was reminded of her absence. Her final solution pressed in closer and closer. I began to hoard my migraine medication. Soon I had one hundred tablets.

Perhaps it was not surprising that in these years, with my mother gone, neither Joy nor Daddy could cope with my increasing depression anymore than they would have been willing or able to cope with hers. They viewed mine not as a first illness of my own, but as a continuation of hers, and were perhaps as angry with me as they had been with her. The fact that I had published six books by then was frightening to them: as an author, perhaps I was just borrowing my mother's life in one more way. I was certain that they cared about me, but their emotions led them to pretend that there was nothing wrong. Unfortunately, I still needed a deep emotional commitment from them both—one that could battle the ups and downs that impacted me more and more forcefully every day.

They didn't want to hear about depression or some crazy idea about a legacy of suicide. Just as my father and my grandparents on either side had urged my mother to "straighten up and fly right," both he and my sister now urged me to be strong, and "get with the program," another indication that they still understood as little about mental illness as they had when my mother was so sick. I was to be handled in the same manner that each had used with her during the last years before her death. Little by little we began to move even further apart.

The depression was pressing me harder into the black recesses of my mind. Each day that I survived, I hated myself for being a coward. Little by little, I was being squashed into a tiny, wasted ball of self-hatred. My medication began to fail.

I persevered, though, remaining alive by obsessing about my children, by worrying about their friendships, grades, drugs, girls; I remembered how I had felt at my mother's suicide and desperately did not want to put them through such a traumatic event. It occurred to me then that if I did succeed, I would also have handed suicide down as a reasonable option for another generation. How badly did I want to dissolve this inheritance for them, even as I wished to perpetuate it for myself?

Awakening in the mornings, I rolled my face back into my pillow and thought, desperately, about how willing I was—no matter the cost—to trade my life for peace. I did not realize how close I was to doing just that.

PART 3

{in the lunatic factory}

What we call the beginning is often the end
And to make an end is to make a beginning.
The end is where we start from . . .
Every phrase and every sentence is an end and a beginning.
Every poem an epitaph . . .
We shall not cease from exploration
And the end of all our exploring
Will be to arrive where we started
And know the place for the first time.

—T.S. ELIOT
"LITTLE GIDDING"

{in the lunatic factory}

I ALWAYS PROMISED myself that I would never wind up on a mental ward. That I would never have to have my stomach pumped. That I would never live, however occasionally, behind a locked door.

There had been a stretcher, rolling, white lights blooming over my head like full moons.

Then darkness.

Then silence. Then nothing.

Dimly I remembered the sludge of charcoal being forced down my throat, swallowing a tube, a glimpse of needle, and thick black thread zipping through the skin of my wrists.

Noise now accompanied the moment of returning to consciousness: people moving up and down the hall, phones ringing, voices calling out, carts rolling and clanking, and a periodic sound that reminded me of the buzzer on the dryer at home. On my right wrist was the computerized plastic bracelet and over both were soft cotton bandages.

Blindly, I felt around for my glasses, but they weren't nearby. I gripped my head in my hands as I stood up: a monster headache was playing twin timpani. The world fuzzy and borderless with my minus 650 vision uncorrected, I crept in bewilderment, tentatively, to the door of the room, my heart thumping with anxiety. While the night before I had not asked myself why I wanted to die so badly that I had chosen a knife and pills, that morning I was compelled to wonder, however stupefied, how I came to be in the hospital. What had precipitated such a crisis?

My mind turned over again and again and came up with not a single answer. The anxiety stopped my breath in my throat and I began to gasp for air. Fear climbed up inside me, rung by rung on the ladder of my ribs.

At last I moved from my dark threshold, squinting under bright fluorescent lights. I headed toward the biggest and whitest, figuring it had to be the nurses' station. Where there were nurses, there might be glasses.

"Linda," a male voice greeted me as I shuffled up in my bare feet. "Why don't you sit over here so I can get your vitals?"

It was a jolt to hear my name, spoken with such familiarity. The way a bartender greets you when you slide onto the stool and he puts your drink down in front of you although you haven't even ordered yet. The nurse led me to a chair, wrapped my arm with a blood pressure cuff, and squeezed the bulb. "I'm Drew," he said. "Your nurse for this shift."

I thought to myself that I didn't care what his name was, I just wanted my glasses. And my purse and a pen so that I could sign myself out of that place.

"How about you get your vitals and I get mine?" I smiled, trying to win him over to my side.

He cocked his head and with his silence appeared puzzled.

"Like my glasses? I can't see a thing."

"We'll check after we're done here. I don't remember anything about them in the chart, but we'll look again." He slid the thermometer under my tongue and I blinked again against the blindingly white light, putting my hands up to shield my eyes. The migraine shimmered at my temples.

My hair was still wet from where I had clumped it last night in the ponytail at the back of my neck; it had made the collar of my bathrobe soggy. Uncomfortable, I looked down and saw I was wearing nothing but a hospital Johnny under the blue and white patterned institutional robe.

Details began to return to me—or maybe I was just filling in the gaps with the most likely, obvious explanations. I remembered white arms pulling me, slippery and naked, from the bathtub. While I was in the emergency room, unconscious, my body must have been exposed, whether or not I wanted that; my body had been beyond my control. That idea shook me. After my admission, someone must have then kindly clothed my nudity. I had nothing of my own with me, not even my wedding band. Stripped of my worldly goods. No glasses. No clothes. No money. Not even my watch. No identity.

I averted my eyes from the door into the unit, on the end of the corridor. Even without my glasses I could tell it was there, buzzing open and shut, admitting and discharging staff and visitors. I was willing to bet that patients didn't go through that door at all. My head continued to thump as memory kicked in: my hand with a pen, signing papers clamped to a clipboard.

In a queasy blur I saw myself, in isolation in a barren room with nothing but a flat bed and a black window. They must have left me to sleep off the booze and drugs.

At some point I was moved to a twin-bedded room complete with a roommate. My brain spun again and landed on a logical thought: how would I go about getting a private room, even for a few hours, and would Jim object to the cost? When would Jim get here anyway? How badly I needed to be rescued: I wondered if my mother had felt the same way—the claustrophobia and the sense of helplessness. I started to cry again.

"Do you want to talk about how you are feeling?" Drew asked, removing the blood pressure cuff from my arm.

I peered at him out of the rabbit hole my life had suddenly become, desperately trying to think of the right answer. It somehow seemed clear to me that to complain of my headache, or my stomachache, or my guilt or confusion, would be nearly obscene. I straightened my shoulders. "I can't see without my glasses."

"Serves you right," my inner voice observed smugly, calling up my mother's predicament long ago with the angry, abusive nurse.

He shook his head. "When they brought you in, it seems you didn't have them on. At least, the chart doesn't list them and it usually would. Maybe your husband will bring them when he comes."

It returned to me, then, the way I had folded them so carefully and set them down, balanced on the edge of the bathtub with my martini glass. An instant later, memory slapped at me again: "You're three times the legal limit," someone in the emergency room had said. Through my haze I had wondered why it mattered—I hadn't been driving.

"A cigarette?" I asked the nurse, his name already forgotten; I could not make out his ID tag. Though smoking hadn't been an urge in over ten years, desire now came over me in a remarkably strong wave. "Can I have a cigarette?" Smoking would feel familiar, would make me feel a little bit in control.

He pointed at the wall behind me where a white board was mounted. Peering at it, without my glasses, reminded me of being in the fourth grade and the shame when I couldn't see the math problems on the blackboard. I had felt desolate then, and I felt desolate now. I moved right up against the board to bring the writing into focus. My name, like the fifteen others, had a column under it: Linda Sexton. Room: 10B. Doctor: Flores/ Marsh. Nurse: Drew. Privileges: 1A. Checks: 15s. Diet: NC. Status: 3-day Voluntary.

What did all the codes mean? I wondered. Nowhere, I noted, did it indicate anything about smoking. Even if I had a cigarette. "What's 1A?"

"Restricted. Until your privileges are 2A or B, you can't go into the garden." He slung his stethoscope around his neck. "And the garden is the only place you can smoke."

"Why am I 1A?" Claustrophobia screwed my voice down into a whine.

"You're on 15s."

Panic iced over the tears that had begun to pool inside me: there's a garden into which I may not walk, there's a door through which I may not pass.

"Mother may I take one giant step forward?" sneered the voice inside me.

"Talk to your doc. Usually they'll put you on 2A pretty fast if you aren't having any problems." He wrote something down on the chart.

"What kinds of problems?"

Shelving the chart, he leaned back against the desk. "Well, you're on fifteens for a reason."

My head buzzed with the migraine, my dry eyes burned. "I don't understand this rule—what are fifteens?"

"Fifteen-minute checks."

I remembered the way some woman had put her head around to check on me while I was on my bed. It dawned on me: that quick glance was no accidental invasion of privacy. "You mean you're watching me?"

"Linda, you tried to kill yourself. That's why you're on fifteens. Only your doctor can change your status to thirty-minute checks."

My humiliation complete.

"How do I get off fifteens?" Despite my shame, I persisted.

"Don't have any problems." He smiled at me.

"But I thought I was here because I've got problems!" I was getting pissed at the pat merry-go-round of his answers.

"They usually bump you up to 2B on your second day." He put his hand on my arm and gave it a sympathetic squeeze. "Ask Flores when he comes on duty."

"Who is Flores?"

"Your doc." He gestured to the white board. "He's a good guy."

"When do I see him?"

"It depends. If you're lucky, around eleven."

"Eleven?" I looked at my watch, which wasn't there. "Why can't I see him now?"

"They're still doing rounds now. They checked on you at six but you were still out."

The curious obsession to smoke intensified. That cigarette symbolized freedom: a walk in the garden, past the door at the end of the corridor.

A stainless steel cart was wheeled past us and Drew gestured at it.

"Breakfast," he said. "And after that, morning meeting—you can come in your robe—and at some point you'll get your shower when we find you some clothes."

"I really want to go home." My voice quavered and I fought not to cry.

"I'm sure you do. That's why we have you sign yourself in."

I felt the sweat start to gather at the nape of my neck. "But I was unconscious when they brought me in. I could have been signing the Declaration of Independence!"

"Don't worry about the next few days," he urged. "One thing at a time—why don't you go on down for breakfast? Start working on getting in good enough shape to be discharged."

I touched my ponytail, feeling soiled.

"And there's a good women's group at two. The time'll go." He stood up. "Let's see what Diet sent up for your meal. After you eat, you can fill out a menu for tomorrow's choices."

"But I can't see," I protested, gesturing at my face. "And my head hurts. I've got medication for it in my purse: where is my purse anyway?"

"I'm sure it's locked up in the on-call room. But you can't have any meds that aren't prescribed by our staff. You'll have to talk to Flores about that, too."

"Don't you know what happens when a migraine starts to build and you don't treat it?" I was in despair. It dawned on me that they were not going to be willing to give me any pain relief.

"I'm sure Dr. Flores will treat it with utmost seriousness. But until then . . . ." He spread his hands, palms toward the ceiling.

"Well, at least, see my bathrobe, how the tie is missing." Even the details of this incarceration reduced me, little by little, to someone with no control over what was happening to her.

"No ties on this unit," he replied, as if announcing something positive. The cheer in his voice was strong enough to burn barnacles off the hull of a ship. "So don't worry about walking around with your robe untied. Everybody does. General rules are: no shoelaces, pantyhose, matches, nail files, polish, or remover. Oh, and no pens." Then he added matter-of-factly, "And dental floss only with supervision."

I stared at him, feeling a surge of anger.

"All packages get checked at the front door and certain types of items are removed—like ribbons on flowers. Also, good news here," he was consulting the chart again. "There's a note that your husband said he'll bring the glasses along when he comes in."

"When is he coming?" I demanded.

"He's away, I don't know when he'll be here." He paused, assessing me. "Don't you remember where he is?"

This was all news from another world, spoken in a foreign language. The language of the woman I had been, not the woman I now was. Now I must obey arbitrary rules and regulations as if I were a child again: let your bathrobe hang open; let the nurses spy on you. What had happened to the rules I had once made for myself?

Don't ever be sick the way my mother was.

Don't ever let the children see you act like her.

"Of course I remember he's away," I said after a pause, lying. "But I don't imagine his flight would even take off until this morning."

"This is the common room," Drew said as we passed from the hall into a room stinking of sulphurous eggs and oatmeal. My stomach flipped. "This is where there are group meetings, the television. Some OT, even an exercise bike." He pointed to a dinosaur of the species. I looked on in dismay.

"But I'd like to eat in my room."

"No eating in the rooms on this unit."

I clenched my hands and hid them inside the pockets of my robe. "For Christ's sake, why not?"

"You need to start socializing with the other patients. Hiding in your room by yourself isn't part of the program here."

I stared at him, finally nonplussed into silence. From the runners in the heated cart, he slid out a tray covered with brown lids. Who was crazy here? The idea of talking to the others—people just as crazy as the patients in the wards my mother had stayed in—seemed nuts just by itself.

"Going to group, that's the kind of cooperation, the kind of steps, the docs look for when assessing your privilege level."

Stunned by the obvious bribe, I followed him to the table where two other women were shoveling food in without speaking. I knew I was definitely not sick enough to be here. This was all a big mistake, and once Jim arrived we would begin to sort it out, because I certainly was not going to stay here for three days.

I poked at a gooey soft-boiled egg with shivery whites and waited for the bell that would release me back to my room. Luckily, my breakfast partners ate their meal quietly and didn't attempt conversation. I drank the cup of coffee on my tray but when I put the little white checklist that came with my meal up close to my nose, studying it as a way of not looking at anyone, I realized the abbreviation "NC" in the blank following the designation "Diet" meant "No Caffeine."

A man sat down next to me. I clutched at my bathrobe and tried to focus on the fact that soon I would leave. With relief I thanked God I had committed myself voluntarily; it should make it infinitely easier to get free.

After a while, the others stood and took their trays back to the cart, everyone clearing his dishes just as if we were all at home. The nurse in charge checked to see what was eaten and marked it on a clipboard, and then she counted the silverware to make sure no one had put a knife in his pocket.

As I walked uncertainly, blindly, down the hall to my room, I passed a man standing in the threshold to his room, talking to himself. As I got closer I could see he was layered in filthy old woolen hats and scarves. He looked like one of the homeless mentally ill people I had served at the soup kitchen.

I was horrified: Now I was one of them.

{the door}

IT LOOKED LIKE an ordinary door, but it wasn't.

After a while, closer scrutiny revealed the synchronicity between the opening of the door and the nurse who sat behind the main desk at the nurses' station, working on charts at the same time she directed traffic with a loud, vibrating buzzer. The door was obviously secured from the inside. Even staff had to wait for permission to exit and enter.

The buzzer stirred a terrible sense of panic in me. Its blurt alerted my claustrophobia. The door itself assumed proportions suitable for Alice's Wonderland: so tiny and shrunken that I knew I would never fit through it.

I had always panicked under tight sheets, or in small, restrictive places like airplanes, caves, and MRIs. The idea that I was somewhere that had no exit terrified me. Once again, anxiety surged in my throat like bile: how would I ever return to the life I had known? I wondered, while an old woman passed by me with her soiled nightgown.

She turned around then, and came up to me, where I stood, frozen in place, at the entrance to my room.

"Do you see?" she asked, pointing at the ceiling. "They're talking to me again. The wolf is the loudest. How do you sleep with the wolf?"

I shook my head and muttered something. I didn't know what to do; I just wanted her to go away. She resumed her shambling walk down the floor and I breathed a little easier until I remembered my own predicament.

How would I return to the safety I used to feel, supported by husband, family, and psychiatrists? Would I ever again function as the mother of two, the writer of seven books, the wife of eighteen years? I had crossed an invisible line—one that, conceivably, I might never step back over again. I closed my eyes against the mire each question brought into sharp and frightening focus.

Right from the start, my life seemed paralyzed in place like the locked-down door. All normality had slipped away, and I remembered the white bleached atmosphere of my mother's incarceration. A host of questions buzzed through my mind, three tumbling out of the chaos with particular intensity: Was I condemned to live in this abyss for a long time, either here on this ward or even just in my mind? Would I ever trust myself again? Would my family ever trust me again? Perhaps I was fated to continue on, just as my mother had: enduring the inner pain until yet another inevitable suicide attempt—until, finally, I achieved my purpose.

A nurse walked by, glanced at me and made a note on her chart. I had a lot of questions about this place, still. I was afraid to ask about so many things, even though I felt a push of desperation as I tried and then failed to approach any of the staff. Shyness overtook me. I wondered what all the other symbols on the whiteboard meant. How did you get another cup of coffee, a hot one this time?

I shuffled back out to the nurses' station. "Is there anywhere I can get a cup of coffee, or a juice?"

"You can keep your own supplies in the common room refrigerator, labeled with your name, and subject to your diet. No caffeine means no caffeine. Coffee is a no-go."

"How come?"

"Too easy for patients on an NC diet to get a hold of the stuff and make it look like soda."

"Mother may I take one step forward," droned the voice in my head.

"I don't know when someone is coming to visit who could bring something to me. Couldn't you make an exception?"

The nurse looked at me with pity. "No exceptions."

I turned away, discouraged. Once again, I was dying for a smoke even though it had been ten years since I was last hooked.

I kept wondering about Norman Greid—did he even know I was there? And what of Ben Berns? Why hadn't they come to see me? Where were the children? The questions were a waterfall tumble inside my head.

Another nurse passed by and I stopped her. "Did they let my private doctors know that I was admitted here?"

"They did that from the emergency room. You probably don't remember giving their names."

Another stab of anxiety in the stomach. Neither had come to check on me last night and neither had been in yet this morning either; soon they would both be starting with their first patients in the office. "It's really important that I see them—especially Dr. Greid. Being without my medications could be a disaster."

"Stop whining," the voice directed.

"I think Drew was looking after that," she said, as she shrugged and walked on.

I leaned back against the threshold and shut my eyes. I was only just now discovering how the system here actually worked: a voluntary commitment was only voluntary when you were signing the papers, i.e., no one else was committing you or holding a gun to your head. Of course, it didn't matter that you didn't even have your glasses on when they put the papers in front of you in the emergency room—or if you were totally blasted. You didn't need to be very aware when the resident sutured your wrists up with the kind of thread Nana had used to mend gloves.

Now, after all the paperwork was finished, I was in the hands of the state, though I would not come to understand that until many hours later, and when I did, my skin itched, and I scratched and scratched, raising a hot red rash across my stomach and arms. Drew had explained to me that if you are admitted on a three-day voluntary you can't leave until the prescribed time limit is over—and, even then, the state or the doctors can refuse to release you if they still think you are a danger to yourself.

When he told me this, I looked at him with horror. I couldn't imagine spending even a night here and reassured myself with the comfort of knowing that when Jim arrived, he would be able to work his customary magic.

But, in the meanwhile, I swung in the breeze with no one telling me when they would discharge me, envisioning myself having to stay there against my will until they decided I was safe once more. Safe—whatever that meant.

"You're terrified, aren't you?" the voice taunted me.

Suddenly I was air hungry again, and gasping a little with each breath I took. For a moment, I thought I was going to pass out. How desperately I wanted the Klonopin I usually took first thing in the morning. I did not care what little good-girl routine I had to fake; somehow, I was going to get out of there whatever it took—but I'd need Greid's help to do it. Right then, standing in that hospital doorway, I was feeling abandoned by everyone.

When I asked again for a painkiller for the migraine, the nurse told me that they could only dispense my former daily "meds" if my private doctor, working through the staff doctors, prescribed them. I had already missed my morning doses of regular psychiatric medications, and they would not treat my headache with anything stronger than a Tylenol, which essentially meant no treatment at all.

I went back to the nurses' station and begged. "Please can't I have my migraine medication?"

"You already asked," Drew sounded a little bit irritated this time. I started to turn away, trapped, angry, and frightened. "I told you that I can give you Tylenol, and an icepack for your head."

"But Tylenol doesn't work for this kind of pain—it'll just get worse until you can't medicate it away at all, even when you finally do get the right medication. If a migraine gets entrenched," I went on, trying to keep from sounding desperate, my tone even, "there's something called kindling. The migraine sets up a pattern in your brain chemistry and the headaches just keep rolling in." I was pleading with him now.

"You don't have to explain it to me," he said. "But I really can't do anything. Why don't you go back and lie down and I'll bring you the icepack."

Defeated, I went in and lay on my bed, massaging my head and trying not to move for fear of stirring it up even worse. Drew brought me the icepack and I lay there gritting my teeth.

I wanted to cry: how alone I was. How much I needed someone to take the time to pay me a visit, despite the inconvenience. Selfish as this may sound, my ego was at such an all-time low that I couldn't even imagine the difficulty an early morning hospital consultation might cause two busy physicians like Norman and Ben. Even though my current predicament was entirely of my own making, I was vulnerable enough to need to see that someone still cared. I did not know then, and would not know until much later, when the doctors began to educate me about the twists and turns of bipolar illness, that the self-absorption a patient feels is yet another classic manifestation of clinical depression on the bottom rung of a bipolar swing. Yet it looked to the outside world—especially family and friends—as if the patient was nothing other than self-centered, with a total lack of empathy or sympathy for everyone around him.

At lunchtime, my new staff resident, Flores, and a fourth-year med student did come to my cubicle to take my history and to define better how I was feeling.

"Please let me go home," I asked, with urgency. "My husband will be here soon, and he'll be able to take care of me."

Unperturbed, he looked at me carefully. "Linda," he said at last. "Do you really think you are ready to go home?"

I fiddled with my hands, sliding my fingers up and down over the place where my wedding ring used to be. "Of course, I'm ready," I said with a quaver in my voice. Suddenly I felt like crying, but I didn't know why.

"Are you safe?"

"What do you mean, 'safe'?"

"I mean can you promise me, to a certainty, that you can go home and not hurt yourself. Can you assure me that if we discharge you today you will be able to keep yourself from trying to kill yourself again?"

I had no truthful answer. I just looked away from him, silently, and longed for my own bed, for Jim's arms around me again, for the bounce and bustle of our kids. "Well, when my husband gets here we can talk about it some more."

He looked at me thoughtfully. "We can talk about it some more, but your husband has nothing to do with my decision. What you say matters a whole lot more than what he says."

Finally they left, but, to my relief, Flores prescribed my usual migraine medication, which Drew brought fairly quickly. As I lay there with my head on the hard pillow, I couldn't help but hear the door onto the unit buzzing over and over. Soon it banged in my head as violently as the migraine had done before the medication began to take effect, and before long it became impossible for me to think of anything else except that noise, over and over again.

I got up and drew the curtains tightly around my cubicle. I sat again on the edge of the bed, its rubber mattress and stiff sheets crinkling under me. The noise made me feel that I was in a prison. Or a coffin. Rocking back and forth on my bed, I felt the panic rise another notch, and I scrambled for some logical progression, like a mnemonic, that would spell calm.

I tried to demystify the door: I would suck away its power by ruminating over all the doors I had known. Doors that were flat and innocent, doors of no consequence. The first I could remember was green with a brass knocker, on the door of the house I lived in as a child in a small Boston suburb, where, on Halloween, I hid behind the solidity of its wooden panels, too shy to offer the candy bowl to the older children who knocked so loudly. Then there was the brown door, flanked by twin iron lanterns, of our more luxurious home in a larger suburb, in front of which I had warmed to my first kiss. And the white paneled door to my parents' bedroom, funneling soft yellow light into the dark hall on summer nights when the attic fan drew in soft cool air that lifted the curtains. I remembered the expectant thrill as I opened the door to my dorm room at Harvard for the first time. And there was the heavy oak door, always left open, in Hilles Library, where I attended my first college seminar and discovered the pleasure of working harder with my mind than ever before. And then the door to Nathaniel's room when he was a baby, swung wide open every night against my newly discovered fear of Sudden Infant Death Syndrome. The door to our second home, decorated with a basket of ivy and impatiens. The door to Gabe's bedroom now, shut tight and reverberating with loud rock music. And last of all, hanging on the wall of my writing room at home, the bright blue door in a photograph of a tumbledown house in Mexico.

"You are the tumbledown house now," mocked the voice.

ABRUPTLY, THE CURTAIN around the cubicle shifted, and was pulled back a bit at the edge; a nurse put her head around the corner. She nodded at me and then disappeared without speaking. I stared into the space left by her exit, pulled my robe tighter around my chest.

How many times did my sister and father and I go to visit my mother, waiting on the other side of the locked ward door? The face of that door was painted a smooth institutional green, and its small window had wires woven in diamond shapes, right into the glass, for strength. The lock was set flush, big and thick. The only way we knew we were about to be admitted was when we heard the brassy ring of the hoop of keys swinging from the attendant's belt. There was no such thing as a buzzer.

There were crazy people on that ward. Old ladies who sat gumming their lunch in front of the television in its brown wooden console. The two men who drooled and played ping pong in slow motion. The young man with a beard and the glittering eyes of paranoid schizophrenia, who tried to corner me to show how he had lined his hat with tin foil to shut out the voices coming down from the phone wires. And there was my mother, knocked out on Thorazine, eyes half-mast as she chain-smoked. Still, she looked nearly normal. Normal enough. I wanted to shake her and take her home, make her well. Wasn't there always a familiar stack of books on the floor, the box of Kleenex on the windowsill as well? Didn't she say she still loved me, as she reclined there on the bed of her private room, her long legs shiny in nylon stockings, crossed under the double-knit skirt of her navy blue suit?

Now my children would stand and look up at that same door; now they would be the ones to wonder what was on the other side of the threshold. Sitting there on my bed, I started to cry with regret. I had thought that my love would protect them. I had always promised myself they would never see the crazies.

"But they've already seen the crazies," the voice interrupted. "They've already seen you."

AFTER LUNCH, DREW accompanied me to the bathroom and leaned against the doorjamb as I washed my face. He'd finally cadged a toothbrush for me and had to observe me because he had floss with him as well.

I spat, toothpaste dribbling down my chin. "Sorry," I muttered, embarrassed.

"No problemo."

"I need to use the toilet."

He hesitated, and I felt horror. Surely he was not going to watch me pee?

But then he smiled, and just reached across me to pick up the floss. "Didn't they teach you to use this twice a day?"

My face red, I closed the door behind him and just sat there on the seat, my cheeks hot against my palms. All these restrictions rendered me ever more helpless and infantilized. Feeling like a child reminded me of Aunt Alison's, where I thought I would be returned to my mother and spent all my time waiting for the magical phone call that would release me. I wondered about the rules my mother had to abide by when she was hospitalized: surely she must have gotten to smoke in her room—but how had she managed to light her cigarettes without matches? Had to go begging to the staff each and every time? Had she, too, had to make do with a tiny sliver of soap and a little bottle of shampoo? Had she been denied an emery board with which to smooth out a torn edge of a fingernail?

Early afternoon and the locked door swung inward and all the girls on the floor went over to the unit next door, with a chaperone, for a "group meeting." Here, movement was enviously free. The patients were allowed to saunter in and out, down to the cafeteria to score better food, outside for cigarettes with no supervisor whenever they wanted, or long walks around the hospital corridors if they felt like it. I didn't understand why I couldn't be on a ward like this one, and I resolved to ask someone. But underneath I was still so overwhelmed about being here at all that I was too discouraged to tackle any of the questions that continued to mount in my mind. Did they think I was so sick I couldn't be by myself for even a minute? And so, sullenly, I went to the meeting, introduced myself and listened to them bitch about their lives; it seemed to me they were only feeling sorry for themselves—perhaps I was, too, but I didn't want to hear anyone else whine. And, once again, the crazies from my unit paced the halls; they reminded me ever more vividly of my mother every time I passed one of them. Tears for her rose at the back of my eyes as I tried to calm myself. Being hospitalized made me feel sicker than I had felt back at home, before my world had come unglued.

I WAS IN a deep sleep that defied the unit's mid-afternoon noise as well as the blurt of the door buzzer, when a stranger, who introduced himself as the director of alcoholism for the hospital, wakened me for an unexpected visit. I was puzzled, as I certainly hadn't requested a visit from any doctor or therapist regarding a problem with alcohol. He sat down heavily in the chair beside the head of my bed, clearing his throat and speaking my name—probably several times as I surfaced from the depths of troubled sleep. I rose up on my bed into a sitting position too fast and with a head rush; startled, I was disoriented and at a definite disadvantage. Silently,

I swore. I hated this invasion of my privacy, a sharp intrusion on sleep as he simply seated himself at my bedside, uninvited. I groped for my glasses in a wild bout of nerves before remembering I didn't have them with me. My heart pounded. In time I would learn that staff often arrived this way, unannounced and unwanted, especially at their daily six A.M. visit, one for which you definitely wanted to appear organized and poised, so that you could ask all the questions you'd been piling up since yesterday. Instead, I was sleepy and incoherent.

"Your alcoholism," the director began. "Probably tied to . . . your suicide attempt."

I squinted at him. His words kept fading in and out as my attention raced; in and out my mind went through all sorts of possibilities.

"Your alcoholism . . . experience withdrawal."

I still didn't understand why he was there. The fact that this heavyset man with a kind face sat at my bedside increased my feeling of disorientation.

"More than sixty percent of people with bipolar disorder also suffer from alcoholism and drug-related problems. Our program is designed . . . ."

"I'm not having any withdrawal," I said, pulling my blankets up around my lap protectively, shivering again with anxiety. "I don't drink enough."

"Well, we can see how it goes, but in any case, your family picture of alcoholism . . . ."

"Another salesman," my inner voice commented in a determined tone. "Who says you're an alcoholic anyway?"

I drifted away from the doctor's patter again and envisioned the kind of family picture I would have drawn when I was in grammar school: stick figures, standing side by side, hands joined like a chain of paper dolls. Now this doctor was telling me it was not only our hands that were linked.

Was I an alcoholic? Over the last twenty years the question had tugged at me with varying degrees of urgency. Once, it even led me to stop drinking for three years. In time, I disabused myself of the notion and started drinking again; alcoholism, I decided, was my mother's disease—not mine.

Over the twenty-three years since her death, I had come to accept, slowly and with resistance, that her alcoholism was part of what had led her down the path toward that lonely and barren ending in the garage. By the time she died, she had begun to drink with her breakfast, and then could work her way right around the clock. Having read through many versions of her life—her poems, her journals, her audio-taped sessions with her psychiatrist—I had learned, painfully, about the progress that alcoholism had made throughout the generations of our family. My mother's father was alcoholic enough to have received treatment in an era when most alcoholism was termed "heavy drinking," and my mother's mother drank at both lunch and dinner. After her father stopped drinking, my mother remembered her mother standing at the kitchen sink, downing straight shots of whiskey so as not to miss her daily ration.

My father, on the other hand, spent much of his childhood being sent into bars to retrieve his father—a sad, sad task for such a young boy. As time went on, my grandfather became a classic drunk, even though he had achieved abstinence at the time of his death in a car accident with a drunk driver. He was fifty years old. Her husband's alcoholism undoubtedly accounted for Nana's negative reaction to our introduction to alcohol, but my parents saw nothing wrong with allowing us to drink early. In fact, they saw it instead as part of their parental duty: "teaching" us to drink was how they phrased it, as if it were an activity where proficiency was desirable.

Right from the start, I had loved the boozy hum that went along with being high, not unlike the warm buzz of grass. With pleasure,

I always remembered the sweetness of my first bar drink—a glass of Sauternes—ordered illegally the summer of my seventeenth year, and the hot spike of my first Bloody Mary—eye-watering with the fragrant horseradish that was my father's trademark. After my mother's death, I hosted frequent sherry receptions in college that I, seeking the sophistication I believed all my new roles would require, converted into regular "grown up" cocktail hours, with Scotch and soda or martinis, and even a cheese plate. Booze made me looser, lighter on my feet, less shy, more able to flirt and joke and get along in a world that continued to loom.

All through my teenage years, when we—and the medical community—addressed my mother's problems, we did so in terms of her mental illness, not her alcohol use. Depression, not booze. Sporadically the doctors might mention her lust for the glass but always after they addressed her lust for death. At the time, none of us questioned the role that booze played in all our lives, even though cocktail hour had often led to those terrifying fights between my parents that Joy and I had to battle through: oddly enough, it occurred to no one in the family that booze might be at the root of the increasing frequency of the problems between my parents as the years wore on.

Not until much later did I begin to believe that without delving into my mother's alcoholism, there was no way her mental illness could be "cured" or even just "improved." As time went on, her drinking problem worsened acutely as she attempted to self-medicate away her depression by imbibing around the clock, rather than using the psychiatric medications prescribed to address her many "illnesses of the mind." There was no one and no way to call a halt, because even then, despite all we could see, alcohol lived in our minds on the same plane as food: civilized folk did not do without it.

"Would you like to join the group?" the director asked, pulling me back to the present.

"I'll have to think about it," I answered, squirming on my stiff mattress, wishing fervently that he would just leave so that I would be able to breathe freely again.

"With your family history, I think our group could be very useful for you. Supplemented, of course, by regular AA meetings."

I looked past him and focused on the blur of my nightstand. "I'll have to think about it," I repeated, feeling the itch of claustrophobia on my skin.

He gave me his card, we shook hands and he left.

Anxiety revved in my chest again.

The door buzzed.

{never be a suicide}

I WAITED AND waited, an eternity it seemed, for my husband
to come and fold me into his arms. I wasn't sure when Jim's
plane would get in, or when he would arrive here. We had not
spoken, even over the phone. I wondered—would he be tender?
Would he feel as I once had about my mother? Would he be
angry, or confused, or wishing with all his might that I were
anywhere but behind a door that locked me in and my loved ones
out? I understood all those emotions so well.

Sometime during the afternoon, I heard my name over the
loudspeaker. I rushed to the threshold of my room and saw him,
standing at the nurses' station, handing over a bag to be inspected.
When they finished, he slowly turned to look around, and saw me.

I was hungry for him, I realized then, anxious for his arms, his
cheek pressed against mine, the link to home, my other life, my
sanity. He held all the keys. The strength of his embrace felt as
comforting as Nana's once had in times of trouble.

I drew him back into my room and shut the curtain. He sat in
the chair, and I perched on the edge of the bed, wishing he would
come sit beside me. The distance between us made me ache, but

I knew I had no right to look for more. I had done this to myself. He took my glasses from his pocket and handed them to me: the world I had only been guessing at sharpened into reality.

"Why did you do it?" His voice reeked with an awful despair. "Why didn't you tell me how depressed you were last night? I would have come straight home. When I think of all the years I tried to make sure this didn't happen——" he broke off; I could tell that the list of questions, all unanswered, petered out when he locked his hands on his lap and looked away from me.

I stayed silent because I didn't really know why I hadn't opened up to him. The impulse to take me out of this life had just seized me, amazing in its strength, and I had failed to predict its occurrence or to combat its power successfully.

"I'm so sorry," I answered, spreading my hands, feeling utterly defeated. Then I realized that the motion of my arms made my bandages show. Quickly, I rearranged my sleeves. "It just seemed to pull me under, and then suddenly here I am. I want to go home. Please take me home." I started to cry, turning my face away in shame. How could I have done this to him—and to the children?

"Don't you know how much we all need you? Not just me—but the kids? Do you have any idea what this has done to all of us?"

My head drooped further. In the background I could hear the drilling whine of the buzzer, but with Jim here it didn't feel so upsetting. "There's nothing I can do to take it back, Jim. Nothing. No matter what I do. How hard I try. But I would—if I could." I wrapped my arms around me and shivered. "The kids—"

"You can get better. Starting right now. You can never do it again."

His face suddenly had a hard edge, his mouth tightening against his teeth as if he were repressing something he wanted to say; was this his anger leaking out? I wasn't surprised that he would be angry with me. I thought of all the times I had been angry with my mother, all the times that we, as a family, had punished her with our distance for being what we considered a weak and manipulative person. He stayed sitting in the chair, upright, as if he couldn't relax against its straight back. "I was worried before this," he said. "All those damn painkillers. I should have said something. I should have done something."

"Are you mad at me? My dad was always angry with my mother." I was scared to hear his answer, but perhaps it would diminish some if it were brought out into the air. I wasn't sure how much anger I could bear but I was willing to try.

"Well, you're not her! Don't talk that way—what happened to her isn't happening to you," he said, with that same set expression on his mouth but a detached look in his eye. "How could I be mad?"

"I was always mad with my mother," I answered dispiritedly.

"Well, think of how many times she tried. This was just a momentary black mood."

"I wish we had some privacy." I gestured to the flimsy curtain separating us from my roommate.

"What does that matter? Everyone knows—everyone will know sooner or later," he corrected himself. "How am I supposed to explain this to my parents? Our friends? The neighbors who saw the ambulance."

"I want to get out of here," I said then, avoiding what he had just said, avoiding the terrible fear that I would never be able to return to the days before the legacy seemed so inevitable. "But they say I have to stay. Can you do something to get me out sooner?" My tone grew desperate as I tried to convince him.

"Are you sure you're ready to come home? Maybe it's better if you're here for a while. We have to think about what's best for the children."

The idea that my return to home wouldn't be best for Nathaniel and Gabe pierced my heart. But, I thought, I deserved nothing more than his doubt.

The fear on his face mirrored the fear I felt about remaining here.

"I'll be fine at home. A lot better than staying here with a bunch of crazy people."

"I'll talk to the doctor," he promised, but still, he sounded reluctant.

"And the kids?"

"I'll bring them over later."

"You think it's a good idea—for them to see me here?"

"They need to see you are okay," he answered with determination. "Already they were asking to come."

I suddenly realized that I knew so little about what had happened to them after the ambulance left. "What—" I swallowed hard, "what do they know?"

"They know it all," he said bitterly. "What did you expect?"

I stared down at my hands. I did remember, how frightened their faces were as I was wheeled out the door.

"What happened to them after—," I broke off, wincing, feeling ashamed that I hadn't even wondered more fully about them before now. "Afterwards."

"The police stayed with them until Julie and Wally came to pick them up."

"That was good of them—Julie and Wally, I mean."

"We're going to owe a lot of people before this is over," he answered grimly.

He stayed for a little while longer and then went in search of my doctors. Jim was a very organized type: if anyone could get me out of there, it would be him. I punched my pillow up behind my back, my mood shifting just a tiny bit. With a book in my lap, I anticipated escaping the rigors of the ward's intense self-examination very soon. Suddenly, I could breathe again. It didn't seem so far off before I would be home once more, and everything would be the same as it had been. I might miss dinner tonight, but I'd be making Worcestershire chicken for tomorrow's supper. How I longed for a second chance, another time to try my hand at marriage and motherhood.

Just before supper, Jim reappeared, this time with the kids in tow. He told me in a low voice that he hadn't been able to overcome the commitment papers I had signed. I would have to stay until the three-day limit was up, and I might have to stay even longer if the staff reevaluated me and judged me unsafe to release.

I crashed, crushed that I would have to stay another day. My eyes watered with tears I would not allow to fall. Because the children were there, I did not bring it up again, as I tried, with no success, to conceal my mounting sensations of sharp claustrophobia while the kids asked for sodas. Jim went to the nurses' station to get them drinks. The thought of upsetting the children any more than they already were was disturbing, and so I tried to throw myself into the visit and wipe my distress off my face.

I tried to protect them from the wandering loonies on the ward by keeping them in my room for the length of the visit: they were reassured by the surface of it—the attached bathroom, the bureau, the window without bars. They were surprised that the bed didn't go up and down. What kind of hospital room was this anyway? My shame deepened: I bit my lip and looked out the window as a way of keeping my expression calm.

In spite of my somewhat muddled state, I knew this: no matter how I might hate my illness and wish to protect my children from it, I had begun the process of handing the legacy along, hand to hand, mind to mind, heart to heart, as if I had a bomb that was ticking away strapped to my chest. Despair rolled in and my depression deepened. One minute I'd been having an extra drink and taking a bath, and the next I was waking up in the hospital, on a mental ward.

Later, the children turned their faces upward to receive my kisses, looking tentative. They had not known what to expect, and

I felt shy around them, not sure how to explain what I was doing in the hospital or why I had committed such a devastating act.

Gabe observed shyly that I seemed okay and I realized then how easily I could fool people. I wasn't sure I ever wanted to hear or understand what they had experienced when they watched the paramedics wheel me out in the early morning hours. I didn't want to hear how hard it had been to visit me behind a locked door. Despairing over what felt like selfishness, I just wanted to push the knowledge down, down into some inner dark cave within my mind: I had most certainly hurt them.

LIFE ON THE ward moved slowly. There was little to do. The day after I was admitted, I showed the kids a drawing I had done during occupational therapy, and gave them the fat candles I had made for them with different colors of swirled wax and glitter. It was the reverse of coming to their classrooms years before for parents' visiting night, when they would show me their artwork. At the time of my mother's death, I still had the wicker basket she had made me when she was doing OT in the hospital, and now I thought of it, probably somewhere in the storage room out back.

How strange it was to feel like a child again, under supervision, as I painted and played with crayons. All of this made me feel so sad and ineffectual; here I was doing more of my mother's gig.

The third day was more of the same. When Jim came to visit, I could see in his eyes that he was a little afraid of me.

That morning, I had been jumped up to 2B and could go with the group for a smoke, albeit under the supervision of a guard. The sun warmed my face: how wonderful it felt to be outside and smell the early blooming flowers so common in Northern California, to feel the air fresh on my face. I felt as if I had been a mole living in fluorescence; and now I squinted against the bright light. My mood lifted a little bit: it was good to see that the outside world did indeed exist. The garden was beautiful even in December but it was surrounded by chain link, as were the walkways, the sides, and even the overhead panel. It imprisoned us all around, like a cage. I went to the guard for his match and bent over the flame of yellow and red.

Susan, a young woman who had identified herself during that morning's women's meeting as a lesbian, came over to where I was sitting. She was wearing baggy jeans and a nose ring. I wasn't lonely right then, I was just sitting back and looking at the sky, happy to be away from the bustle of the ward, but still, I didn't have it in me to be rude and tell her just to go away.

"Are you a cutter?" she asked, gesturing to the soft gauze bandages on my wrists.

"A cutter?" I was mystified, and drew hard on my cigarette, down until the ember glowed.

"You cut yourself?"

As I thought about her question I realized that there must be a whole group of people who cut themselves all the time, maybe not for suicide, but just to cut.

"I tried to kill myself," I answered, with a flush of shame, still embarrassed by my ineffectual scrapings of the kitchen knife.

She smiled mildly, unsurprised. "I cut to keep myself from killing myself. It feels good, doesn't it? The pain goes away for a little while."

I nodded, a little reluctantly. I wasn't sure I wanted to be talking to this girl. Nevertheless, I found myself intrigued. Even if the cutting itself hadn't been the point, cutting was surely part of what I had done. To find relief from inner pain. I thought about it for only a moment, remembering the sensation of pleasure that came every time I had stroked the blade across my skin. It mystified me that I could feel both emotions at once.

The guard announced that our fifteen minutes were up, and we jumped as if we were adolescents huddled over an illicit magazine, and then tramped up the stairs. Back inside, I unwrapped my wrists. The stitches would come out, the cuts would begin to heal and eventually disappear, and the silver tracery would be forever carved on my skin, proof of my failure. I was deeply ashamed that I had been such a novice, and I was growing angrier and angrier with myself because I had made such a botch of it.

My friends came to visit, like ghosts who reminded me of my old life, but I hated it when they put their faces around the curtain into my cubicle. I was glad that I had on the long sleeves and thick socks that covered the raw meat of my arms and ankles. No one knew about the pills I had taken: they seemed to me not to count in the final tally of events, even though the doctors kept harping on the fact that I had been unconscious when I came into the emergency room and had to have my stomach pumped.

My friends were studiedly cheerful, trying to pretend this was just any hospital floor. The truth was staring us all in the face, but we rewrote it. They brought the ordinary things I needed because I had nothing: clothes, shampoo, lotion. Cigarettes, even though Julie told me she had never bought a pack in her life; I had to tell her where to get them. And, of course, books. Books should have given me solace, but I discovered that I couldn't read. My mind raced and I couldn't focus. The meds sometimes helped me to sleep. They were the only way to get unconscious, but mostly I felt so agitated that I could not stop rocking on the edge of my bed.

That night, the violent agitation inside me started up again, and I couldn't control or stop it. I went outside for a smoke at nine, but when I came back in, I was terribly restless. My body felt as if there were high-voltage electricity running through it. Once out of the hospital, I would learn from Norman Greid that what I was experiencing was called a "mixed state," or "dysphoria," a condition particularly common in bipolar illness. I was feeling both depressive and manic symptoms simultaneously, creating a state of extreme agitation. I went back to rocking myself on the edge of the bed, sitting upright and clasping my knees to my chest.

I felt like I would explode.

Suddenly, the urge to hurt myself was overwhelming. It was not a desire to die, but an imperative to lessen the pain. However, there was nothing on hand to use, not even a sharp edge against which to rub my arm. I kept looking, crawled under the bed to search for a metal protrusion. At last, I spotted it: the metal prong that hitched my watch closed.

I got up on the bed and with one eye on the door in case a nurse came to check for thirties, unwrapped the bandage on my right wrist and started there, despite the fact that the recent cuts were still painful. I scratched and scratched, digging the prong down in, as deep as I could. Then I stopped, sated. The aching and stinging there now felt good, a release from the agitation. If I hurt on the outside, I couldn't hurt on the inside.

But then I began to worry. I would lose my privileges. I could not even ask for a Band-Aid. I was supposed to be evaluated the next day for release—now I would have to stay longer. There was no way they would let me leave now.

The nurse on duty was kind when I wandered out onto the hallway, my wrist in front of me like a badge, and asked for a Band-Aid.

She took a look at my arm, and then applied some antibiotic from a tube. She wrapped it with gauze and tape.

"I feel so stupid," I confessed with a despairing shake of my head. I wanted to hide my hand behind my back, as if I had only been a naughty child. "I was just so agitated. I couldn't sit still— it was as if I were being attacked by a swarm of bees."

"I know what you mean," she said comfortingly. "We have a lot of patients who have agitated mood swings. This isn't the worst I've seen." She disappeared for a minute and then returned with a paper cup.

"Here," she said, shaking the pill into my palm. "Your doc ordered it for sleep."

I took it, gratefully.

Because she was so empathetic, I did not feel guilty; I did not hate myself for what I had done. It was as if my new wrist slashes had come as a sort of given. I had cut myself before, I might cut myself again. And now I had better insight into why I had done it. I thought, hopefully, that maybe I never would do it again.

"I have to take this away now," she said, unstrapping my watch from my wrist.

I did not protest. Her kindness filled me with warmth that, for this moment, took away my desire to bang my head against the wall. Her gentleness reminded me of the way Nana would cleanse a skinned knee, slowly, just a little bit at a time. I went back to my bed and dropped into a deep, exhausted sleep.

THE NEXT MORNING, my roommate looked over at me, when, for the first time, I pulled open my cubicle curtain. Her visitors had just left, and I was sitting on my bed trying to read. As I had expected, I had bought myself several more days on the unit because of the stunt with my watch the night before. I had been castigating myself for being so stupid, but I tried to smile at this new friend. We introduced ourselves, and then qualified our names with our disease. For three days we had been listening to each other brush our teeth, wash our faces, pee and shit in our communal bathroom, but still we hadn't met. There was an absurdity to such close quarters when the corresponding need for privacy was so crucial. Only the curtains separated us and all discussion, whether from visitors or doctors, was plainly heard.

So now we laughed at the irony. Laughing with someone felt good.

"Tell me about the ward?" I asked. "It seems like there's an awful lot of different patients here."

"Oh, we've got two ECTs—that's electric shock therapy—and I'm one of those, one schizophrenic, that's Ed—you've probably met him—he's really worried about his penis."

"Yeah, last night he wanted me to check his size out—not much different than most of the sane men you see."

She laughed again. "Yeah, size is his obsession. That's what he says to everyone who comes on that's new."

"No special preference for me."

"So, going on from there, there's one MPD, that's multiple personality disorder, and three bipolar disorders. That's the family on Unit 4."

"It's such a load of bull. All these As and Bs and garden time and smokes or no smokes."

"And there's a lot you can do to earn better privileges, how you can please the doctors so you get better status."

"Like what?"

"Like going to morning meeting and talking, even if it's about nothing—they just want you to participate. And always going to the women's meeting on 2B."

"I hate that meeting! But I don't see why I can't be over on that unit."

"Cause they can't watch you well enough. They can't even really do that here—you're just too clever. Who ever heard of cutting yourself with a watch strap."

"How did you know?"

"The ward's a pretty gossipy place. Not much is private."

I looked down and fiddled with my blanket. "I feel so stupid."

"Hey, you never know where your illness is going to take you." She shrugged.

We talked for a while longer until it was visiting hours, and she had a load of family coming in. I sat and stared at the wall for a while, feeling disappointed, even though my family had stayed for a while, and only left recently.

As the shifts changed and new med students, interns, and residents came on board, I put up with their continual stream of redundant questions with a disingenuous smile. I was faking cooperation like mad.

The night after I had been, once again, promoted back to status 2A, I had just fallen asleep when I was visited by a new resident. I had shut off my light at about ten o'clock, going to bed early in an attempt to foil the late-night agitation I had been experiencing. On waking, irritably, I asked him for a Risperdal, which was the drug Norman had prescribed for those times when I couldn't conquer the out-of-control feelings any other way— but this was a teaching hospital, and in order to get a tablet I had to explain my condition all over again to him, and then he had to track down the attending physician to obtain the okay for the new prescription.

The particular resident who had interrupted my sleep that night seemed to fancy himself Sigmund Freud: he asked me about my cutting in great detail. He grew stiff with disbelief when I told him that the occurrence with the watch strap was the first time I had ever cut solely to cut myself. He insisted I was lying. I'd never been accused of lying, not once, since I had come onto the unit, and his proclamation made me furious. I stared at him, with his big fat face pinched under his too small tortoise-rimmed glasses, and suddenly wanted to laugh. What did I care what he thought—I knew the truth.

Suddenly then I felt frightened: what if he wrote down in my chart that I was deliberately lying? Would they reassess me and commit me for another stay? This time I would face an enforced three-week commitment, a determination they could make regardless of what I said or wanted: the state could then authorize them to hold me for that length of time. If my insurance wouldn't cover staying at this hospital, I would then be sent to a different facility, run by the state. Once again, visions of ghastly institutions played through my mind, the old pictures that I had gleaned as a teenager watching gratuitously exaggerated movies. Fear clutched at my chest. Talking with him renewed my sense of having been a naughty child who now must confess and apologize, and I was relieved when he left.

Of course, I could not then return to the welcome darkness of sleep.

I waited a while, fighting the urge to hurt myself once again, and then went out into the hall and sat down next to the desk. My night nurse sat beside me and listened as, for the first time, I began to talk about my newfound desire to cut myself: how it helped the painful numbness of my depression on the one hand, how it alleviated my anxiety on the other. After a while, my Risperdal began to take effect, and I shuffled back to bed. For the first time talking with someone about my destructive urge had prevented acting on that urge. For the first time, despite my dark feelings of despair, I felt a little hope fill me. A precious golden liquid, not to be spilt.

{a cool distance}

IT WAS JIM who brought me home from the hospital. He was as
solicitous as a nurse, tucking me into our bed and plumping my
pillows as if I were an invalid. He left me alone. I didn't tell him
that the best thing for me would have been to get up and be with
the bustle and company of my family.

Once I was on my feet again, the children seemed to accept
my apology for everything that had happened. They trooped off
to school each day, and then came home after working on the
school newspaper or lacrosse practice to do their homework.
Still, at night, as I sat on the foot of their beds as we talked
before sleep, Gabe repeatedly asked me to promise that I would
never hurt myself again. I began to understand what they had
endured on that night, with the police swarming through the
house, their mother carried off screaming, strapped to a stretcher.
It never occurred to me that they, too, worried that they might
be the ones to discover me if I hurt myself again.

Jim was quiet. Too quiet. Day in and day out, I felt only a cool
distance emanating from him. I had expected him to be angry
with me; perhaps on some level I wanted him to be angry. I was

certainly filled with more and more self-loathing as the days slowly moved onward. A new sort of awareness began to dawn on me, as I awoke once again to the pain of living, day following day.

I had allowed a suicide attempt to touch my children, and I still didn't really understand why I had done it. There were plenty of other times when I had been depressed, but never before had I taken such an extreme action. And so I remained numb a lot of the time, still speechless, still without explanation or expiation.

As the time passed, I began to understand that Jim was not going to have any overtly angry reaction at what I had done. I welcomed the idea of his potential anger because of its familiarity: I had once been angry with my mother for just this. It was something I knew how to handle, so instead, his silence mystified me. I knew neither Jim nor the children owed me answers about how they were feeling; it was I who owed the answers to them.

My hospital stay haunted me, fraying the edges of my days as if I were a ragged sheet put through the spin cycle of the dryer too many times. Several times a week, I went to see Ben Berns, who had given up his sterile university office for the one at his home, a small cottage set on the edge of his property amidst winter-blooming perennials. Several species of lavender outlined the curving path of gravel. At the end of that path, a cup of herbal tea and his nurturing approach awaited me every Monday and Thursday. I was overwhelmingly grateful for his compassion.

December went by with a subdued Christmas. Then the rains of January began in earnest. In early February the daffodils bloomed, in early March the cherry and magnolia trees unfolded, but I noticed inside me a distant feeling: that was the outside world and I was locked in my own tiny room.

Jim's remote demeanor was exacerbating my depression. I was reaching out to someone who kept backing away from me silently, as if I were contagious. Despite his retreat, he continued to deny that he felt anything except love. I had expected that being back at home with him again would salve the wound the suicide attempt had made, but though Jim remained friendly, I could still see cool, dead space behind his eyes. I wasn't reaching him, which brought me to a state of despair. He refused to discuss any of it. That, too, was familiar.

One night several weeks later, on our way out of our favorite Italian restaurant, I stopped on the macadam of the parking lot and spontaneously reached up to embrace him. He jerked his face away from my lips. I just stood there, stunned and hurt, my handbag drooping off my shoulder. In all the eighteen years of our marriage, he had always responded to me eagerly, whether in private or in public.

He started walking to the car as if nothing had happened.

As we buckled our seatbelts, I turned to him. "Why won't you kiss me?" I asked, at last sickened by pretending nothing was wrong. I was giving voice to my strongest fear: did he still love me?

"I don't feel very sexual about you right now," he said at last.

His answer was like a punch to the gut. After a minute I recovered my balance and decided that, while it wasn't good news, it was better than silence.

"Are you still angry with me? You know I don't think about 'that' anymore."

"I keep telling you I'm not angry," he said with exasperation. "I just don't feel like kissing you right now."

"I don't understand. Why are you so cold?"

"Let's just drop it," he said, turning the key in the ignition.

Acute anxiety now: he was fleeing to some place I could not see or understand or share; he simply wasn't going to let me into his world anymore.

That night in the car he had given me something far worse to worry about than anger.

Time passed uneventfully—but I continued to feel on edge, ready to tip over even as I strove for health. We visited my father in Boston; in the basement I stood and eyed the package of razor blades he had handy for scraping paint off the glass of the windows he had cleaned that fall. Numb, numb—wishing once again that I could let the bad feelings out by cutting myself as I had in the hospital. But I knew that would send Jim even further away. I climbed the cellar stairs and went to sit in the den and watch television with everyone else; the banality of it stopped the waterfall of my destructive thoughts. Still, I did not sink so low that I wanted to kill myself.

While I had originally thought that discussing Jim's feelings might ease the problem, as March turned toward April, he still would not embrace me, cuddle with me, make love. He only relented once from his continued silence to explain that my suicide attempt had come as a betrayal of our marriage because he had struggled for so many years to ease my depression. He felt frustrated and, most importantly, hurt that I had not confided my desperation to him that night over the phone. "I don't know if I can ever feel the same way about you again," he said, matter-of-factly.

Suddenly I felt as if I had crossed some indelible line with the suicide attempt, dragging him behind me; I didn't know if we could ever turn around and cross back over it again. Would we ever be able to resume our relationship as a couple? My uncertainty deepened as he grew more and more distant. I didn't know how to fight for him or for the marriage: I was afraid any attempt I made would only alienate him further. He had painted a protective glaze over his pain and I could not crack its surface.

Trying not to cry at night, I wrapped my arms around myself and waited. And waited. There, trying to stay awake on my side of the bed, I hoped that he would traverse the distance between us.

Several months after I had come home from the hospital, Ben Berns tentatively suggested that perhaps I would be better supported and happier with a man who was more emotionally available. I discarded his suggestion violently, panicked at the idea that I might have to live without the stability of Jim. In the face of my resistance to the idea of separation, Ben came up with the idea that couples therapy might help us work out Jim's anger and distance, as well as my depression and desperation. Maybe with the aid of a mediator and an interpreter we could learn how to talk to each other again.

But Jim had always been adamant about the lack of efficacy of "talk therapy" (at least as far as his own life was concerned), and I doubted that he would be willing to see a therapist, even with me in tow. Later that day, after work, I put out Ben's suggestion and, to my astonishment, Jim readily agreed, despite his fear that he would at last speak his true feelings about both me and our marriage.

Ben found us Rose Kramer, who specialized in marital therapy. We shielded the children, not letting them know that we were going to see a marriage counselor. Once in Rose's office, the two of us seated together on the yellow couch, Jim gradually began to pour out a litany of fury and alienation.

"We have nothing in common," he said. I couldn't believe that he thought this to be true. I could have listed so many feelings and activities we had shared over the years.

As the sessions rolled along, increasingly my breath would freeze in my lungs as I heard the many ways in which he felt I had failed him over the last eighteen years. After having spent so much time in a marriage that had seemed solid, he now revealed how much time he had spent furious with me and hating my instabilities. I tried to explain how I had been totally ignorant of his distress because he had always hidden it from me.

"You wouldn't have been able to handle any of it," he retorted.

I grew angry. He hadn't even given me the opportunity to try and rectify my mistakes: I felt blindsided, because many of his complaints predated the suicide attempt by years.

"I hate her depression," he went on, talking to the therapist as if I weren't even in the room. "And her migraines are totally out of control. She just grates on me constantly."

"I don't understand," said Rose, lifting her eyebrows. "Depression is treatable these days and so are migraines. Why are these two things such showstoppers for you?"

He only shrugged, unimpressed with her logic. He felt how he felt—and that was that.

After a month, we stopped sitting on the couch together. Every time I reached out to him, he backed further away.

A new and strong fear invaded my mind. I heard finality in all his words.

My inner voice was direct and unnerving. "He's moving away from you, and you know it. You're going to have to do without him."

But Ben, Norman, and Rose all reassured me that I was worrying needlessly—Jim was, they promised, still very much committed to the marriage; it would just take time before he could work out his anger and relegate it to the past. It would take a while before he could trust me again. In our therapy sessions, Rose reminded us both that usually her patients left her care to continue their marriages once again, and that generally they were successful.

Though Jim could finally vent his feelings about the past, he could not listen when we discussed the present, or break through to his deeper emotions of anger and betrayal surrounding the suicide attempt. Rose finally dealt directly with his recalcitrance to introspection over these issues. "Hey, come on," she admonished him. "I'm not a dentist—this isn't supposed to be like pulling teeth."

But, whether true or not, I was sure I knew why Jim was so distant. It had always seemed as if he just wasn't mentally wired for the kind of analysis that would enable him to make the necessary connections; it would be very difficult for him to achieve an insight that might help us work through a difficult period. Perhaps he was holding me at arm's length with excuses about not having things in common as a way of preventing being abandoned by me again. He must have wondered: December had been the first try; who could say if it would be the last? He desperately wanted to be neither present nor responsible if I should make an attempt again. In the end, however, it was all guesswork on my part. Rebuffed by his silence when we were alone, I relinquished my attempts to articulate my need for him, and he began to move into a phased abandonment that confused me: he was there for doing homework with the boys, but he wasn't around to hold me or even to talk with me. We had never been so physically distant.

Overwhelmed and frightened, finally I began to perceive, for certain, where we were headed; I started trying to hide my real feelings from him, terrified that he would use something—anything—as ammunition in the therapy sessions that had quickly become a torturous exercise for me. Each time Wednesday came around, I had to force myself to remember our lunchtime appointment, set up at that hour because it was difficult for him to lose time at work. Often I grew distraught and couldn't control my emotions or my tears; sometimes I raised my voice to fight off my panic. I wanted to try and convince him that whatever he was accusing me of just wasn't true, but he always kept a dispassionate expression on his face. If I became upset, he would lift his hands in a shrug, telling Rose, "I hate her when she's like this—do you see what I have to deal with?"

Often I began to sob, loudly, my nose running. Rose always sent me to the bathroom to recover, but regaining my balance was only temporary.

By the spring, Jim was working into the early hours of the morning on his computer in the bedroom, making certain that we wouldn't have to face—or touch—each other in bed. He had always thrived on working seven days a week, but now, even as he complained of being exhausted, he allowed his inner engine to drive him harder than ever before.

Nothing ameliorated my pain and fear over the deterioration of our marriage. Daytimes I wandered through the house, a terrified ghost, loaded on meds and thinking once again of cutting or killing myself. Only my concern for the boys was keeping me from jumping over the edge.

Jim had been more than a husband to me—I had helped him grow from a boy into a man, and from a graduate student into a respected business executive; he had helped me mature from a girl into a woman and from a fledgling novelist into an established writer. Sitting in Rose Kramer's office, as he claimed that we had nothing to share any longer, I could think of many things that we certainly both enjoyed. From my perch on the edge of my chair, I reminded him that we had traveled together just a few years before, delighting in the long walks among the ruins of Pompeii and swimming in the blue grotto waters of Capri. At crucial points in our lives, we had held each other as we cried, and then as we laughed, and we were able to respect each other's need for silence.

We had created a family against all the predicted odds. We had helped each other find our strengths as parents. We had reveled in our children's achievements. He loved my cooking, and it was a high point of every night when he returned home from work, the family gathered around the kitchen table: brisket and potato latkes, marinated pork tenderloin, veal chops with saffron rice. Settled in our new home, he and I had even stopped fighting and seemed to have rediscovered our love for each other. Every evening we had helped the kids with their homework—an arduous but imperative task in the highly competitive academics of our area. Yes, to me it seemed as if the number of ways in which we were bonded was too many to count, but in his eyes their importance had dimmed, or perhaps had never been strong enough to combat the angry emotions, always unspoken. Perhaps they were no longer a blessing, but a curse, emphasizing all the ways we were tied together and all the ways he ached to break us apart.

BY THE END of June, I finally understood what someone with a clearer mind would have intuited immediately: he was seeing another woman. A month later, though we were still in therapy, he gave me two choices: either I could look the other way or he could just leave.

Concealing my despair and my continuing sense of confusion, I didn't know what to do—would begging him to stay and work with Rose do any good? Despite the onslaught of furious revelations that had felt so cruel in our therapy sessions, I finally heard the truth. And it was then that I discovered that a tiny bit of pride remained in me: I drew its tatters around my shoulders like a moth-eaten sweater.

"Is this separation really what you want?" he had asked me at one point, clearly torn emotionally.

"Will you break it off with her?"

He shook his head.

"What kind of self-respect could I have?" I responded, spreading my hands for emphasis.

Neither of us said a word more.

Clearly, he had not walked through in his mind what this move would cost us all. For the first time, it seemed to me, he was deciding to do something solely for himself, no matter how it affected me, or, even more strongly, our sons. Yet, I believed that somewhere behind the concrete wall he had erected lay a pool of love, and that with time, he would dip a ladle and return once again to the man I knew. Even the attorneys we would eventually hire kept advising us to leave our marriage intact, as, sometimes, we still seemed to care so much about one another.

The idea that he might refuse to come home terrified me increasingly, and I didn't even touch the telephone. The voice in my head was insistent, getting louder and louder and more and more frequent

"Fool," it said. "You're too late."

IT WAS A warm and sunny day on the Fourth of July weekend. I was lying in the backyard, pretending to be working on my tan, but really I was remembering other holidays, like taking the kids to their first fireworks and watching their awed faces light up under the explosions of blue and red and white over their heads. For a moment, Gabe had been scared by the noise and had buried his face in my breasts. It seemed a very long time ago.

Six months had passed since my suicide attempt, and Jim was leaving the house for good. A legal separation was now in place. His departure broke something in me that day—my sense of self-confidence and the safety our marriage had promised—integral elements of my life that could never be repaired. Once again I was standing alone and abandoned. I felt as if I would not make it through this repeat of my childhood history. As I lay there pretending I had no care in the world, anxiety filled me and overflowed into a terrible ditch of despair.

I kept thinking about all the times we had entertained in this backyard. Only last year on this same day we had thrown an enormous party that lasted from noon till eight o'clock because people were having such fun and didn't go home until their children fell apart one by one, their sunburned faces and chlorine-stained red eyes a testament to their total exhaustion, until their fathers flung them up over their shoulders like sacks of flour. And then there was the first year we had moved in. We had known no one, but a neighbor was determined that we not be alone for the holiday and so invited us to the fireman's parade. The boys decorated their bikes with avid first-timers' enthusiasm and we all went off to follow the fire truck up and down the main streets of town. At that point the idea of suicide felt as remote as the idea that one of us might die prematurely—death being a threat but an unlikely one, one with which all people live.

I was hiding as Jim went through the house. He had rented a U-Haul, and cajoled a friend into helping him with the heavy lifting: the project wouldn't take too long to finish, and as much as I wished it would be over quickly, simultaneously I wished it would take forever—that Jim would remain forever—that he would change his mind.

I was afraid there would be many empty spots throughout the house we had furnished together. The closet we shared, big enough to have been a baby's nursery, would be hardest hit, and the bookshelves as well, because he intended to take much of what belonged to him, though nothing of what belonged to "us." That would come later, if he decided to leave me permanently.

Memory assaulted me and surreptitiously I brushed away the tears that were collecting in the hollows beneath my cheeks and then spilling down over my chin into my cleavage. I wanted to sob at the pictures memory drew: I remembered the early light falling across the white skin of his back as he stood and stretched on the balcony of our room in Positano overlooking the Mediterranean; I remembered our transfixed appreciation of the Gutenberg Bible in the British Museum in London, with its elaborate gold leaf and perfect penmanship, protected in a glass case; I remembered the way he would never shine his shoes and I had to burrow into the closet to retrieve them, secretly, for the cobbler. So many scenes built on love.

Jim called to me. Reluctantly, I got up off the chair. At some point, I would appreciate the reserve he had exhibited in terms of what to take with him: the house appeared nearly normal, except for his clothing and some of the bookshelves, which were pockmarked with empty spaces. In the kitchen, I selected a few pots and pans for him, the cookie sheet that had been my mother's (used solely now for French fries because I never baked sweets). This offering was made with the hope that he would change his mind and come back to us.

He had taken many of his books, a little furniture, and some plants I pressed on him. Somehow it felt imperative to be helpful and loving: maybe he would remember this when he considered whether to return. Maybe it would break through the ice that I still saw behind his eyes.

He didn't want to change the way the house looked in any major sense, for it would continue to be the boys' home and mine and he was sensitive to that. Yet, despite my efforts to put on a strong front, I could not help but feel that he was just washing me off, like the dirt and sweat after a bike ride. It appeared to me that he had no need for me, or for our memory-filled possessions.

I kept reminding myself that this was only a trial separation— that he might come back in three months or so, satisfied to have hurt me in the way I had hurt him with my suicide attempt, and after he had cleansed himself of the lure of his "other woman." I believed he would come back, and sat down at the kitchen table, struggling against my anxiety.

And then we walked through the rooms and he pointed out what he had loaded onto his U-Haul. His huge mahogany desk in the bedroom had been uprooted, leaving a big hole in the room, its outline set deeply into the rug and rubbed in shadow against the white wall. Modem and phone wires were left dangling in colored disarray.

"Where will you go?" I asked, suddenly a little wobbly, imagining some empty motel room with a bedded down twin and only a television set for company. I was feeling a little protective for him, even though he had angered and hurt me so deeply. Compassion, it seemed, was not so difficult to achieve.

"I've got a rental right off Knightly."

Knightly was only a few streets away from our house.

"I wanted to be close so the kids could bike back and forth."

"A rental apartment? Already?" I was now nonplussed.

"A house. A small one," he amended, clearing his throat. "A three bedroom."

The blood roared in my ears. There I was, picturing him sad and alone, when he had already set himself up. He was well on his way to being totally independent. Suddenly I was terribly angry. "How did you manage that in just a week or two?" I heard my tone turn sarcastic. "Or were you really looking for a while behind my back?"

"For Christ's sake, Linda, I started last week, after I left here. The hotel was getting too expensive and I could hardly take the boys there when they get home from camp next week. So I jumped on it. Do you want to see it?"

I knew it would upset me, but I was upset anyway. As my boys' mother, I should check out the place they were going to be spending half their time, as the temporary custody arrangement dictated.

We took two different cars, and even that felt strange. It was eerie: going to a house I'd never seen, where my husband would be living without me after we had been together for nearly twenty-five years, including those four we had spent after college, living together in that tiny studio apartment, before our engagement.

He was right about the boys needing a real home away from home, I thought as I walked from room to room, hiding the fact that, once again, I was crying. I wiped my eyes on my sleeve viciously. I wanted to look strong but here I was crying in the place where my husband would entertain his new girlfriend.

There were single bedrooms for each one on the ground floor, albeit covered in revolting floral wallpaper, and a small bath they would share, complete with deteriorating grout. Upstairs there was a large master bedroom with a huge Jacuzzi tub in the recently remodeled bathroom, and a king-sized bed with a new, expensive-looking duvet.

Later that night, when I went into our closet, I stopped short.

Jim's closet poles were totally empty except for one suit he had mysteriously missed during his exodus. Nothing else remained except old wire hangers knocked askew, nothing but black scuff marks on his shoe shelves. I might never again see the clutter of his shirts, the rows of suits and jackets, pants folded sloppily over their hangers, the snaky tangle of belts on their preposterously tiny rack.

I started rummaging in the drawer where I kept my minimal supplies for sewing on buttons. Finding a large pair of pinking shears inherited from Nana, I snatched up the single suit he had forgotten to take and cut off both the legs and the arms. Maybe I was sending him an unconscious message: what kind of man would run away when his family needed him?

Then the emptiness hollowed a crater inside me, and for the first time all day I let myself sink to my knees and let out the big heavy sobs. This was all that remained of nearly two decades of marriage.

IT WAS JIM'S idea that though we were now officially separated and he was seeing another woman, we could still remain in therapy with Rose Kramer. I trusted Rose like a grandmother, so that, even though I spent most of my time in our sessions crying, she counseled me privately to be patient and non-demanding. I dropped five pounds in the first week I was alone. Was I about to lose another person I loved? Was this situation, truly, all of my own making? This time to a kind of living death? I did not think I could survive another separation. Despite our situation, however, our visits to Rose Kramer were predicated on the idea that he might change his mind.

I was willing to do anything to keep alive the hope that our marriage could be salvaged, even when it was humiliating to know, without any direct information, that he was spending time with another woman while we were still working in therapy. At last I got angry with him and the situation: why was I bothering to undertake the work of therapy if he was involved with someone else—no matter how preliminary the stage of the relationship? In a turn that would later seem preposterous, Rose suggested that we begin dating each other as well—in spite of Jim's outside romance. She still held out hope that we might get back together, and told me in private that men who had high-powered careers often returned to their wives. She suggested, strongly, that I not give Jim any ultimatums.

I kept waiting, hoping that Rose's predictions would prove out. We went to dinner as a way of trying to rebuild our relationship, Jim providing the small courtesies like opening doors for me or pulling out the chair at the table in a restaurant: these niceties were so out of character that I could only conclude he had learned them from someone else. Our dates were a disaster in every way. He obviously loathed being with me and barked at everything I said throughout the evening, or else he was ominously silent. Only going to a movie was safe because we could not start an argument when we were in the dark of a theater watching a film.

Nothing I did was right—everything I said "grated" on him and he didn't hesitate to tell me so. Through others I learned my female nemesis was stable and steady with a flourishing career.

Beautiful. Ideal. In my mind, my own accomplishments paled beside hers: who could compete?

In the autumn, Jim took me to Arizona; we went to Los Alamos, to see where the atom bomb had been created and exploded for the first time. I could only feel that the place he had chosen to take me was a metaphor: he had set off another explosion in my life, and now the landscape was a desolate crater. We ate at several good restaurants, and took in many of the shops, looking at the artwork and pretending we had common walls on which to hang it.

That night he didn't even put his arm around me in the bed.

All my fragile striving to right myself in the aftermath of his departure toppled like a pitifully crooked tower of blocks. Just as at other times in my life, I was alone, abandoned. I alternated between shocks of needled emotion and periods of dull, numb emptiness.

After our trip, I couldn't stand the indecision any longer. I confronted him in Rose's office: what was he going to do—come or go? He looked at me long and hard, and with that look, the anger I felt transformed into a sorrow that would become, over the ensuing months, permanent. He was ready to move on. A short time later, the legal machinery started up.

And so we met for the last time as husband and wife over a round conference table in a lawyer's office—rather than in our own home next to the boys, with Jim carving the holiday turkey.

{pretty red stripes}

SMOKING A CIGARETTE, I sat in my car in the parking lot at the edge of Oak Manor Park. Valentine's Day had come to California and there was a warm wet rain streaking down my windshield. It was a year and counting since my suicide attempt. I had been without Jim for all that time, if I counted his departure from when he began to withdraw and shut me out. The rain was having a curious, prosaic effect on me: it summoned up old memories of my mother and how she had toilet trained me by running the tap.

But I wasn't there to think about the past. I fastened my mind on more recent events.

The large area of well-tended grass was bounded by a fence of lattice design, and enormous oak trees waved their leaves in the wind like women shaking out their hair. Immaculately kept, the profusion of shrubbery gave off an air of serenity, as if someone ought to be playing croquet next to the gazebo. Before my separation from Jim, this was where I walked my two Dalmatians, Rhiannon and Tia. Now I had only my young dog, Gulliver, and I never brought him here, a place too haunted by memory.

After I had been discharged from the hospital in December of 1997, I had at least tried to keep both the thoughts of suicide and my internal voice tamped down under a cheerful surface, tried to keep up with my friends and persevere with my activities. But slowly everything normal began to drop away. I missed Jim as fiercely as I had supposed I would.

In my mind, suicide was obviously off-limits, never to be experienced again, but as the months passed, moving into the new year, I acted increasingly upon the education I had received at the hospital: Cutting 101.

For the eight weeks following the anniversary of my first suicide attempt, my thoughts had turned obsessively on the axis of death; just surviving blanked out the red hot touch of passion, the blue of cool comforting hands, the celery green of that new spring's energy. Once again, the world was black and white. And so, that day in the park that had once been ours, I ruminated about the terrible engulfing dark of Rhiannon and Tia's death; I wanted to cry, but could not. Jim was gone, my mother was gone, two of my dogs were gone. And despite my mother's promise on that wintry day when my kitten had died, "living on" in my heart was not nearly enough.

Back before my empty weekend days began to extend themselves into some kind of twilight sleep, back before I'd thought I could escape the legacy by simply looking away from that abyss into which I could so easily fall, I was like the drunk who thinks he can get clean simply by avoiding the bottle. Yet, here I was, returning to a place that was familiar and filled with good memories. Sadness prevailed nonetheless. I felt only grief at discovering myself once again, right here, right where the dogs and I had been so united.

And so I promised myself, like a drug addict, that I would take only one bump of death that rainy day.

And this was why I had sought out such a solitary location; it suited my intention, a small treat right there in a parking lot.

I had become a true cutter, feeling better each time I sliced into my skin. I had already cut myself earlier that week, despite the fact that after my first bout with cutting following the suicide attempt, I had promised Ben that I would never do it again.

"Why do you hurt yourself this way?" he asked.

"It's a way of letting the poison out. Taking control again." Desperately I tried to make him understand how I felt. "It makes the voice in my head shut up. To bleed is a way of knowing you're alive."

He shook his head; he plainly did not understand the miraculous power cutting had to make me feel better. Ben drew up a contract requiring my signature, handwritten on a yellow-lined piece of paper that I carried in my wallet. In it, I promised that I wouldn't try to hurt myself, not even to the smallest degree, because he warned me he would not act as a therapist to anyone who was actively self-mutilating. I signed, but I knew in that moment, exactly then, that it was not realistic to believe that I could simply decide to stay in sufficient control; I could not promise that I would abstain from this kind of enjoyment—no matter how small it was—and so I lied. Death and its near misses had a power all their own. It seemed to me that the urge to cut controlled me, rather than the reverse. The punishment for breaking my contract with Ben would be the forfeiture of therapy with him—but in that moment, I didn't care.

I had also promised him, specifically, that should I cut myself, I would confess immediately. I knew, of course, that following such revelations he would refuse to see me any longer and I would be alone once again. The consolation prize would be that he would help me find a new therapist. These conditions did not promote honesty between us; his rigorous rules simply drove my behavior underground. The price for restraining myself was too high—just as the price of cutting was in and of itself very high. The guilt over lying to him paled next to the urge to bleed myself. And so, that week and the week before, I had broken our contract and then remained silent in our sessions, bringing to a close the code of truth that must exist between therapist and patient for true work to continue.

For four days that week, the threat of his withdrawal had kept me from cutting again, but that day in the park, the buzz wanted to get out, and I couldn't hold it back any longer. I didn't care what he would do or that I might be required to lie, or what I would have to do in order to cover my action. I was wresting control in my internal chaos. I had decided to cut my ankles because the wounds would be easier to hide: bandaged wrists would alert Ben immediately.

It was my first time with a razor blade.

An hour ago at the hardware store, I had bought a transparent plastic container of ten, each wrapped in brown paper, each with an edge sharp as a wasp's sting. Carefully I unwrapped the creased paper jacket in which the first lay, savoring in advance the ready-made high it would bring, as if I were sitting down to a roast beef dinner.

I could still feel the high anticipation as I settled into the cushion of my seat and pulled my ankle onto my lap, adroitly fashioning a lotus position beneath the steering wheel. I made a light test run. After a second, delicate ruby beads strung out along my skin. And then a deep breath before I made the first straight controlled shot, its length just two thumb's lengths, maybe a few inches. The sound the blade made as it moved through this level of my skin was something like cloth ripping; it made me grind my lip between my teeth. On the inside of my ankle, the straight white lips of the cut opened and there was a quick rush of blood from the wound.

"Nice color," said my inner voice. "Go back and do it again, a little deeper this time."

I felt the next sharp sting and took a deep breath; my face

flushed. In my life, in that moment, nothing was happening except this. I hated doing it. I loved doing it. I paused then; tears watered in my eyes as I trembled in the blank purity of the instant. Exhaled then, a long blow outward. Flooded with pleasure. With my windshield running rain and the inside windows steaming up, I was in a cocoon. Unobserved. My despair seeped out, if only for a moment. I was bringing Death close, drawing him deep within the circle of my arms.

I HAD TIME to ruminate between cuts, and my mind tipped backwards, to the days of other more, many more, pleasurable things: to the walks I had taken with the dogs here. My family had had five Dalmatians and one litter of eight puppies when I was growing up, and all of us believed that dogs were something to celebrate. Dogs kept us alive, sometimes even when my mother was making a bid for death. In February of 1966, she wrote a poem called "Live," using as inspiration our new puppies, who bleated out little hungry cries as they crawled around, searching for the teat.

When Jim and I moved to California, we at last had a large backyard; with the children in school full-time, it was easy to reinstate the happy legacy of Dalmatians in my life. In this way did the one-year-old show-quality bitch Rhiannon, named after a Welch witch and the Fleetwood Mac song, become ours. I was disappointed that she wasn't a puppy, but we bonded almost immediately and I put my desire for a dog in its earliest months aside.

For the next several years, I took lessons in dog handling and obedience training two days a week, practicing on the back lawn every night after supper, while Jim threw the baseball around with the boys. We spoiled Rhiannon shamelessly, and slowly she developed into—as parlance in the trade called it—a "special" dog: one who had rare depths of understanding for the humans who owned her. She did everything I could ask of her, and then even more. As we practiced in the backyard, I realized that I hadn't had such fun since summer camp, where I loved to ride and show horses.

Later that year, I brought a new puppy into our home. The calm of my two years alone with Rhiannon was shattered by the arrival of a rambunctious bombshell, Tia, just twelve weeks old. The kids were thrilled.

When Rhiannon turned two, I carefully chose a mate for her, putting genetics first to make sure I had a litter of lively but quiet, obedient dogs, those who would defy the ubiquitous stereotype that Dals were hyperactive. We sent Rhiannon to Minneapolis to be bred and decided we might perhaps take another pup from the litter, scheduled for January. Jim had rolled his eyes at the idea of a three-dog household, but I wanted a male this time around. As the time of Rhiannon's whelping drew near, I laid out the instruments, the towels, the scale, the rickrack that would encircle every puppy's neck as he or she arrived so that I would be able to track both weights and well-being.

One by one the puppies slid out, still encased in their watery blue bubbles. My hands shook and nausea erupted at the bloody mess before me. A particular smell, coppery and pungent, pervaded the warm room but I couldn't have named it—something that hovered, perhaps, between life and death.

In a few moments all the nausea and the shaking of my hands stopped, as I lost myself in helping Rhiannon open the membranes. I tied off the umbilical cords and then weighed the pups as they came. It was an experience I would never forget. I held beginning life cradled between the palms of my hands, and perhaps this was the reason I had done it to begin with. Perhaps I had needed to rediscover the magic my entire family felt when our litter of puppies pulled my mother away from her instinct to die, and returned to her a desire to live.

Rhiannon whelped eight puppies while I was alone in the house early that January weekday afternoon. Nearly all were girls. Eventually I would place "Ashley," the most striking female of the litter, into a home from which I could take her to dog shows. Over time, my co-owner, Pat Maciejewski, would become a deep and valued friend with whom I shared much joy and laughter as we toted the dogs around in her sleek RV. Later, I would breed Ashley to my friend Dawn's best stud. When her litter arrived there was a beautiful boy I immediately claimed as my own, and in this way Gulliver joined our household.

Things were not relaxed between Rhiannon and Tia, however, and soon we were locked into a downward spiral. Though the two dogs initially got along well, when Tia reached adolescence, she made a bid for being the head of the pack, and the two of them also became jealous of their time with me. Nevertheless, I began to train Gulliver for the ring.

One night Rhiannon and Tia grew aggressive over a dropped bagel, and went at each other in a quick, sudden confrontation. It was a dance of unrecognizable, unanticipated hatred. They growled and rose quickly to their haunches, locking on, muzzle to muzzle. When they broke for a moment to establish a new grip, Gabe and I, terrified, managed to drag them into separate rooms. Oozing red gouges and gashes marked the snow of their coats.

After our trip to the vet, I called a recommended behaviorist in desperation. I was afraid to let the dogs together again. She made a house call, and established order. From that point on, as instructed, we hung from every doorknob trash bags chock full of soda cans that were filled with pennies—the loud rattling that came when a bag was shaken was one of the only things to which the fighting dogs would respond. I worked with her several times a week, practicing submission exercises so that the dogs would look to me for their cues, rather than relying on their own instincts as to who was the leader.

Six months went by and it seemed as if they had relented in their sudden hatred of each other—but then, suddenly another fight: Tia's teeth missed Rhiannon's left eye by inches; Rhiannon needed twenty stitches for the slashes in her muzzle, through which blood bubbled as she struggled to breathe.

The gateway had opened. And so it went, fight after fight, the behaviorist arriving, new electric shock collars strapped on, the terrible hatred between them continuing. At last it seemed there was no help for us. Yet I was determined to keep both of them, determined that my love for them would conquer their hatred for each other, just as I had once thought that my love for my mother would conquer her hatred of life.

We were counseled by the behaviorist: never put your hands into the middle of a dog fight. She knew people who had lost fingers, or even, a hand. Gabe in particular grew terrified, and we learned to keep the dogs apart, each confined to her own crate and allowed out only when the other was safely shut away. We lived with an expanding fear that billowed outward into our lives.

There were a total of eight fights, with the bills mounting into the thousands. I didn't remember all the wounds. I didn't remember all the veterinary bills, the surgical packs, the endless visits to the behaviorist. I just remembered each dog's face, so important to me, so destined to endure in my heart.

"If they have another fight," the behaviorist told me at last, "you'll have to put them down."

It was those words, catching me with a gripping nausea, that made me realize how bad things were. I asked her, with desperation, for her opinion on placements, but she shook her head. Even if I could find them other homes, I could not be certain they would be dependably safe—with other dogs, or even with people who might try to separate a fight. I asked around, desperately seeking another solution, scrolling through the pages of names in my membership booklets of the Dalmatian clubs. Not a single other breeder would take on even one of them.

But then, luckily perhaps, a year and a half of peace passed and I relaxed. I got sloppy. The shaker cans were relegated to the closets. And, at last, the dogs slept together on the same bed again, ate side by side again, romped and played and even "mock-fought" from one end of our green acre to the other, under supervision. At six, I supposed, Rhiannon had mellowed. That autumn, when I brought Gulliver into our family, interestingly enough, both older dogs perked up with a youngster around. They had come to an understanding, it seemed.

Hubris led me to complacence, to the belief that I could overcome their instinct for the jugular. And I was also very preoccupied: I had reached the point when I finally understood my mother's wish to die, and saw that the wish had at last become my own. I believed that if I understood, I ought to be able to control it all. I got cocky. With the dogs' lives as well as with my own.

In late November, just before my suicide attempt, I came home from shopping with Gabe and let the dogs loose from their crates. For no reason I could discern, Rhiannon came full blast into the room, snarling and ready, and Tia met her full bore.

In a fury, they fought across the bedroom and knocked over a table, a lamp, and a chair. The blood began to spray across the white sheets. I couldn't stop them. Both Gabe and I stood to one side as instructed, unable to intervene, terrified and useless. I turned to the door for the shaker can bag that should have been hanging on the knob but was not.

At last Tia squirmed under the bed where Gulliver was already hiding. Rhiannon stood panting, her legs splayed, her left ear torn from one side of the pinna to the other, hanging on by only a thin thread of tissue. Blood dripped down the side of her muzzle and onto the carpet.

I bundled them into their crates in the van and sped down the highway to the vet. I didn't want to face the inevitable but my inner voice was virtually clamoring with the obvious. Once in the office, Rhiannon lay down beside me where I sat on the linoleum, and snuggled her head deep into my lap, despite the pain she must have felt from her nearly detached ear. She looked up at me with the dark soulful eyes that had first convinced me to take her home, those dark eyes that had always relied on me to protect and care for her. The blood pooled on the floor.

The vet wound the tourniquet around Rhiannon's leg and located the pulse of her vein beneath her taut white coat. The tech handed over the syringe. My dog looked up at me, right into my eyes, still trusting, and I numbly repressed the words that would stop everything. The minutes had slowed and it was hard to breathe. My hands shook. And so, I simply held my dog because holding her was all that was left for me to do. Her tail was wagging, hard, left to right and back again, but suddenly, like a motor running down, it slowed, and then she was gone from me, away from the touch of my hands and the love in my face. Her eyes stared into mine, empty. I had killed her. Death was in my life, this time in my hands, once more.

Sitting in the car with my razor blade that day in February, I remembered Rhiannon's face with longing, and drew another line across my ankle and watched it bleed, using a tissue to sop up the blood. There were several such bloodied tissues scattered on the passenger seat of the car, and I felt proud that I had been able to cut deeply enough to need to staunch the bleeding. My inner voice was bitter and loud about my inability to keep my dogs alive, and I had no answer to gain relief except to draw another cut.

The bright red of the small perfect incisions on my ankles reminded me of the way the dogs had drawn the blood that stained their snowy coats. I had killed them just before I had tried to kill myself by cutting my wrists, blood blossoming then into the water of the bath. Blood for blood. November to December: the arrival of death twice in the span of a month.

And yet, where they had died, I had failed.

Fourteen months later, in the car now, punishment beckoned. I hated myself for what I had done to them. I tugged my ankle closer and bent over my work, using the forward edge of the blade and following with the center, just as smoothly as a skater cuts circles on fresh ice. I'd dig to China maybe. Down through the layers. Here was sinew. Here was fat, muscle, tendon. What secret lay hidden, here in the strata of my body?

When I was finished, my ankles buzzed but my insides did not and there was relief in this. Still, a sense of letdown suffused me: the petty tidiness of my cuts disappointed after all.

I sat back in the seat, my sense of dissatisfaction growing: for this I would have to powder my wounds, wear thick socks, create a lie for Ben. While cutting might suffice for a while, I could see that one day soon I would grow bored with these pretty red stripes, set back to back like the careful ruler lines of a long-ago grammar school copybook. After a while, I would have to get back to the big time.

{round two}

EVERY DAY I thought about suicide—sometimes seriously, and other times desultorily. I was fragile and felt that I could snap, like a thin stem of a wineglass, at the slightest provocation. I began to stumble around in the deepest tunnel of depression, riding on that familiar conveyor belt in the dark.

I took to bed, ostensibly for a light case of the flu, but when my temperature returned to normal, my mood did not. I didn't push the covers back and get up: as I hid beneath the blankets, both my body and resolve weakened. Any kind of movement reignited the anxiety gnawing on my gut, reminding me, as always, of the bleak totality of all my losses: my mother, Jim, Nana, Poppy, Joannie, Gaga and Grampa, Rhiannon, Tia. My failing work. The unhappy faces of my children at supper when the fourth place setting, empty, made itself so poignantly felt.

Right then, I just wanted to go to sleep.

"What kind of mother are you, wanting to lie down and close your eyes to the world?" the voice recriminated me.

I didn't need the voice to answer the question. I knew the

response and dread grew large and powerful. I had to admit it to myself—I had become a mother like my own.

A good mother gets up and makes the soup; she drives the carpool, goes to work, folds the towels; takes her son's pain and rocks it away. She puts on her best wise face along with her lipstick so that she can deal with whatever the day dishes out.

Folding the negative feelings deep inside me, I feared that to admit the depth of my depression would make it even more real. Sudden bouts of tears and emotions slammed through me on a tide of hypomania, alternating with periods of silent numbness and then an agitated rage—the latter mostly over the divorce. I took the family photo collages made by Rachael and, with one of my sharp razor blades, cut Jim out of every one.

There were some serene moments between these outbursts, when I would remonstrate myself for my temper—despite the fact that I had kept much of it private. I tried to calm myself with the knowledge that at least Jim had left me financially secure. Yet, I concentrated compulsively on the fact that when my marital support terminated in 2009, I would be on my own—and most likely, still writing, which would pay not even a single month of expenses. I worried, constantly, that I would lose my house.

As I looked around at the plight of others—the homeless man on the street corner near the market, the battered women hiding in shelters, the pregnant teenagers who braved the protestors to enter abortion clinics—I was ashamed, but even so, the shame did not wash away the anxiety. And then I would think of the African child whom I had "adopted" through Childreach, living in a village with no running water or toilets. I had pictures of her hanging over my desk, going back at least ten years to when she was a toddler. Now she is a young woman, educated only a bit, but nevertheless able to contribute to the economic well-being of her village by working in the fields. Even she was more productive than I. And what of the soup kitchen, and the Meals on

Wheels program—everything for which I had given so much of myself in a joyous burst of enthusiasm. All gone now, abandoned, as I tried so hard just to keep on living.

I huddled beneath my blanket and I wondered how I could justify my moods—all of which might be construed by others to be self-pity—to those friends and families who had no education on the plight of depressed people? How could they cope, any more than I? Even my love for Nathaniel and Gabe could not keep me from ruminating over my cutting, that lesser cousin to suicide. How I hated being a parent then, because once again it seemed as if being a mother could predetermine whether I lived or died.

The tunnel became blacker and blacker, tighter and tighter, claustrophobic to the point that all I could do was to scream, silently. Even with Ben, who might have helped mitigate my negative affect, I was silent about the increasing intensity of the depression, and canceled several appointments, exaggerating the malaise of a flu long after it had passed. When we did meet, guilt overshadowed every session.

My inner voice pulled me down each time it spoke. I pretended to be deaf and blind to the inevitable crisis approaching me. I spoke of it to no one; I did not even let myself think of it, desperate to pretend it was not happening. Wondering if I had somehow created my own misery was one more reason not to confide in others, or to let myself think clearly about the situation. In this way, doubting my own inner resolve to get better, I unintentionally severed myself from friends and family. The outside world receded from my life. I wasn't a writer. I wasn't a wife. I wasn't a mother.

My identity as an author spiraled away further and further in my mind, like an article of clothing dropped into the blackness of zero gravity. Finally it seemed as if nothing was attached to me in any way at all. Had I ever written or published anything of worth? Or was that, too, as much of a lie as the idea that my marriage had once been solid and good?

Some days the world was all slow motion, and I was a swimmer on the other side of the glass in the aquarium, gone out of my head and heart. I just kept pressing against the current in my struggle to stay upright, my face averted so that no one would know how far down I had sunk.

I thought of my secret cubby, complete with its bottles of medication. Knowing it was there comforted me. The prescription bottles were lined up, full, like penny candy pots, plenty to carry out this job. It reminded me of being nine, when I hoarded my Halloween sweets in a file box, to be eaten one precious piece every day. At forty-six years old, I had prepared a lethal stash of pills, a way out of pain and into pleasure, just as cutting often flooded me with a similar emotion as I tried to obliterate my pain that way. In my hidden cache, I had a box that held my book of instructions from *Final Exit*, a self-deliverance manual for terminal patients, and the small brown jars of drugs.

I had an idea about where to do it, and the proper way to take so much medication successfully. I had found a gigantic pill crusher in the pharmacy one day, which would speed things along. I pictured myself as a good Girl Scout, prepared to bring about the end.

THE LOSS OF my children—for two nights during the week and full-time every other weekend—nearly overwhelmed me. Later these separations would worsen when Jim began to take them more, except when he was traveling, that old arrangement where I raised the children without his presence. Ironically, this time I was expected to tolerate both the separations from the children, and still also be endlessly flexible about the extra days I took over custody from a busy ex-husband. Though perhaps I should have resented that, I was quietly grateful: on the days and the nights the kids were with me, it was much easier to stay afloat.

Jim and I worked out the custody arrangement for the children ourselves. As our "fair and equitable" solution evolved, the attorneys were not involved: we were proud that we had not had to resort to legal intervention. It did not occur to me at that time that Jim could have tried to win sole custody of the boys. Who knew whether leaving them with me was even safe? But he seemed to intuit that if he had taken them from me, I would have totally disintegrated.

He continued to be a father involved in the minutia of his children's lives. In some ways, I hated him for being such a loving, attentive parent because I wanted the kids to complain about him, to hate him for having left—to take my side. But, as Jim and I had promised each other as we drew up the custody arrangement, we would try our very hardest not to put the kids in the middle of our problems or badmouth each other. We strove toward this goal, though sometimes we did not succeed and the children grew surly at what they considered our manipulative behavior. Nevertheless, it seemed to me that we managed this reasonably well, expressing accusations and anger at each other only on occasion, though the children would later disagree with this assessment.

Their own emotions were still in turmoil: my theory was that they felt abandoned by Jim, and that they blamed me for his departure. The children felt totally unprepared for the divorce, and that they had been lied to. Gabe said his life had been ruined—both by my suicide attempt and by his father's absence. Nathaniel argued with his father over why Jim had left.

The situation worsened for them as they watched me wrestle with the depression. The fact that I hadn't written anything in many, many months was becoming more and more frightening to us all.

The children and I continued to hold each other at the edge of their beds. Both still cried inconsolably on some nights, and I was put in the awkward position of attempting to skim over the surface of the problem, hoping to blink back the inevitable tears, to which I felt I had no right.

But, over time, they began to return from his place on Knightly with equanimity: they were unhappy we were separated, but, slowly they had become used to dealing with each of us, alone. On the days when the children were at my house, I tried to be brave and not cry or mope around; I tried to cook pancakes from scratch at breakfast and make their favorite dinners nearly every night. I tried to keep their home changed as little as possible. In the grip of a delusion that Jim might ever cook for them, I sent him a few recipes. Even separated, I still felt intent on making us seem like a family.

Some of the time, even when I tried my utmost, I failed at all these attempts to keep normalcy. Some of the time I just broke down and cried, and the children wound their lovely young men's arms around me in comfort, and—despite the guilt I felt in accepting that comfort—I took it anyway. They kept me breathing. They kept me alive.

Their laughter. Their needs. Their desires. I had never in my life lived so totally for someone else. Inside I was hollowed out. If it had been up to me, I would just as soon have been dead.

When they looked at me with certain expressions, I could see the ghost of Jim's face and I would start to cry again. Then I would have to explain that I was crying with love, that I wished Daddy would come back, and they would tell me, quite perceptively, that he would not, that he was happier now that he was away from me. When they socked me with their truths, despair would suddenly surface like a whale breaching for air. Then they would hold me for a little while longer. Only later could I admit what I knew in my heart all along: that though I had promised myself that my children would never play this role of the adult in our relationship—because I knew the burden of that role through my own mother's dependence on me—that was exactly what I was doing. Once more an aspect of the family history made itself felt.

I TRIED VERY hard to let no one else see my continuing distress, especially not Jim, because it seemed imperative to keep up a front—to make myself look like a buoyant, confident, and desirable woman. My anxiety and weight loss continued and I began to look haggard. Still smoking after my hospitalization, I felt entitled to just this one bad habit. The odor was repellent to Jim. As hard as I tried to stop, it was a stubborn habit that I wasn't able to relinquish in light of the pressure I was experiencing every day, and I felt that staying alive was more important than overcoming my nicotine addiction.

I still do not know how I endured those first few months following Jim's departure without trying to kill myself. I certainly had more reason than ever before. Family and friends kept saying, "Don't leave your children the legacy of suicide, Linda," as if it were possible to control my emotional state, like some sort of simple decision I only had to make. I was poised on the brink— just one small shove and I would be over the edge, spiraling down into darkness. But somehow, for many, many months, for some reason I could not name and still do not now understand, I beat back the suicidal feelings and held on. There was just enough strength in me.

EVEN THOUGH JIM could no longer live with me, he did not cease to care about me. He paid my health insurance. He returned to the house to teach me the computer software program that would enable me to pay the bills online—even though he grew angry when I couldn't quite catch on. He demonstrated the tricks to dismantling the spotlights on the front gate so I could change the burnt-out bulb—but became exasperated when I could not manage the strength to turn the screws in the socket. He helped me to unscramble the complicated phone system when it broke down—but was certain that I had messed it up in some way and thus he had to spend his precious time attempting a fix that should have been handled by someone else. He was trying to be a friend when he could no longer be a husband, but my pride made it difficult to accept his help, and yet never before had I needed it more.

Underneath all the cordial maneuvering, we both stifled our true emotions. Me: bitterness. He: an increasing sharpness with me as he found it difficult to be supportive in a gracious fashion. Later my analysis of his behavior became keener—had he only been trying to assuage his guilt, which made it difficult to be pleasant?

Up and down we went on the continuing seesaw of surface affability on the one hand and repressed hostility on the other. And of course, in the background, was the ongoing march of legal drafts of marital settlement agreements and divorce papers. In all our meetings he never once touched me: not a pat on the shoulder, not even a handshake. I began to feel more and more toxic.

Nevertheless, it seemed to me that our divorce was developing as thoroughly differently from my parents' as possible. My mother had cut my father off and there had been terrible enmity between them. Neither had shown brave or courageous colors: my mother actually accused my father of homosexuality and infidelity in the papers she filed with the courts—both of which she knew were untrue.

It appeared to Jim and me, however, that we were embarked on a different course, perhaps because of the boys, or perhaps just because of the deep nature of our relationship: our divorce bore an intimacy that would outlast the early pangs of animosity we both felt when he first moved out. Though the boys felt that the divorce was an acrimonious one, they had never before seen how bitter and terrible a divorce could become.

THE SEASONS CHANGED and nearly a year passed. I was never without the gnawing in my gut. I often got migraines that lasted for days, the throbbing in my eyes and head as steady as bad rainfall; I felt I would go mad from the pain and frequently went to the emergency room or the doctor's office for shots of morphine. At home, I started using Vicodin around the clock. Nothing anyone could do helped, not even my sessions with Ben. I saw him three times a week and his kind face and wise words supported me for the fifty minutes I rested in the warm womb of his office, but as soon as I left him I was shivering and unprotected in the outside elements again.

I hid from Jim any feeling that was even remotely depressing. I saw him often, as he came by every morning on my custodial days to pick up Nathaniel and Gabe and drive them to school, even though we lived only a bike ride away. He was determined to remain as close to them as he had been when we were living together. Despite my anger with him, I wanted what was best for them, which was to remain in a loving relationship with their father.

Every day I forced a bright demeanor and a smile on my face. I did not want him or the boys to know how depressed I truly was; I was still operating under the delusion that his leaving was solely caused by me. If so, wasn't there some hope of reversing his decision? I clung to the idea like a pit bull.

My despair went unmarked and my life continued to unravel, because, at that time, like an evil genie, it defied me to define or communicate about it. In fact, however, this "mental pain" did express itself physically, in secret, internal ways: I had a constant stomachache; my migraines had worsened; anxiety made it hard to breathe or get enough air into my lungs; my heart pounded and my palms were continually sweaty. Overheated and nauseated, I felt as if I were locked in a tiny, hot, black closet without a doorknob, my skin burning and itching with a rash I could not reach to scratch. I was smothering to death, but no one could see that. It was perhaps inevitable that I thought obsessively about delivering myself into oblivion.

I found it impossible to listen to phone messages, much less to return them, and so my world turned further inward as I slowly but surely cut myself off from my few remaining friends. I couldn't explain to them—I didn't want to explain to them. My feelings were too raw to bring out into the light. I wanted them to remain shrouded in the dark. Soon only Dawn, a close friend from the world of dog shows, and Myrna, a divorcee herself, remained. Myrna was a therapist as well, and I could be with her and feel understood. Even Rachael, with her abundant love, receded.

I couldn't concentrate to read a newspaper or a book; I couldn't decipher either my bank statements or my bills because the numbers turned upside down and sideways in an untranslatable code. Worst of all, I believed that I had nothing left to give to the people I liked and loved—and that I never would again.

Alone in the silent house, which now was alive with laughter and the rock music of The Dead and Pink Floyd only every other week, I wondered what I should do with all my empty time. I missed the kids' love and companionship. When Jim came to pick them up for his custodial week, I would stand at the front of the house and wave goodbye, watching the taillights of his car go down the driveway. Then I would shut the door and press my face against the wooden lintel as my entire family drove away, the shiny silver car sleek as a hearse.

MIGRAINES ROLLED IN like the tide and I used increasing amounts of drugs to force them to ebb. Sometimes such head-aches lasted for days, the stabbing in my head like burning stars. In this way, I first began to use narcotics regularly.

My mind stuck upon the image of the small child, standing desperately alone on a strange sidewalk, her parents having driven off and left her with no shelter and no money; that image was pressing enough to become the emotional scenery of my story. It hurt enough to bring the idea of suicide in front of me repeatedly. It was like working on a jigsaw puzzle: the edge pieces first and then moving inward. I had calibrated the dosages I would need and, taking them from my plentiful migraine med-ications, stashed them under my pantyhose. I was relieved to see that there were more than enough. One rainy day, I drove through the mountains, looking for a secluded place where I could park and swallow the pills. To be sure of success, the car must go unnoticed for at least twenty-four hours. I wrote a draft of a will that covered small bequests of personal items: a ring for Dawn, a necklace for Myrna; bracelets for Julie, my mother's diamond bar pin to Joy. I was determined that my children would not have to deal with mess or a body, especially one that was limp, or cherry red, or worse, mutilated by gunshot.

At last, a brainstorm: no romance this time around, nothing dramatic that could be foiled.

"Oh, you were being practical, is that it?" taunted the voice. I nodded to myself, this time agreeing with what the voice had observed.

I wiped from my mind the lures found in a seaside setting, or the beauty of the woods, intuiting that discovery would occur too soon for definite success.

In choosing overdose as my method, I was borrowing one of my mother's escape routes, even though it was one she ultimately rejected because it had failed her too many times. Her tolerance was too high for the number of pills she could swallow before falling asleep. Her switch to carbon monoxide in the garage worked for her because she didn't need to worry that anyone other than an adult would find her. I, on the other hand, had the boys to consider, and so I focused on the impact of discovery rather than the impact of death.

My mother's legacy of suicide solidified inside me like rebar under concrete—strong and yet concealed to those around me—and I no longer resisted it. On the contrary, it felt satisfying, almost thrilling, to surrender to it in this way. To be making plans. To know that when the time came, I would be prepared.

FOUR A.M. THE house had an eerie calm so early in the morning. Nothing moved. No one spoke. I remembered two things from the past: the sound of Jim's footfalls as he padded through the house, getting ready in the dark to go to the airport; and a summer from childhood—when all of us woke in the breaking dawn of our Cape Cod rental to get up and go clamming on the vast, bare tidal flats, pail in hand, jeans rolled up around our calves.

I hadn't been able to sleep. My mind was off and racing double speed. My wrists and ankles were beginning to heal now and cutting, in any case, seemed too inadequate. As sun stained the horizon, I paced through the living room, counting my footsteps, and then circled through the family room and kitchen—still counting—until I returned to the living room and wondered if the piano would look better on the other side of the room. With an agitated, untapped energy, I swapped the pink chenille love seat and the long chintz sofa, thinking there would be a totally different look to the room—far from the decorating Jim and I had done. I pushed and pulled until I was sweaty and it was time to wake the boys for breakfast.

I made matzo brei, surprising the children with my fervor, as we watched the day rising through the big kitchen window: a sunny warm blue April. Well-established Northern California spring. Magnolias, plum, and cherry spread pink and white through the gardens and matched my sudden, happy mood.

Later that morning, when the kids were off at school and I was still rearranging rooms, furniture, bookshelves, I began to feel terribly restless and agitated. Inside, the pain of my loneliness was coiling and uncoiling again, like a provoked snake. Quite suddenly, I was once again air hungry. I sank down on the sofa and gulped for breath.

As I sat there, my eye fell on an Eliot Porter photograph Jim and I had bought back before we were married, and I remembered then that just last Sunday he had asked for some of the art still in the house, and that I had agreed, quite amiably. It seemed only fair.

I went into the bedroom and pulled on my jeans. Beginning to run through the house, I grabbed framed art off the walls, making the choices I thought he would like. Why was I doing this? I wondered. Why should I want to give him anything? I was like an engine revving up, and I wasn't going to stop to question or to answer.

I piled the paintings and photographs in the back of the minivan, and then unlocked the storage room. Here there were all sorts of items that belonged to him, and to our old life together, things he'd left behind. He'd abandoned these items because it was more convenient than taking them to his new place. He'd reported feeling remarkably unburdened now that he had simplified his lifestyle, and I had thought to myself furiously several times that he hadn't simplified anything—he'd just left it all with me.

So into the car went his sleeping bag, his golf clubs, a friend's suitcase and banjo, boxes of photos and books, a non-working lamp, a CD player with a disc stuck in its maw. Working furiously, I crammed the car full of as much as it would hold. By then I was even sweatier but still feeling elated, bouncy, a little bit high. Tired of taking his crap, tired of lying in bed like an invalid—how good it felt to be doing something!

When I arrived at his house, whistling, a car parked right in front stopped me. Was someone home? Was that someone "her"? I decided that it wasn't, simply because I didn't want it to be, simply because I didn't want even to contemplate having to unload the car back at my place and then haul it all back here another time. I was ready *right then*. The sensation was urgent.

I pulled over to the sidewalk one house down the block for safety's sake and crossed the front lawn, knocked boldly on the door. No answer. Reassured, I went to the place where Jim hid the spare key behind a brick. When I swung open the door, a female voice called out a tentative, "Hello?" This certainly wasn't the Spanish-speaking cleaning lady.

I shut the door fast, a reflex, and sprinted across the lawn in a state of high agitation, praying that she couldn't see me from the upstairs window. I flung myself into the car and peeled out of there. Halfway home, however, my heartbeat slowed enough for me to wonder why I was running away. *I* should run from *her*? Why not face her down instead, the way I would a nightmare. I pulled up in my driveway, went into the house to change my clothes, put on makeup, and fix my hair. Then, heart hammering so hard that I felt as if I were going to choke, I returned and backed the car down into his driveway.

At first, I unloaded everything directly in front of the garage, actually hoping she was watching. But if she was, she didn't come out and introduce herself, or face me. Once the car was empty, I stopped and considered: what if it should rain? It would be unlikely here in April, but it was definitely possible. I decided to cart all the stuff inside, where it would be safer. This, of course, was just an excuse to go into the house, but I was thinking less and less clearly. My decisions were now dominated by strong, pressured emotions, and what I felt most strongly was my desire to confront her.

I knocked one more time, but still no one came to the door. I retrieved the key and opened the door and again heard the same feminine voice call out from the upstairs bedroom.

"Hello?"

This time I did not flinch. "I'm just dropping off some of Jim's things," I shouted back casually, as if I had a perfect right to be there, using his key. "It won't take me long." Now surely she would show herself, and I would be able to tell her exactly what I thought of her.

I marched back and forth self-righteously, with the vigor of Joan of Arc. With each box, each picture, every item, I could feel myself expanding, growing bigger and stronger. I was no longer afraid of her. Each second she didn't come downstairs from the master bedroom indicated that she was scared of me and the power that emanated from that, from experiencing her weakness, was delicious.

Somewhere in the back of my mind, unacknowledged, probably not even conscious, there was the thought that if she came down the stairs I would pull her hair, kick her, scratch her. Never in my life had I hated anyone as much—not even when I was little and the word "hate" carried with it such power.

At last I had brought everything in and there was no other reason to prolong my stay. She still hadn't come down. I strode to the foot of the staircase so she would be certain to hear me.

"I'm finished," I called out, my deprecating tone laced with sarcasm. "I'm leaving—so you can come out of *hiding* now."

No answer.

The melodrama of this would have made my mother proud.

Back in the car, I pounded the steering wheel with exultation. I phoned a friend from my car phone, screaming as I pulled out of Jim's street, "I got her, I got her! She was just like a trapped mouse! She didn't dare answer me! She just hid up there!"

My mind was speeding but I didn't care. At home, I danced around the bedroom, buzzed around the house picking up the standard mess at a furious rate, piling up plates and glasses for the dishwasher, getting all the work done with a ferocious intensity. I didn't want to calm myself. I was swinging upward, feeling high, higher, highest.

However, sometime during mid-afternoon I began to sink like a helium balloon losing its gas. The ground was coming up at me, fast. I was so high, it was a long way to fall and suddenly I was afraid. How angry was Jim going to be? I had gone into his house without permission and yelled at his girlfriend. Suddenly I felt chilled: the old flu-like feelings reasserted themselves and the thermometer showed the same low-grade fever I'd been battling for weeks. Over me like a blanket, depression descended, muffling the air and the light.

AT FIVE O'CLOCK Jim came by to pick up the kids for their weekly Thursday-night supper, but he didn't just honk out front, he came into the house and stormed into the bedroom that once had been ours. Following his usual pattern, he didn't yell or raise his voice; he was just icy and enraged beyond belief. "You had no right to go into my house that way." His teeth were clenched.

"You said you wanted some of the photographs and paintings. I put all the stuff next to the garage but then I worried about rain."

"Come on, Linda." His tone grew ever more bitter.

At his recriminations, something inside me exploded. Rage was all I could feel. Rage bursting out of my body like the birth of some alien species. "It's all my fault again, isn't it?" I shouted. I was totally out of control, crashing to the ground, broken and bent, not even human anymore. I felt like a loathsome vermin that had been poisoned and flung onto a garbage heap.

"Just like always," I went on. "It's *always* my fault. Like the kids' problems are all my fault. We know whose fault everything is. Never perfect Jim's." There was enough sarcasm in my voice to fill an ocean. "Fine. I'll take *all* the blame."

"I hate it when you say things you don't mean!"

"What difference does it make? I've apologized. I'll never do it again. I can't take it back. What more do you want?"

"I want you to understand how you trespassed on my privacy."

My anger deflated into despair. How little he understood. "Can you take the kids tonight?"

"That doesn't work for me."

"I've got a migraine and I'm upset. I don't think they should be around me."

"Look, it's your night with them."

"Please, I need you to."

"Why?"

"Just because. It's personal."

"Well, I'm sorry but I can't."

That's when I remembered: *she* was over at his house. Of course he couldn't take the kids.

The three of them tromped off to McDonald's and I leapt from the bed as soon as the front door closed. At last I felt ready to find the end of all the pain, the impetus on me like a fury. I knew I had very little time and I would have to work quickly. Fortunately I had rehearsed everything in my mind several times. I knew exactly what to do.

From the box under my pile of nylons, I pulled out my stash of pills. I dumped one hundred Fioricet and one hundred Tylenol with Codeine into my food processor and let the combination of tablets run until the pills were powder. While it was grinding, I scrambled for as much applesauce as I could find, and added it.

Because there were so many pills, the paltry amount of apple-sauce (an item I had forgotten to have on hand) merely made a thick paste of the drugs and was terribly bitter. I swallowed two Phenergan—a strong anti-nausea drug—to help me not vomit, and then scribbled a note to Jim, jamming it inside the front door. I paused for a minute. Sudden calm descended over me, though the urgency remained. Doubt did not exist for me because I believed with all my heart and mind that this was where all my anguish would finally end.

I snatched up a pillow and blanket, a soda, and the bowl of medication I had made, took a plastic spoon and then got into the car; it was a race against time, I had to leave before anyone could come home and stop me. Before the kids could see another suicide attempt. My fervent hope: to be successful this time.

Because the chief problem with using pills was discovery, just the week before I had hunted out a location where no one would find me until I was long dead. I did not think about what I might hand on to my sons—I thought of nothing but ending the pain. One day I would look back and understand that I had deceived myself, that I had never accepted the fact that I was indeed building a legacy of my own—a legacy that my children would therefore inherit, whether or not I ever succeeded. It was enough that I had introduced it into their lives. All I could feel in that moment was the terrible urgency to act and end the pain. No one and nothing mattered more than that.

In the car, the Phenergan began to make me drowsy. I hit rush-hour traffic on the freeway and as I crawled along I began to drift off to sleep, even though I hadn't taken much of the medication from the bowl yet—still, I didn't anticipate that the Phenergan would have such an immediate effect. I scraped the guard-rail several times with the side of the car. I drove the last mile and swung off at the ramp for the airport. With my head nodding, I made it the last hundred yards into the parking garage.

I had felt jubilant when I first found this perfect place: I could crawl into the back seat and lie down under the blanket; with the dark-tinted glass no one would see me for a long time. I had left my car here for over a week when I was once on a book tour, so I knew very little attention was paid to cars left alone for days. In my secluded spot, I started shoveling the acrid paste into my mouth, alternating with swigs of soda. How ghastly it tasted, and I kept gagging, but I kept spooning it in mouthful after mouthful; I would not fail. *Final Exit* had suggested that the dosages I would need could be further enhanced by alcohol, but I was determined not to die with a drink in my hand, as had my mother. The world began to whirl and I had just decided to climb into the back seat when I spotted the car phone, mounted on the dashboard.

I hadn't had time to leave notes for the boys.

How I longed to say goodbye, the way my mother had not. To tell them that I loved and believed in them. I lifted the receiver off the phone and somehow managed to dial. I spoke to both boys but remember nothing of what I said. Apparently Jim then got on the phone, begging me to give them my location, but I refused.

At this point I vomited. I needed to eat more paste and lie down. When I hung up the phone, it didn't click into place and thus fell, unnoticed, onto the floor. I quickly passed out behind the wheel. At that time, car phones could not be traced.

Armed with news from the California Highway Patrol that someone had been driving erratically on the freeway near the airport, the police began to circle the roadway that runs in front of all the airlines and the parking garage. Past United and American, past Lufthansa and British Air, all the while with their sirens turned on. What I could no longer hear, they could. The wail of those sirens eventually became audible over the cellular connection back at the house where Jim and the boys waited, and after a short time the police at the house were able to direct those cruisers to my car's location.

Unlike the earlier episode, when I was at least partially conscious of being rescued, this time I had no recollection about the arrival of either the police or the ambulance. I had managed to take a lethal dose, and I had done it in an out-of-the-way spot from which I shouldn't have been rescued. I had definitely intended to die. And I'd almost made it.

PART 4

{time passes}

The defects and faults of the mind are like wounds in the body—after all imaginable care has been taken to heal them up, still there will be a scar left behind.

— FRANCOIS DE LA ROCHEFOUCAULD

{the door, part ii}

I HAD NO memory of having my stomach pumped or signing any commitment papers. I had no memory of anything at all. Later I would be confused, and yet somehow strangely numb with an extreme lack of emotion. Or perhaps, the truth was that I didn't really care about anything other than simple escape: I just wanted to rewind time so that I could succeed where I had failed, and this was all I could concentrate on as I woke up in a strange ICU. There was no one there to tell me that this sense of numbness, of focus only upon myself—rather than on those whom I had hurt—was another profound symptom of clinical depression. I did not know that I was simply sick rather than being selfish and so I excoriated myself for my unacceptable feelings. Eventually a nurse—putting her head into my cubicle and checking her watch in a way that reminded me of other times in another hospital—did tell me that the ambulance had brought me to the nearest hospital's intensive care unit, rather than the one I had been in before, because the paramedics were afraid I would not survive the extra twenty-minute drive. This time I wasn't on the psychiatric ward for some seventy-two-hour hold.

This attempt was serious enough that the doctors refused to tell me how long I would have to stay; they concentrated in an annoying fashion on trying to push me to the point where I could be happy to be alive.

When I regained consciousness, however, I was as mad as a raccoon hissing in a trap. I didn't want anyone to see me in bed. I was supposed to be dead, and I hated having been rescued. I loathed everything and everyone around me. Jim brought the children to see me in the ICU. I did not gather them in tight against me and apologize, but instead turned my face away. Even at the time, I felt how cruel this must have seemed to them, but I just wasn't ready to see anyone—not Gabe, not Nathaniel.

There was no way around the fact that this second attempt was worse and less forgivable for the children. Jim had been gone for over a year and a half, but still, even then, I had kept alive the idea that he might somehow return to our family constellation. Both Nathaniel and Gabe could sense his happiness and relief at having escaped me and all my problems. Now I knew, all was lost.

I got transferred the next day to the hospital nearer our home, where I had been before, so that I could be closer to my doctors and my children—but most of all I wanted to be someplace where I knew the routine. I had already experienced the trauma of confronting that locked door at the end of the hall. I wanted to be by myself, as I confronted my own stupidity and indifference, and I berated myself for not flinging the car phone from the window.

In my small, curtained room, I paced back and forth, my head full of plans, as soon as I got out, as to how I would liberate myself by finishing what I had so badly mangled, despite not wanting to hurt the children one more time. Unsure where I would find more drugs again, I nevertheless couldn't stand thinking that I might have to wait three days, let alone a week or more at home. The pain inside me ramped up with vicious, metastatic intent.

I was on strict fifteens. The chief resident categorized my attempt as "fatal" and the staff treated me differently this time around. They watched me as if I were a dangerous animal. Or was my imagination just running wild? It was frightening that I couldn't tell; reality seemed to fade further and further away.

On the third day, the kids came to visit and I made myself smile, but I didn't want to see them.

On the fourth day, a few friends came with flowers and books, and I made myself smile, but I didn't want to see them.

My shame was intense. I felt full of hate.

Being alone with my thoughts was all I could manage. My feelings and ideas went around and around, doubling back on each other, trying to discover a way out of my predicament. The doctors upped my Risperdal: it dulled the pain somewhat but it made me fatigued and thick-tongued. Despite the drug, all my impressions were flooding in from the outer world, a waterfall, as if I were filling a glass and losing control of the pitcher. I was living with no filter, no "off" position, no way to stop the noise, the smells, the touch of everything around me.

The few friends who braved coming to visit seemed, simply, at a loss. How to approach me now? Were they supposed to mention the attempt, or ignore it? How sick, really, was I? Should they bring some kind of gift or just arrive with empty hands? Because, after all, what could you bring to someone on a mental ward?

Getting free to kill myself, or at least to cut, obsessed me. If I could cut I would at least ground myself, set myself straight—make the pain outside match the pain inside. I was just waiting for my opportunity, all the while following the rules and smiling and sucking up to the staff so that at least my privilege status would go up and I could go outside and smoke. I had passed the legacy on to my childrens' shoulders.

The idea dug into my heart, and it was the only thing about which I did care.

THIS TIME AROUND, I made friends with my roommate. It seemed both useful and prudent. Margie had been admitted for severe anorexia, even though she hardly looked the typical picture of a starved adolescent. In her thirties, she was the mother of a three-year-old, and worked as a social worker for troubled teenage girls. Eventually, Margie confided to me that early in her life she had been forced by her brother into an incestuous relationship, and she had recently confronted her mother with that particular truth. Her mother hadn't believed her, however, and shortly after their discussion, Margie found that the smell of food made her ill. She was going to disappear, just the way her mother had made her problem disappear. I felt sympathy for Margie. I knew all about disappearing tricks.

This was when she began to refuse food. Or perhaps "refuse" is the wrong word. Shortly I began to recognize that her inability to eat was not a "refusal" any more than my agitation was a symptom "of my own creation." She literally could not get food past her mouth into her throat without choking on it, just the way I found I could not control the electricity that forced me to pace back and forth, or to rock myself on the edge of my bed, as nighttime approached. Even though Margie could understand the synchronicity between the events in her life, the gagging reflex continued. Even though I knew my behavior was due to hypomania, the rocking continued.

The nurses kept a chart that noted every calorie consumed, every anxiety pill needed. Each day Margie's tray in the day room was returned to the nurse on charge with only a few items picked at; as her condition worsened, they resorted to allowing her to eat in her room, hoping the privacy would aid her. The nurses kept tabs on me, checking me again and again. I didn't care what they wrote in their charts. All of these maneuvers changed nothing for either of us.

She sat in her wheelchair listlessly, too weak to walk. I talked to her from my bed. As we got to be friends, we began to sit together at our doorway, watching the corridor's traffic, while she sipped her Boost (a high-calorie liquid) and I chugged a Diet Pepsi, looking for caffeine. With her dry sense of humor, she joked that even the name of my drink had "die" in it. Often we went out into the day room to see what was going on; I rolled her from place to place in her wheelchair because she could not stand without her blood pressure dropping precipitously. It felt good to have a compassionate comrade on the unit, someone I could confide in. Little by little, she began to eat small morsels again. I had grown attached to Margie and her severe illness worried me intensely as I cheered her on to graduating from the ward; I felt the tug, just below the surface and never voiced, of how her exit would affect me. Eventually, she, too, would leave me, as all the others had done.

Her anorexia and my self-mutilation built a common bridge between us: each self-destructive behavior bonded us with its own beauty and logic. The lure of our diseases was invisible to the majority of the outside world, where people worried about mortgages and menus, children's grades and friends. Cutting and anorexia were incomprehensible to our families and friends—but they were a secret Margie and I shared. Nights we lay in the dark and talked about the thrill of it from our beds. It reminded me of camp, except that now we didn't have to whisper.

I thought to myself that I had made Margie into a sister because my own still seemed so distant and unavailable. And right then, Joy's reasons for retreating from me felt too distant to ponder.

THE FIRST TIME I tried to kill myself, my father and sister were as stunned as they were angry. They didn't expect one of the standard-bearers of anger against my mother's suicidal tendencies to turn suddenly and become suicidal herself. It caught them off guard and that hardened their response. Perhaps some pocket within their minds and hearts held a question: how they could be asked to endure this sort of pain again, this time at the hands of a family member who ought to know better, one who had also endured my mother's attempts with them? I was sure it felt like a terrible betrayal to them. Their anger had an unconcealed, raw tenor, tempered neither with empathy nor forgiveness. I didn't really feel surprised by this, but still, it startled me—my father seemed to believe depression and suicide were an adolescent stage I should have outgrown. After the second attempt he said to me, "Linda, I thought we were all through with this."

I was profoundly humiliated. I had wanted so badly for him to put his arms around me and let me cry, to comfort me in all the ways Jim had when we were married. But I was too ashamed to ask and I needed a mind reader—someone who would know that I was lying when I told him that I was fine once again.

The situation seemed as if I were still living in that past we all had shared and remembered well, but now Joy and my father distanced themselves by treating my suicide attempts as they had treated my mother's repeated efforts. I didn't get to begin at my own starting block—I just inherited hers, and all the emotions they had in place for her. Yet, I was also standing in my own desperate situation, too. Nature vs. nurture no longer seemed to matter. Regardless of where the legacy had emanated, and no matter how hard I fought it, I felt as if I were just spinning in space, never moving out from under it.

To them, I was doing my mother's dance, one that was a well-orchestrated tantrum. Initially, I, too, had been unable to understand what was happening to my mother. I had seen it as a childish loss of control. But when I entered the hospital for the second time, I began to understand all the facets of her desperate situation: I stopped blaming her. My father and Joy, on the other hand, couldn't bring themselves to understand her illness or mine, because that might mean they would have to forgive us, and they were not yet ready for that.

I was ashamed of all I had done, and I was needy as well. Vulnerable and naked. Suicide exposes you, shows the world what you really think about yourself and how weak your self-image is. I wanted someone to rock me and tell me everything was going to be fine. I wanted Jim to come back, I wanted my father to visit, I wanted my sister to come and hold my shaky hand in her competent one. I wanted to be someone's little girl—I'm not sure it mattered whose. Nevertheless, I quickly began to dismiss friends, even those who had come to visit and who seemed willing to be supportive, at some level, at least; I couldn't bear to keep explaining myself and what I had done. I felt like an uncoordinated bear, lumbering in a zoo, being scrutinized and watched with curiosity and a very real lack of understanding—and thus empathy—for my situation. It was inevitable that no matter how caring the friend, most days I concentrated mainly on how to get through another twenty-four hours of pain.

Initially, during the first days of this hospitalization, my father had surprised me by announcing that he was canceling his plans for an anniversary trip to New Orleans: his place, he said, was in California. He'd be out as soon as he could arrange it. I wanted nothing so much. But I knew that if he did, most likely he'd feel resentful over his lost vacation, and, in any case, I would be stuck on the psych unit for a while. Looking at it sensibly, he ought to take his vacation now and come to visit afterward for a long weekend, when I was out of the hospital and really in need of companionship.

After he and his new wife returned home, they settled back into their Boston routine; their perception of the crisis, it seemed to me, had passed as soon as I had left the hospital. They finally came to visit during the summer months, when I was less obviously "sick," but my step-mother, Marty, told me that my father worried about me incessantly the entire time they had been away and for a long time afterward. I wished I could have felt that worry from him, but once again, I thought, I was probably being unreasonable.

My sister, told by Jim that I was back on the psych unit, sent word that she would call me in a few days but that it was too difficult for her to speak with me right now; understanding her reaction did not make it hurt any less. Once, when I was nineteen, I had told my mother that I wouldn't come to visit her at a mental hospital because that would be too much like "supporting her sickness." What had seemed an important step in my separating from her now seemed a cruel rejection: I had been angry at what she had done and I had punished her the only way I had at my disposal—by withholding myself.

I didn't blame Joy or my father, but still, I hated what they did. Some part of me didn't want to accept the fact that my family was refusing to help me overcome the disease that had wrapped itself so tightly around me. I crouched alone in my room, and felt as isolated and lonely as I had as a child.

Two weeks after I had returned home from the hospital, I called Joy and begged her to come visit, promising that if she did we'd have fun together visiting Muir Woods and Big Sur; we wouldn't just sit around listening to some funeral dirge. Having thought up every enticement I could muster to convince her, I eventually broke down and told her how much I needed someone from my family right now. She said no, citing an old reason she'd used before: no vacation time available from her job, and no money available for the flight.

I was stunned into silence: I'd thought my frank plea would

move her. For a minute, I considered buying her the ticket, but suddenly I didn't want to offer to pay her way and then be rejected yet again. This kind of interaction had become a pattern between us since I moved to the West Coast. Now I wondered: if I had had a stroke, for instance, would she have made an effort to find the money and come? What would it take for her to spend a few days with me? I asked none of these questions because I didn't want to hear the answers to them.

Joy's refusal was a much harder blow than when my father went to New Orleans, perhaps because I craved so much the emotional bond we once shared as children. We had survived the shipwreck of our mother's illness through so many years, and now I felt that Joy might understand what I was going through as no one else could, but it developed that this was just too difficult for her. It cut too close to the heart. On the telephone, if she would ask how I was doing and if I went into any detail at all, she would always terminate the conversation with a phrase oft repeated, "I'm not comfortable talking about this."

I believed I didn't want much—an embrace, some laughter with someone who shared the same childhood. And yet, I wanted a great deal: to be forgiven for having taken a step I believed I was entitled to take, but which would inevitably alienate me from those I loved, even if, most especially, those actions emanated from a disordered mind. I had to accept the fact that I would be blamed by those who could not—or would not—understand me. Even worse, they didn't want an explanation about it all; they didn't want to know how such a situation had come to pass. Once again, mental illness and depression were on the list of unmentionables. My family and friends just wished it would all go away and Linda would go back to being Linda, the way we had all once wished that Anne would go back to being Anne.

Ultimately, the bare bones fact is that no one wants to deal with a suicide.

Part of my rehab was to make amends to those I had hurt, so immediately I humbled myself to all my family members, especially the children, who accepted my mea culpa with good grace, regardless of how they truly felt about it. My guess was that they might not understand how they did feel until they were older, and even then, maybe not: perhaps it seemed that they had to acquiesce to my overtures in order to help me recover. To be forgiven mattered to me very much, but I knew that it might take a very long time. After all, I had needed more than thirty years to begin to forgive my mother her illness and the impact it had had on me.

Eventually I wrote letters to the police officers who had been so ingenious in saving my life. I tried to explain the tunnel of depression and the drive toward suicide at the end of that tunnel. The police chief wrote me back, saying he had always considered suicide to be a selfish act, and that it had never occurred to him that a suicide could be driven by intense pain. I had helped him, he said, to see that terrible aspect of the act. He would never again look upon it as he had before. To have helped even one person understand suicide better made me feel infinitely more useful, and perhaps it was then, without even recognizing it, that the first true seeds for this book fell on the thick loamy soil of my imagination.

MARGIE WAS THE only one to whom I had confided the truth about trying to kill myself again: I was really just marking time, waiting to make another attempt. At the same time, my confession troubled her. She thought I ought to tell my psychiatrist about how I was feeling; I explained that when you confess your suicidal impulses to the doctors treating you, they immediately stash you in the hospital. Letting them know how desperate you feel becomes just another way of handing them the key to stop you again.

If you really want to kill yourself, really want to, you don't go around broadcasting it to the mental health professionals involved with your case: they are obligated by the state and by their code of ethics to foil your attempt. Of course, if you don't tell them, the untreated depression and confused state of mind can lead to another try at self-annihilation. This is how I began seeking death, rather than calling Ben or even Norman Greid. Or Myrna or Dawn or Julie or Pat. Certainly not my father or my sister. No one could help me stave off the longing. It was a conflict of interest to let anyone know I had the slightest "suicidal ideation," or to ask for help that, really, I wanted only on my terms.

After the initial seventy-two-hour hold had passed, I had a meeting with my assigned house doctors (from my previous visit I knew that my private physicians would not visit or control my treatment while I was in the hospital). Without Ben and Norman, I was experiencing a withdrawal of their support—which felt like another predictable abandonment. The attending doctors and the residents coerced me to sign myself in for two weeks by explaining that they could take me to court if I tried to sign myself out against medical advice, and the scuttlebutt on the unit was that if you go to court and lose, sometimes you can get confined longer than the initial request. I knew my insurance would not pay for any more than two weeks, so I'd be sent out of my well-appointed teaching hospital into a state facility. Suddenly I was very frightened, because I felt I had little control over what became of me.

Exacerbating my emotional state was the fact that, for the first time—and unlike my mother—I was in the hospital entirely on my own, without Jim to mediate for me. I had to navigate through each and every decision alone. So I missed him even more desperately. Even then, I refused to let him see how much I needed him and how the divorce had devastated me. Determined that he have nothing to do with my hospitalization because I wanted him to realize, unequivocally, that he would have nothing further to do with the upheavals in my life, I insisted he just drop the kids at the hospital entrance and then come back later to pick them up. My pride and my fury forced me to say I didn't want him coming onto the ward at all.

Nathaniel and Gabe came to visit nearly every day. They didn't talk much, but I knew they felt supportive. In the full bloom of adolescence now, naturally enough they were angry. I reassured myself that it was natural for them to be gloomy and silent. At my insistence, we had a family counseling session. In my little curtained cubicle, the three of us tangled our legs together on the bed while the therapist maintained her distance by sitting in the chair. I realized that this time something had really changed: they didn't trust me anymore. And I didn't blame them.

I remembered what it had been like with my own mother after her suicide attempts, and so I told my boys that I understood how they felt. And, I believe, I did understand: I was empathetic to their feelings, and, in fact, I was surprised that they weren't angrier. Perhaps this lack of anger stemmed from the fact that I had only tried to kill myself twice, in contrast to my mother's many attempts, of which they had no experience. I used the memory of those emotions as a blanket to layer over my heart and to ease the bonechill that remained inside me like a frozen pond. Once, I'd vowed that my children would never feel the same pain as I had when I was little. Now, I was horrified to see how easily I had hurt them. Even as I reassured them that I was better now, in my heart there still lay—coiled and ugly—the urge to die. Successful suicides were only part of the legacy in my family—even an attempt was a curse to be handed down. And so I had passed the legacy on, and now it only remained to see what they would do with it.

Meanwhile, I was just waiting for another shot at death. I loathed myself and the foul mother I had become—masquerading as a person trying to get well when really I was a person still fascinated by the end of life. When Gabe pleaded, plaintively, "Promise you won't do it again, Mommy," I lied in order to reassure him and that lie made me tremble—not with fear for my children or their loss, but with the fear of being discovered. While I was able to lie convincingly to the doctors, it was nearly impossible to lie to my children, who seemed able to read intent through my eyes.

I felt a tsunami of guilt as I knew, in my heart, that good mothers put their children before themselves: I believed that I should always have been able to say, with conviction: "I will live for my children's sake."

But the intensity of my pain and depression during this second hospitalization was radically different than anything I had previously experienced. Never before had I encountered anything that so totally engulfed me, and under its obliterating presence, I felt that I had ceased to be. It was not a question of pain *versus* love; in this equation the two different levels of sensation were never in competition because they were as different as a skateboard and a Mack truck. For love to have been big enough and strong enough, I would have to have spent a lifetime learning to harness my suffering, to become adept at how to funnel difficulties of the soul into peaceful and productive channels so that its energy flowed out in ways that did not ravage.

I didn't stand a chance.

The belief that love can conquer immense pain in the life of the ordinary person is another way in which the legacy of suicide continues to be handed down generation to generation, damaging all family members. This misperception traumatizes those who experience the loss of someone close (certain that if they had only been more worthy, their friend or family member would have loved them enough to bear the suffering), and it also becomes an obstacle for those who survive the attempt to end their own lives. I would guess that even now my father and my sister must still suppress some rage at this idea in a private, silent way: they are angry that my mother did not care enough to put them and their feelings first. It became an issue of love, when really, it should have been seen as a barometer of pain. Despite my former fantasies about dedication and worthiness, I now believe that by committing suicide, my mother simply bowed out from under the hurt in her life.

I was still a novice at dealing constructively with my depression—if such a thing were even possible—and, despite my desperate attempts to combat it, I lay at its feet, day by day, feeling unbearable guilt that my love wasn't strong enough to help me to rise.

I hope my children will someday learn to trust me again— even though I have admitted, in print and in public, that there were times that I could not love them well or wisely enough, that there were times when I was not a "good mother," or even a "good enough mother." But I hope they will remember the times I tried so hard and that those attempts will count, at least a little, even if they did not always succeed: how we spent many afternoons, chicken noodle soup on the stove and long conversations at the kitchen table; how I always offered a ride to their nearby school, even on sunny days; how we shared the many bedtime cuddles and songs and stories that I made up to lull them to sleep. Throughout all those days and months and years, I gave them everything I had to give. I emptied out my shelves, and I begged God for it to be enough.

AS THE DAYS passed at the hospital, Margie drank more Boost, ate a little bit more solid food, and her blood pressure stabilized. Her doctor began to talk to her about returning home, using the outpatient treatment clinic the hospital offered as a baby step forward. Still, she was terrified that she wouldn't make it in the outside world again.

I'd been on the unit for nine days when the staff finally decided that it was time for her to leave the hospital and try it at home. In my precarious emotional state this, too, felt like another abandonment, and when I first learned of it, I fled from a group therapy meeting to a corner of the day room, where I stood shaking, tears running down into my collar. One of the nurses discovered me, a glazed look in my eyes, and my chest heaving up and down as I tried to get enough air. Despite the fact that I was attempting to hide from this extremely intense anxiety attack, I knew I needed help: I felt the bottom collapsing under me, and this time was overwhelmingly grateful for having been noticed. She handed me a paper bag.

"Breathe into this," she said, her calm face bringing me back to myself. "You're just hyperventilating."

When my breathing returned to normal, I sat on the sofa and held her hand while I cried. "I know I'm being ridiculous," I apologized in gasps.

"Don't worry, Linda—a lot of the feelings you have while you're on the unit are painful—it's part of why you're here to begin with," she said quietly. "I know it's hard, but here you can let out whatever's hurting you, rather than just sitting somewhere all alone, engulfed by those things in your life that just never seem to go away. Rather than talking about how you feel, you could be cutting yourself. Isn't this way better?"

On the day Margie actually left, after our goodbyes, I was in line at the meds closet, waiting at the window for my paper cup of pills, and I turned to watch her, just for an instant, walk down the corridor toward the door, which appeared to open like magic. Then she passed through it into freedom and I went to my room, empty by half, and sat on my bed for a long while, concentrating on not having another anxiety attack.

My time on the unit had been longer than any other patient's except one, who was expected to stay for quite some time, months perhaps. Liberating myself had initially seemed an impossibility, because I was unable to show the doctors proof that I was happy to be alive, and saved, and without the intent to try to hurt myself again. For some reason it didn't occur to me to lie; but, on the other hand, if I didn't lie, they weren't going to let me go. I was running perilously close to the end of my insurance coverage, and I couldn't see what I was going to do, but then a friend suggested to me that I conceptualize staying alive by just thinking of it as only one day at a time.

It was a brilliant strategy. I knew I could do it. I could promise that for today I would keep myself safe, neither building a stash of pills, nor making any suicide plans, nor attempting suicide. Sitting at the desk in my cubicle, I worked on a strategy of that way of living, creating a list of warning signs that could predict a decline: poor hygiene, messy dress, staying in bed, not cooking, avoiding the grocery store, prolonged depression, not returning friends' phone calls, crying nonstop, wanting the kids to mother me, restless agitation. Next came a list of possible people to call for help. The following morning when the doctors came in on rounds, I skillfully made out the case in support of my release, and they bought it.

And so the doctors said, miraculously it seemed, that the time had come for me to try the outer world again. Flooded with fear and anxiety, yet happy with the knowledge that I would once again be in control of my life, I realized that for the first time in three weeks I would be able, once again, to choose my fate. I concealed, one more time, my continuing urge to self-mutilate or die, and congratulated myself that I had succeeded in making myself look presentable to the doctors who governed my next move. Obviously, I seemed increasingly stable to them. Of course, I didn't really believe that I was.

This time, however, I wouldn't just be going home. The unit staff had made a requirement: discharge was dependent upon my attending a partial hospitalization program; it ran from nine to three, five days a week. It was the same outpatient program that Margie had gone to, and I thought this would be a small price to pay for my freedom. The two week "course" in living in the outside again seemed stupid to me, but as the day of my release neared, the world beyond my window felt dangerous and my fear increased. To go back to my empty house and sit there all alone after the structure and companionship of the unit would have been a disaster.

I was trembling at the bus stop, three days later. Without Jim to bring me even a suitcase, I had stuffed all my possessions into two supermarket paper bags, and I clasped them to my chest as I waited for the shuttle, with one of the nurses from the old unit who was accompanying me. The world around me seemed lit with halos of light.

After the first day in the clinic was over, my friend Julie came to pick me up and drive me home. She waited while I unlocked the front door and then walked in with me, setting down the paper bags of clothes on the kitchen table. I felt myself strangely out of joint—new and inexperienced in this old and familiar space.

"Would you mind?" I asked her, "if we went outside and just sat in the car?"

"Think you need to face it again?"

I nodded, grateful that she instinctively understood what would have been embarrassing and difficult to explain.

I unlocked the car doors and sat in the driver's seat while she went around to the passenger side. I was trembling. How glad I was that she was with me.

She reached over and patted my hand.

I swallowed and nodded. "I think I'll be able to drive myself in tomorrow."

She smiled and I smiled back.

The next day I drove myself to my day program as if nothing had ever happened in that car before. But I knew that I would never really be able to forget what had transpired in the front seat.

I don't believe that my mother had ever participated in an outpatient program, had ever taken this new approach to recovery: going in for structured therapy full-time during the day and then back home to the family at night. For me, this was a new model of how to get well and it did give me the structure I needed to face each day. I wasn't left alone long enough to be cooking up my suicide plans. I was by myself just long enough to be frying a chicken for the children's supper. Returning home, however, was much harder than the last time because Jim was no longer by my side, either as a supportive husband or to help me parent our sons. Fortunately, he made sure the children were with me that first week so that I could get the routine down. As each day passed, I felt a little more surefooted.

On my second morning at the clinic, I drove into the parking lot just before nine, my hair shiny and freshly washed, dressed in pretty, clean clothes. I was trying to keep my mind open to the idea that behind these orderly walls there might be redemption for me.

With its dingy and dark red brick, the place certainly didn't look it. The building stretched several solitary storeys into the sky, a monolith that would later remind me of my stay there every time I drove down the main street in town. To me, it towered over the countryside like some grand and influential castle, in which lived the kings and queens who could send you home, or send you back into full-time patient care on the unit. Yet, thousands of other people drove right past and didn't even know what it was—they didn't really "see" it.

The day at the outpatient clinic began with check-in. As the patients filed in the door, each in his or her own state of mood

disarray (we had everything from depressives to multiple person-
alities to anxiety disorders and so on), they were scooped up by
one of the staff members—psychiatrists, psychiatric nurses, psy-
chologists, and an art therapist—one of whom went over the
hours you had spent outside the sturdy walls since yesterday.
Being on half days meant you began at noon, but for those on
full days (like me) it meant ending at three o'clock when the
program finished for the day and turned you loose to your own
dangerous devices. All those urges I experienced in my hours
away from the program, whether acted upon or not, were what I
was meant to bring to morning check-in.

I told the chubby blond psychiatric nurse that yesterday I'd
left and gone to the supermarket to pick up milk, peaches, and a
broiler, had cooked my kids supper on the barbeque, had watched
television, and gone to bed early. I didn't tell her that it was not
early enough to prevent me from thinking about cutting myself.
These were the details they wanted to hear about and these were
the details I wouldn't give them.

One of our exercises the previous day had been to fill out an
hourly schedule for the approaching weekend, and then trade
your sheet with the person next to you, who, hopefully, would
have some good suggestions. (Why the staff thought other disturbed people could provide answers to questions as large as
these escaped me.) It made me feel depressed.

In art therapy, I drew images from my life: a baby in a crib, her
cries going unanswered by a mother who stood to the side with
eyes that gleamed with insanity. Next I drew the toddler I had
been, crouched and hiding in empty space, while my mother
typed away, while the neighborhood children my age went to the
nursery school right next to our house. Nothing I drew had any
happiness. It was all thematically stark, with lots of black oil
pastel smudged in with the edge of my fist. My mood was bleak.
As I drew scenes from my childhood, I realized I was also angry.

We meditated. We wrote in journals. We did group therapy. We ate lunch, alone or with a partner—whatever we chose, a step up from the rules on the ward. To my delight, Margie appeared after my second day, and we hung out together. When my insurance rebelled at my continuing stay in the Partial Program, I had to leave but she remained. This time I went first, and it was difficult—but much easier than being left behind. As I walked out the last time, I was frightened: the world outside waited. I still felt it was a hostile place.

At home, the children seemed happy over my return. They marched in and out, off to school and back again, arms heavy with books, sports equipment and projects for the literary magazine, their minds already preoccupied with friends and wishes for girls. I wasn't writing, so I tried to read. It took only a week before I stopped making out the daily schedules, but I did stick to trying to reach out to the friends still by my side. I tried to keep busy and to look nice each day, and I went back to my exercise routine at the gym. And all that helped, even though following a chart made me feel like a child again. Still, I knew it was the only way: it taught me techniques in how to live with depression—things I hadn't known, such as making my bed immediately on rising so that I couldn't get back into it.

But all the routines available couldn't erase the fact that the depression remained active, hungry, and eager to feed. I still had not been able to lay it totally to rest. Alone, I still remained in pain in the black black tunnel. And despite all the help, I still wanted to die.

{in the land of the bed}

AFTER JIM LEFT me, I had begun to sleep during the day on some days; after my rehab wore off, I began to sleep nearly all of the day on many days. In the end, the months added up into years—four years—with intermittent periods during which I did manage to rouse myself. Those times felt as if I were standing under an umbrella of depression with spikes of occasional mania that would at last drive me up, in a fever, from my bed. Up, in a burst, for Gabe's latest theatrical production, and then for Nathaniel's graduation from high school. Up, eventually and for what felt far too soon, to take Nathaniel to his first semester of college, losing his empathetic support. Up with concomitant reluctance and anticipation, to move from my house of fifteen summers and winters.

Yet, despite my occasional bouts of optimism, the loneliness did not really ease. Sometimes I sobbed, the pain too intolerable for me to continue. The days passed, many alike and emptied of everything except gray light, the cold and unyielding hours. Nothing to cushion anything. Just the voice in my head, a constant companion, talking to me louder than ever before, reminding me of what a mess I had made of my life. Feeling desperate, I tallied the years, adding and subtracting and arriving at a spooky parallel: my mother had divorced my father in the same year of her life as Jim had left me in mine, minus one. Once again, my life and my moods still seemed inexplicably tied to hers.

It was during the last two of those years that I really regressed from my stint in the hospital in March of 1999. Often, I was not sure of what year I had passed into. The year 2003 felt nearly the same as 2004, regardless of the changes that might have occurred in the reality of my daily life, like the kids passing forward into new grades, or the car needing repairs. On the weeks they were at Jim's, I was once again sweating out being alone in the house. My anchors had broken free and left me victim to the tides of each day.

Even now, looking back, it feels difficult to remember what it was like to be in my bed for an entire day. Yet, simultaneously, it seems as real as my life does now, sitting here at my computer, summoning up all these old emotions. One day simply followed another, and then another—and then the nights came on the same as all the days. The air in the bedroom was tinged with a sepia tone. None of the furniture or the objects in the room had any defined edges. It was as if I were trying to live without my glasses. Everything out of focus.

I fed on the nectar of pillow and blanket. Smooth and soft, the sheets hugged me. The electric blanket spread its coiled warmth over me; the lamp cast the only light in the room—a yellow glow across the bed. But with the curtains closed, it seemed the boundaries of the walls had tightened down and given the room a stuffy feel, as if it needed to be aired out.

Craving the sweet buffer of sleep, which had become the whitewash for my soul, I felt like a bird in my nest. Sleep would drown out the voice that constantly judged, constantly recrimi-nated me about what I ought to be doing, what I ought to have achieved. This was a daily exit from life, not unlike suicide, but one from which I was still able to wake.

I turned the phone off and would not come to for a long time unless someone rang the doorbell and the dog started up a racket. Then I would go to the door in my bathrobe, stinking of morning breath at noon, feeling humiliated, but not humiliated enough to get dressed before the laundry man delivered on Tuesdays at one o'clock. My cocoon provided safety, but the king-sized bed felt empty with just one, so I had permanently shifted to the center. I had long since abandoned the lists I had made at the outpatient clinic about getting dressed and washing my hair. Now, on those days I did manage to dress myself, it was only in jeans and a sweatshirt gone baggy, due partially to my weight gain, and partially because I just didn't care. My closet overwhelmed me with all its infinite choices: colors and patterns blurred, creating a confusing sense of indecision and defeat. All the pretty silk shirts and leather skirts hung untouched, and the boxes of shoes remained closed. With my hair stringy and limp once again, there was no question about applying the makeup I never used to do without. The depression was still keeping me prisoner.

Some days I stayed in bed all day and then lied to the kids when they got home, telling them I had been overwhelmed by another migraine an hour ago, and so had just that moment laid down. I never said anything about the fact that I wasn't working, but they knew anyway. Sometimes my days revolved around the schedule of medications: Vicodin for the headaches; Lamictal for depression; Neurontin for anxiety and chronic pain, along with Klonopin as well; Abilify also for the mood stabilization of the bipolar disorder; Topamax for the weight control I needed so desperately as I ballooned up forty pounds with the addition of the Seroquel, which was also a mood stabilizer—not unlike Lithium or Depakote in its side effects of weight gain; Temazepam for sleep.

Every so often I dragged myself back into my writing room.

My computer was asleep, too. Its keys had grown dusty and the screensaver had become a blank, black hole that challenged me whenever I crept through the door. My dictionary lay open, its tissue-like pages untouched from the last day I had worked. Capsicum to carbonara. Under the blanket of depression, my mind had forgotten its treasury of words.

Bit by bit, I forgot about that book, or revisions, or anything else I could have conceived of or begun to take notes on. All I could manage now was to stare out the window at the intricate garden I had planted with such love in that other part of my life. One day I noticed how the hydrangeas drowsed under the relentless summer sun, drooping, the indigo heads standing out in sad relief over the limp green leaves. In winter their branches would be cut back to the soil and the stalks would become stark bare sticks. I moved away from the glass quickly. The bareness of the hydrangeas would be only temporary. What about my bareness, my barrenness? I shuddered and returned to my bed, where I curled my body into itself.

I spent a lot of time crying, even when it seemed there was nothing to cry about, and I was mortified every time the tears started again. I remembered my mother had cried just this way, and I closed my eyes against the shame that I hadn't understood her better, that I had blamed her for giving up. I felt like a traitor.

PERHAPS IT WAS mid-week, perhaps Wednesday, or Friday, or any day. But noise was coming from the kitchen. Angelina must be here for my weekly housecleaning—and so I knew that it was Thursday. Her broad smile felt to me like a teaspoon of joy. She was running water and turning on the dishwasher and humming.

Angelina was from Mexico. At one time, in the land of her birth, she was a medical doctor. She liked the US enough to stay here as a cleaning lady, enough to get her citizenship, and sever her legal connection with a very poor place in exchange for what seemed a better life. When I heard her coming down the hall, I closed my eyes and pretended to be asleep.

Angelina was not fooled—anymore than my mother had been when I tried to elude her prying eyes by pretending to be napping. With my mother, I had to hurriedly sneak my book under the covers. Books required only time back then; they provided me with a place to which I could have escaped. But during these years of depression, I could not read at all; I felt my head buzzing with the letters, keeping them from becoming words. I had been so ignorant when my mother was ill. I hadn't known that depression could gut you and leave you there like a flounder, useless, your one eye staring up at the ceiling.

Angelina crossed right to the edge of the bed and put her hand on my shoulder. "Linda, when did you last eat?"

"Maybe breakfast," I muttered, hoping she would believe me, my eyes still closed. Angelina did not know how many days I had been lying there, and I didn't want her to know. Next to her sturdy work ethic, my incapacity to live a normal life was embarrassing.

She rattled the spoon in a yogurt container and looked at the crusted remains. Clearly it was a remnant left over from yesterday's effort to eat a little. Disgusted, she made a little sound in her throat. "You need more. Especially for dinner." Shaking her head, she took the container back to the kitchen along with the dirty glasses that crowded my night table. I loved Angelina, but she wasn't enough.

Gulliver's sweet warm weight stretched out beside me. He indented his body around my curves. Since the separation, he was my constant companion, keeping watch, only going outside occasionally. I turned to hold him tightly as he babysat me. Stroking the skin of his ears, I knew that he loved me despite the fact that

I had become disgusting and bedridden. His smooth wet tongue lapped away my tears and I loved him even more for it.

Gulliver was much like Rhiannon; he followed my every step and my every hand motion. He had been only six months old when his two other companions disappeared, and less than a year old when Jim left us. Quickly he graduated to being the only one—besides the children—receiving the heap of love I had in my heart. He had become my therapy dog. When I took to bed in the midst of my depression, so did he. It was as if he could read my mind, see my tears, and understand what they meant. He became my guardian.

I curled my body around him and he pushed his back hard against me, entwining us in the embrace that would extend for hours if nothing interrupted. I couldn't put my head down on the chests of my children to cry (too similar to what my mother had done with me); I couldn't explain to anyone how I was suffering the effects of the legacy, but I could lay my cheek against Gulliver's soft white coat, and let the tears spill. Stoically he accepted my grief and took on its burden. He simply encouraged me, for a moment, to lay down my pain.

The doorbell rang and he ran straight as a shot to the front door, barking his head off. In my pajamas, I turned the lock and the door swung wide. A process server handed me a packet of final divorce papers, filed now, with the court's official stamps. I slid the fat envelope to the very bottom of the tall shaky pile of mail in the kitchen, and resolved not to think about it. I hoped, still, that Jim would call me and tell me to tear up the documents.

ALONE IN THE silent house, which was alive now only every other week with the children's noise and life, I mostly roused myself just to drive to my fifty-minute therapy appointments on Tuesday, Thursday, and Friday. Afterwards on at least one of those days, I ought to have gone to the supermarket, but usually I scurried back home instead.

I gave the kids money so that they could eat out at pizza shops and burger joints. I stopped eating anything except junk that only needed reheating in the microwave or caloric things like ice cream straight from the container. The drugs began to pile on the weight and in the space of only a few months I had gained more than when I was pregnant. I went from a size six to a size twelve. I used to love to cook but when I was on that walkway in the recesses of my mind, every pot in my kitchen was cast concrete and the vegetable peeler looked like a foreign object. All notions of being a good mother "via the stove top" fled. No longer did I involve myself in the children's school events. I was a mother without that vital connection to other mothers. Parents' night felt like a slough of loneliness. No longer did I help on the occasional field trips to which parents were invited. Working in the library, as I had done previously, required an insurmountable effort, one beyond me. Once again, I was hibernating from life.

My new psychiatrist, who had replaced Benjamin Berns, kept telling me that one day the depression and anxiety would stop, and I tried to believe in those words as if they were talismans, lucky charms that I stroked continuously.

Each by each, slowly but inevitably, my old friends receded. Hard as I tried, I was helpless to make them understand the pain I was experiencing. They could neither imagine nor picture such relentless incapacitation. Perhaps, somehow, without realizing it, I had begun to drive them away: Isabel, who had always asked for my advice with mothering; Vicky and Ellen, my two roommates from college, who used to listen intently to every intimate secret and emotion; the neighbors who had often asked me to lunch parties, baby showers, weddings, and dinners; Adrienne and Julia, my literary companions and mentors; Ellen and Jeanne, with whom I had had a weekly workshop for our novels and memoirs. Inexperienced with the kind of depression I was enduring, they understood nothing about the rectangular box in which I lived. There was no avoiding the fact that the phone rang less and less often; the message service had grown quiet and empty.

To my friends, it all just sounded like an elaborate excuse. "How hard could it be to pick up a telephone?" they asked. I did not answer. I did not say, it is very hard, when you have nothing to say, when daily your self is shrinking down as tight as a snake's new skin. Just the thought of calling someone made fear rise in my throat like bile.

I had never needed my friends more. No one seemed to understand that being withdrawn and somehow helpless, especially when there is no visible physical illness, is the crux of the isolation my mental illness fed upon.

One afternoon, I awakened to find the phone dead: the telephone company had terminated my service for nonpayment. A trusted friend, in whom I at last confided, helped me dress and then took me to a superette where one could pay off the bill and get service restored immediately. I felt like a bum.

I avoided bookstores, which, I assumed, had long since stopped carrying *Searching for Mercy Street*. It was just a gut feeling. One day I summoned the courage to go into our local independent store, which had always had my books on the shelves, and where I had given several well-attended readings. I found, as I had feared, that the memoir was no longer on the shelf, but—as my inner voice pointed out with satisfaction—all of my mother's books were there, including the biography.

I had stopped reading the *New York Times Book Review*, a bible for all writers, and so had lost track of the publishing world as well, all the arrivals of those highly touted books I had so eagerly sought out previously, week to week. I was used to being invited, several times a year, to write long reviews. But now I was cut off to what was out there that was new and good, or even new and bad.

MANY WRITERS WRITE just because they must: the muse is so strong that they have no choice. I had always counted myself a part of the many for whom this was true, and felt that being within that community of people, who understood all that I accepted about this art of ours, was as comfortable as it was safe. I had never written just for publication, and I had often emphasized to my students at the Berkeley Adult Extension course (which I taught right after the memoir was published, before my depression settled in) how important it was to write for oneself. Yet, there I was, damned by my own advice—my muse had turned her back on me.

Worst of all, I believed absolutely that I had nothing left to give to any of the people I liked and loved, and that I never would again. When I was back at home, even Gabe, who had more compassion than anyone except Nathaniel, asked me why I hadn't cooked a meal in two weeks. "After all," he pointed out, "you're not working. You're just sitting around all day doing nothing."

My father used to tell a story that I, in turn, then told to Gabe, hoping it might help him, feeling desperate to make a connection with him. Apparently when my father was traveling, he used to call my mother from the road to check up on her and ensure that she was all right. All day long he worried about her, especially when she was depressed, and especially as long afternoons drew to a close. Dusk fell and the highway's gray miles changed into the home stretch, and he'd pull into a filling station and use the pay phone to tell her to put the potatoes into the oven. She'd promise to start them baking, but when he got home, there the potatoes were, just the way he'd left them that morning, waiting neatly scrubbed on the counter—and there my mother was, just the way he'd left her that morning, lying in bed. He would put the potatoes in to bake and dinner would be late, but my mother's helplessness with something as simple as a potato filled him, like me, with frustration, loneliness, and fear.

From the expression on Gabe's face, I could see that he was trying to be empathetic as he heard this story. However, it was too much for him, a young teenager, to really comprehend.

RACHAEL WAS THE most difficult to tell of my second suicide attempt, and so, with dread, I procrastinated about calling her until the very last. I knew I had to let her know about my deterioration and not leave the task to somebody else. I felt unable to return her increasingly frequent phone messages because I knew I had to confront the truth with her. I decided I must call her no matter what: I felt I owed her an explanation about what was going on, even if I loathed making the call.

"Why didn't you tell me?" she castigated me. "You didn't give me the chance to help."

I didn't know how to answer her. She had always been one of the lynchpins in keeping the legacy at bay: if Rachael believed in me, then I must be a good mother and a good writer; like my father, she wanted me to push myself, and somehow this failure of my strength made me even more ashamed. I fell silent and she took that silence to mean that I didn't care about our friendship any longer, which was so far from the truth.

I was back in the tunnel, buried too far underground, with my skin on fire.

ON THIS PARTICULAR Wednesday, I had no appointment with anyone and the best I could do was to sit on the edge of the bed after Angelina left the room.

She had brought in three days of mail and newspapers. I hadn't walked to the end of the driveway for several days. I let the newspapers slide to the floor, still folded in their blue plastic wrappers. I glanced at the mail (I worried that the town might put a lien on the house for the taxes now in arrears) and then I tossed the stack of it onto the piles of paper junk that were growing up the walls of my bedroom.

"Just ignore this mess," I said as Angelina reappeared.

"Can I do this room? Maybe you want to go into your office and work on the computer."

"Gabe's room." I kept my tone short and clipped, not wanting to engage her in conversation.

As I pushed myself to the edge of the bed, I saw a bright piece of lime-colored paper in the mass of mail. From Gabe's class parent, it was a reminder notice for a classroom presentation of the students' current photography journalism exhibits—an event I must attend, ten thirty on Wednesday the fifth. Frantically I scrambled to push up my pajama sleeve and look at my watch for the date and time.

Too late.

The original notice was probably in one of the paper stacks that surrounded me. Self-loathing stabbed at my head, signaling the beginning of a migraine.

"Dumb shit of a mother," the inner voice berated me.

All I could think about was Gabe, just last night, asking me if I were coming. How could I have forgotten so easily? These days my memory was slick and wily, simply skipping over large parts of my time awake and refusing to record it. I didn't remember people's names or faces. I didn't remember the date or time. I didn't remember what television movie I saw the night before last, not its title, plot, or star. I didn't remember the few phone calls I did get. My doctors suggested to me that I was experiencing short-term memory loss as a result of the medications I was taking. I felt, with dismay, that this was just one more reason that I still carried Jim and the memory of our marriage inside me, and in this way I had built up a scarred wall that prevented me from moving on.

I closed my eyes against the picture of my son's face as he waited for me to come through the classroom door. Yes, he would be standing there, in front of his exhibit, being polite to other mothers and their sons, waiting, his boy-into-man face revealing nothing, his deep blue eyes searching, the brave smile never wavering. From the depths of my own childhood's despair, I remembered the infinite loneliness of waiting and watching for someone who never came. My absence that day was a wrong that might never be rectified, neither with lots of love, nor with lots of consistency in the future. I could hope that, in time, he would push the memory down deep to a place where forgetfulness helps, in part, to erase disappointment over an important moment.

That day, I did not remember all the times in the past when I had not missed the piano recitals (standing in the corner so he could see me, wishing he would get through "Twinkle Twinkle Little Star" without a mistake). Or the lacrosse season (standing for hours on the edge of the hard frosty field, my feet and butt growing numb). Or the school awards ceremonies at the end of the year (hoping Nathaniel would get chosen for something so that one of my particular friends—also a team parent—wouldn't gloat when her son won yet another prize). Or the parent-teacher conferences (sitting in student chairs with attached writing desks that took me back to my own adolescence) where I prayed that both my sons' hard work would be reflected in their grades, and then the back-to-school night (a single parent alone amidst couples). I did not remember, just then, the ways in which I had been a good mother and then some. I felt too saddened by what I had become.

Angelina reappeared with the vacuum cleaner. I took a tissue from the bedside box and blew, hard. Reluctantly I pushed my body up and walked down the hall.

Gabe had decorated his bedroom with posters of the movie and rock stars he admired, and on the shelves there were numerous athletic trophies. I lay on top of the bed and stared at the ceiling blankly. Once again the tears were urgent, hot, ready to overflow; once again Gulliver was there to comfort me. My head drummed with the rhythm of the migraine.

I turned over on the small bed. Gabe was beginning to grow out of it with his ever-escalating push upward. He was already nearly six feet, and I knew that all too soon he would be off at college and I would be missing him. Gulliver settled into a new position. Feeling anxious again, I clutched my stomach and tried to breathe out; I tried to surrender to it, and sometimes I daydreamed, trying to distract myself with pleasurable thoughts.

I picked up *To Kill a Mockingbird* from Gabe's nightstand and shuffled through it. I remembered the sweet discovery of this book, and *The Yearling*, both of which I encountered for the first time when I was about twelve, with passionate delight. How I wished that I could read it again—it might have helped the time pass, it might have given my day some shape.

After a while I went back down the hall to my room again. Angelina had finished dusting and vacuuming. The stacks of papers that climbed against the wall had been straightened.

"Thank you," I said politely, feeling embarrassed once again at being in bed on a day when this hard-working woman took over caring for my home.

"De nada," she responded, as she hefted the laundry basket and disappeared from the room.

I got into bed and stretched my toes down into the cool smooth depths of new sheets. Angelina came in after me, and pulled open the drapes; she turned off the electric lights without comment about me resuming my spot in the bed. A little sunlight grew long in patches on my rug. I remembered how Nana would come into my room when I'd been sick for a while and open up the curtains. She was a shadowy black figure against the light from the window. I was a child who craved nurturing. She sat on the edge of the bed and pressed her cool palm against my forehead.

"Fever's gone," she said. "Time to get up."

"But I still feel sick." I put on my most doleful expression.

Nana put her hands on her waist for emphasis. "Come down to the kitchen for lunch. I'm making French grilled cheese sandwiches and chocolate frappés."

Scooting out of bed, I put on my bathrobe and brushed my teeth.

The sandwiches were as good as promised. We ate together, smiling across the table at each other in the freeze-frame of bright sunlight. My frappé even had a straw.

"You sure you won't get up?" Angelina was back at the door. "Or I could make you something on a tray."

"No, thanks, I'm fine." I remembered the hospital food served on orange plastic trays, a section for the meat, a section for the green vegetable, a section for the starch. Low sodium diet. Caffeine free. All of it awful.

I pretended to read, my eyes glazed with the letters. As I anticipated, Angelina came in to wave goodbye, and once again I lapsed into sleep, away from my headache and away from what I felt to be a low, low mood.

I dreamed of the tunnel again.

Waking, sleeping, it was always there: the conveyor belt and the despair.

There was a jiggling at my shoulder, a voice interrupting the dream that had weighed me down. "Wake up," said Gabe. "Mom, wake up."

I rolled over, feeling groggy and disoriented, my eyes full of sleep, my glasses painfully pinching the bridge of my nose. "What time is it?"

"Almost five."

Angelina left at two thirty, so I had slept for nearly three hours, not counting the ones earlier in the day before she had gotten there.

I swore silently. Not only had I missed his presentation, but I had never taken the meatloaf out of the freezer, a meatloaf lovingly prepared in another time. There would be no home-cooked dinner tonight. "Why are you home so late?"

A hurt look crossed his face, and he gestured toward his clothing. "Look like anything you recognize?"

"Oh, God, you had a soccer game today, didn't you?" I had promised him that I would get to the next game, which had obviously been played while I was sleeping. He had grown so much in the last year it seemed to me that he would no longer belong to me: soon he would be his own independent person.

I saw his expression cross from hurt to disgust.

"Gee, can't you even get straight what I play? It's not soccer— it's lacrosse!"

"I'm sorry, Gabe. I just keep forgetting," I answered contritely.

"Well, I wish you'd get it right. It's not too hard to remember your kids' athletics."

"And I'm really sorry that I missed your project in school this morning—I just had such a bad headache."

"Liar!" the voice accused.

"That's all right—there were other mothers who told me how great it was," he said, looking as if it had been anything but acceptable. He paused. "Why are you in bed?" He passed a cool hand over my forehead.

"A migraine," I replied, cringing at his reference to "other mothers."

"What's for dinner? I'm starved."

"Pizza."

"Great," he said glumly. "Can you call it in right now?"

"Of course." I nodded, feeling guilty. Knowing the number so well I didn't have to look it up, I gave the order. "Forty-five minutes. Do you know where Nathaniel is?"

He shook his head. "He took off with some of his friends."

Once he was out of the room, I closed my eyes for a moment, filled with maternal worry. More and more often Nathaniel disappeared with his friends after school. Were they off in the parking garage of some mall, doing drugs or drinking, as I once had done? Or even, it occurred to me, at his father's house, empty on afternoons. He swore not, but my suspicions grew with every passing week. His grades were still solid and his college applications finished, but still I worried. I pushed my legs out of the bed, getting ready to set the table. At least I could be mother enough to pour Gabe's glass of milk and pull out a stack of napkins for the greasy pie.

The doorbell rang. The dog began his flurry of barking. The pizza man with his cardboard box of pepperoni and cheese had come to my rescue again, arriving at my front door for the third night this week. I went to answer the bell in my bathrobe. Nathaniel did not come home for dinner, and he did not call either. When he came in at seven o'clock, I yelled at him and sent him in to do his homework. He had already eaten supper with his friends at a local hamburger dive.

Afterwards I cleaned up the cardboard box and Gabe's milk glass. I had eaten a few greasy slices and sipped on a Diet Pepsi, feeling dazed. And then, from my bed, I pretended to watch the television for the next two hours, waiting until the children's homework was done in case they needed help. At eleven o'clock I turned out the light: it was now legal to sleep.

PART 5

{waking}

Although the world is full of suffering, it is also full of overcoming it.

—HELEN KELLER

{contours and excavations}

I REMEMBER HOW I interviewed new doctors that late April of 1999, not so long after my second release from the hospital, trundling along with my fat medical file, the history of my head out there in front of me like an overloaded grocery cart. I had to keep forcing myself out of bed: it was discouraging how the rehab had faded, with its precise answers that were so difficult, so impossible, to follow. I felt guilt about the ways in which I had regressed, but as usual, depression trumped all. Rehab had only helped me stay healthy on the surface for a short time. Once again, I was still obsessed with death.

In a session that would catch forever in the net of my memory, nearly word for word, Ben Berns had urgently reminded me that he could not (or would not) continue to see me any longer. He had decided, though, that he would help me out, until I could find a new therapist to fill the void. While I was disgust-ingly grateful for the assistance he proffered, I still resented his brisk and efficient exit; I still resented how easily he was able to push me away, as if I were an old stack of newspapers ready for the dump.

There were only a few possible doctors on Ben's unmercifully short list, but he made certain that I knew how hard he had worked on this search and how much time it was absorbing. It was difficult, he explained, to find doctors willing to take on suicidal patients.

Apparently I had been officially given a new label, one with a negative connotation. I wondered: If he had been seeking a new therapist for a patient who suffered from a vanilla variety bipolar disorder, would he ask that potential source of help whether she accepted a patient with such a condition? Why wasn't I still, just, a bipolar mess? Or a deeply troubled person with a variety of symptoms? To put it another way, it felt to me as if my suicide attempt was what I had done—but it was not a definition of who I was. And so, when I asked him why the distinction of being "suicidal" was such a showstopper, he told me that most physicians don't want to put in the extra time such a patient requires, especially because some of it is often spent in the hospital. This attitude seemed to me incredibly backward and callous. A suicidal patient needs therapeutic help more than any other, but because she needs it so much, she was very likely not going to receive it. The suicidal patient breached the levees of acceptable behavior. A family could hide from what suicide "meant" or "symbolized," but a therapist had to cope with its confrontation of death and make a decision about whether to interfere—a judgment call of the highest order. Both reactions left the suicidal person adrift and alone.

To HAVE A patient exit so abruptly by taking his life must be the worst event a psychiatrist can experience—a rejection so traumatic that it has to reflect, in the therapist's mind, his failure to keep his patient alive, which is every doctor's primary responsibility. Ben had not been able to safeguard me, a patient who had trusted that someday, led by his astute and comforting guidance, she might get well. Suicide allowed for no real goodbye for the doctor, just as it did not for the family, or for the patient.

Whether or not my insights were correct, I was once again left shivering in the draft of everyone's disapproval, dancing like a marionette in rhythm to the old black tune that had haunted my life ever since my mother first kicked me out of the house when I was two. Living in these shadows of the past, it took me many months to accept my feelings about Ben's decision to leave me behind, and several years to come to the conclusion that he wasn't the Godlike doctor I'd painted in my mind; he was only a man, and a flawed one at that. But when I was released from the hospital and had to confront his cold face during our first session, I hated him, on some level, for his lack of compassion. Suddenly he seemed undependable, cruel, and uncaring. I could still see that he was a gifted therapist, but his shortcomings were now overwhelming. In self-defense, I decided I wanted to leave him as much as he wanted me to leave, but, really, this was only a lie I told myself.

And so there I was on that sunny April day, booted out on my ass like the unloved child, the naughty but uncertain teenager, the unwanted wife I was. I was about to "interview" Dr. Barbara Ballinger, who had passed two board examinations in both psychiatry and neurology, just as Norman Greid had, the difference being that she did "talk therapy" in addition to prescribing psychotropic drugs. Her qualifications fit my needs extremely well: she treated clinical depression extensively, as well as bipolar disorder; perhaps best of all was the fact that patients who were suicidal didn't seem to faze her. What I worried about, of course, was exposing myself yet again to another doctor who might have the same sorts of rules Ben did and thus might back away from treating me.

Being early by twenty minutes, I lit up another cigarette as I paced on the sidewalk in front of the small beige bungalow. My mother never had to go through this: she was always lucky enough to have shrinks who did not abandon her over an episode of manic craziness or a suicide attempt. It was always at her own instigation that she terminated with a therapist and moved on to another. I thought about how many more psychiatrists would have revolved through the Sexton household had my mother been forced to switch doctors every time she made an attempt.

I remembered how she looked when she came home from the hospital after a suicide attempt, bruised like the petals of a flower that have been bent and creased, browning around the edges. Despite my repeated watering, in time those petals would droop and scatter, one by one. This metaphor swayed inside me and I felt flooded with a very strong fantasy: if my mother were there at that moment I would stop in the middle of the sidewalk, set my purse on the ground, and very gently, very wearily, put my arms around her. And she would put her arms around me, and the two of us would make one complete circle.

Instead, without my mother, I had to accept the idea that the best I could do was to forge an intimate circle with a doctor, work transference, and see if I could tease apart the tangle of unconscious emotions—to work hard enough to stay alive. But I didn't want to remain in this world. If you had asked me then, back in May of 1999, "Are you glad to be alive?" I would have answered, "No." I was still feeling angry at having been thwarted in my bid for death.

Nevertheless, I worked furiously to obfuscate and thus avoid revealing my negative mood. I concentrated on telling my family, "Okay, the sky is blue, today's a good day," or some other such fabrication. All of this enabled me to make progress toward the positive: the lie was sufficient to keep me from making a new plan that had nothing to do with unobtainable pills and every-thing to do with location and opportunity—but I could only do it for that one day. This was all I could promise my children, and myself. Just one day.

As the hands on my watch hit two-thirty, I dropped my cigarette butt down the storm drain and went, with trepidation, inside to meet Dr. Ballinger. Despite a somewhat cold first interview, she turned out to be "the one." She didn't have a teapot like Ben did, but neither did she require a contract about cutting my or making suicide attempts. It seemed as if I had found a psychiatrist who could empathize with my illness.

She had a wonderful tousle of silver hair that she drew back from her delicate face with a variety of silly or beautiful hair ornaments (depending on her mood), and she dressed uniquely, which is to say no ordinary suits or dresses. Not the hippie California Birkenstock and dirndl skirts type, she followed her own eclectic tastes: silks of wonderful colors and cuts, pants of all lengths, tops that looked as if they came from the thrift shop one day and Neiman Marcus the next.

Her office was a mess, and initially I found I had an aversion to that aspect of her care. How could someone with such a chaotic workplace ever guide me to some serenity? For the first two years of my treatment, Barbara's fax machine was continually jammed, the paper always stuck cockeyed in the feeder. Her desk was strewn with files, and, with its pencil drawer open, it often looked as if it had its mouth agape. There were books all over the place, however, which made me feel at home, and even a dictionary so that we could look up words when we disagreed on a definition—perusing the synonyms, antonyms, and etiology quite frequently, to my intense pleasure out into the light and air "which I had discovered after I moved to California."

I sat on one end of a leather couch that had an afghan over its arm, which I used nearly every session because I was always freezing while doing work that brought me to a cold sweat, even though her office was comfortingly warm. She sat in a leather chair, quite close to me, having kicked her shoes off so that she could stretch her feet out on the ottoman. She and I mapped out all the contours of my suicide attempts, gently excavating around all the emotions, needs, and desires that had arisen during that total breakdown of my life.

I went for four appointments a week initially, and then, as things began to calm down, three times, then two, and finally, magically, to once every other week. It was Barbara who introduced the concept that suicide could be passed on as a legacy; the idea was initially new to me, never before named or examined with any therapist. Barbara went right to the heart of the matter, and old interpretations were torn apart as we probed the legacy's nasty roots: why, when I turned forty-five years old, did I still so identify with my mother—despite her death twenty years before—to such an extent that even in the year of my life at which she had died, I had my first real breakdown, caused by urgent and uncontrollable emotions: I did not want her to leave; I did not want to leave her.

Barbara's questions were difficult initially, largely because I had no answers. She was patient, waiting for me to make the necessary connections. Little by little, I began to allow into my consciousness a new idea: with her suicide, my mother had deserted me once again, and no matter how hard I had tried to reconcile myself to her eventual death, no matter how desperately I had tried to forgive her, I was still running from these continuing abandonments, each of which echoed every previous incident. They added up one after another into a huge pile that would inevitably begin to sway and, eventually, fall. Each time she tried to kill herself, those old injuries I had experienced kept repeating—from my cradle to her casket and then, quite unexpectedly, beyond—into my life without her.

Gradually, I learned that I couldn't outpace this specter, but had to turn and fight. As my mother shut the door on living, the entire family—and those still close to her, as well as those already alienated and angry—rocked with the repercussions of her suicide, just as I had done. The emotion I heard most about was guilt: guilt at having survived, guilt from those who remained, guilt over the loss of their mother, their wife, and their friend. These emotions often leapt from the anger they felt at the final and permanent separation she had chosen, or, in another twist, from the way they had withdrawn from her and her mental illness in the last few months of her life. I felt sorry for all of us: for those who mourned in silence and in loneliness, and for the others who expressed their pain through writing the newspaper articles and eulogies and poems that enabled them to hang on to their memories of this woman they had loved so much. I, too, struggled to keep her alive in some way.

Barbara was the second to suggest that I write a memoir about suicide, two years after a friend had done so following my first attempt. Feeling that it would be impossible to write about such raw material, I rejected the idea, but made a few notes anyway. Perhaps, despite all my failures, there was a tiny hope, buried deep inside me, that, even from the refuge of blanket and pillow, I might still have a story to tell—one that could help thousands of the mentally ill and their families, who often have no voice of their own.

Yes, it always came back to the story—no matter how humiliating—because the story was just another aspect of my mother's life and therefore of my own. Yet I doubted, and worried that I would never grow strong enough to let it loose on the page. As J. M. Coetzee writes in his novel *Elizabeth Costello*, some experiences are too dangerous to be put into words—too dangerous for the reader, but even more dangerous for the writer, who may feel overtaken and undone by them. Determining to dip into a life experience that might be difficult in its telling but uplifting in its conclusion, the idea of helping other people—as Barbara had suggested—took precedence over worry about baring my life and demanded to be expressed in the only way I knew how. And so, every once in a while, I picked up my pen.

EARLY ON, IT was Barbara who kept me afloat. We talked about my mother ad nauseam—that old and powerful identification, the one I thought I had conquered, the one that was really just lying in wait for me. The legacy took that identification, turned it into self-destruction, and brought me to the brink of death.

Barbara was one of the few people who helped me begin to pull myself out of the hole I had unconsciously created; it was a lengthy, difficult process—one made possible only because she was, quite literally, taking care of me in ways I'd never experienced before. It was not just love she offered, but crucial insights into my own past, present, and future.

She also forced me to grapple with the idea that lying in bed for days was another symptom of depression, but that in my case it was also another behavior handed down to me, fist over fist. I had watched my mother linger in bed, an invalid of sorts. If I were to reclaim my life, and re-enter the land of friends and normal living, I had to get up and fight. I couldn't just lie down under depression's weight. This symptom did not leave me for several years, but each year it did get a little better. Throughout, Gulliver stood watch.

I was not alone, even though Joy and my father and I were still estranged, and Jim and I barely spoke. The children were still my quiet supporters. Without them, I might not have made it—not because I loved them enough to restrain myself from that old suicide beat, but because they loved me enough never to give up on me, even when they left and went away to college. But it was Barbara's intuitive instincts that led me along the path to health. She stayed by my side, throughout my tears and regressive outbursts; she was an anchor that helped me begin to get well by allowing me to express whatever I felt, even if it was childish. She knew that until I worked through all those emotions, I would never get well.

I could tell Barbara everything, even when I was thinking about suicide. We had made a pact: if I came clean about any suicidal feelings, she wouldn't shut me up on a psychiatric ward immediately—she would listen to me quietly and deeply and only then, if she were truly worried that I might hurt myself, would she try to convince me to enter the hospital under my own power. Most importantly, she did not require that I tell her what my "means" might be, or my plan, or even where I had the necessary implements stored.

This agreement between the two of us freed the therapy so that I could talk to her about feeling suicidal rather than hiding it for fear of her intervention. Although I am certain that this was a risky path to follow (perhaps she could even have been excoriated by her peers and colleagues), Barbara encouraged me to express all my self-destructive urges in my sessions. At home, I began to look out my window and wonder what the world might bring to me next. By the fourth year of my therapy, my life no longer felt quite so bleak. I thought that perhaps there was a chance of another day, another week, after all. Brick by brick, Barbara was helping me rebuild the house of my soul and mind, even though the very idea was a contradiction: we tore down the old at the same time we built me up, back to where I once had been, out into the light and air. She played by my rules, but she still ensured that I would win.

I continued to be worried about being deserted, just as I had been by Ben, and by my mother, and by Jim. I strove to look attractive on the days I had an appointment with Barbara. I forced myself out of bed and into her office. She, in turn, was gentle with me: eventually I was able to drop any pretense of normalcy and allow her to see the dirty underside of my world with its constant urge to get away from life. Gratefully, I discovered that Barbara wasn't alarmed or threatened by my suicidal thoughts or my cutting or my occasional manic bouts. At the end of each appointment, she stood at her door and shook my hand as I left, intuiting that I needed some kind of a nurturing touch at the end of an emotionally difficult session. Afterwards, I often sat in my car, motionless for a while. I knew it was all part of getting better and returning to life, but that didn't make it any easier. As much as Barbara was with me during my sessions, I had to face the outside world on my own.

I told her about the cutting right from the start, before we even decided that we could work together. Over time, she would ask with quiet gravity to see the damage I had done, and I would show her. We discussed whether the wound should have been stitched, so that I would know what to do in case there was a next time. This was in sharp contrast to the way the subject had gone in Ben's office. I did not want to show him my cuts. I felt they were private, meant to be hidden, and certainly not to be seen by a man. Yet with Barbara, I could tolerate the intrusion. Barbara would inspect my cuts and then bind them back up the way a mother would. After all, it was a mother's tender touch I longed for, and Barbara was providing it in abundance.

I couldn't believe it had taken me so long to discover cutting as more than an occasional activity. Perhaps my slow arrival at this obvious conclusion stemmed from the fact that my mother hadn't ever cut herself, and all my self-destructive impulses had been so exclusively modeled on hers. But now that I had found it as a method to discharge the restlessness and anger I some-times still felt, it seemed impossible not to cut. If my arms and ankles were healed and bare, the urge to scar them again was powerful, and sometimes not to be denied. When the skin became smooth, it was time to act once more. My ankles, inner arms, and even one breast were now marked with short white scars, running their pain through the pink of my skin.

I was embroidering on what I'd inherited, making it truly my own by adding to it. It helped create originality in a world where I lived daily with the idea that I was only an imposter. Ambivalence personified: I felt proud of those marching white lines—and yet I was simultaneously and acutely ashamed. I did not boast of my injuries; I covered them over with Band-Aids and makeup. I knew being able to see them as beautiful meant there was something twisted in my mind, as twisted as an anorexic girl seeing the imaginary fat on her body. And yet, the cuts were beautiful to me. As well as indelible. Their scars would always remain.

After a while, Barbara began prescribing my psychotropic drugs because it was better for us to be able to discuss their effects and the impact they had on my moods in our therapy sessions: this way medication and "talk therapy" worked hand in hand—a better prescription for recovery. I began to see a new neurologist for my migraine medications—leaving behind Norman and his outrageous rate of three hundred and fifty dollars per half hour. She persevered through the medication roulette until we found a successful combination of drugs. And she also gave me a new diagnosis: borderline personality disorder, a disease that was rapidly coming to be seen in the medical community as a subset of bipolar disorder. She explained to me that borderline is characterized by an enormous fear of abandonment, to the point of incapacitation, as well as including, nearly always, self-mutilation. Patients also typically idolize loved ones until they fall from the axis of their grace and power, and then demonize these same people: if you don't live up to expectations of a powerful intimacy, a borderline patient may reject you vehemently. Myrna said that no therapist wanted to take on a "borderline" as they were so demanding. But, once again, Barbara defied the stereotype.

This diagnosis illuminated more of my illness, and it became clear, over time, that the restoration of my mental health depended on a delicate balance between medications and therapy. We fiddled with some new drugs, adjusting up and down, and it was a challenge for Barbara to find the correct concoction.

In the initial years of my therapy with her, a lot of my time had passed in a coma-like state, one which cost me yet more years away from my friends and family and work. I was dreadfully overmedicated due to the interactions of my migraine and psychiatric medications. I walked and talked like a zombie until Barbara and I managed to get all the drugs straight, and this took many months to achieve. Even then, all the medications had severe side effects and I had to learn to live with them, even ones such as extreme weight gain, cognitive impairment, tremors in my hands so severe that I couldn't even sign my name on a bank check, the short-term memory loss, and sleepiness during the day. But, of course, Barbara was at my side for every bump up and down, working hard to regulate the meds as well as monitoring my mood.

On some level, I wanted to be overmedicated: it was easier to live in a painful world if I didn't have to be fully present each day. With time, however, I let go of the crutch. I used less pain medication, and when I told Barbara about the cognitive problems I was experiencing, she cut back on my Abilify and my Seroquel. I felt as if I were a locked cabinet of secrets—Barbara had turned the key and opened me up. She said I could bring all of my problems and all of my anger, and yes, all of my love, into her office and let it rest in her lap. All of my emotions were welcome, even the most ugly, and I was welcome, too.

{a new voice}

LONELY SOULS SOMETIMES commit desperate acts—and joining an online dating service surely qualified as one for me. Six months had passed since my second suicide attempt and when I signed on, I craved only a companionship that might curtail the loneliness wrapped around my ankles like a chilly fog every day the kids weren't around, and even those nights when they were. It seemed they didn't even need help with their homework anymore. I felt, often, that they didn't need much of me at all, so I turned my lights out, some nights, before they did theirs.

My choice seemed the safest online dating service at that time, as well as offering a superior smorgasbord of different types of men. Despite my depression and my dirty hair, I wrote up a care-free profile from bed, accompanied by what I judged was a pretty photo; in fact, it was one taken from a happier time in my life, for the book jacket of *Searching for Mercy Street*. To my pleasure, I was deluged with replies.

It gave my mood a boost. After the long months of Jim's rejection, here were other men who thought I had something to offer.

Eager to respond, I wanted to have "dates" on the weekend instead of sitting home by myself with the dangerous, narcotic pull of sleep. Of course, I told not one of them about my bipolar disorder or those many days when I still hibernated in my bed. Still, I bragged to Myrna that I had one computer jock after another asking me out. She looked at me, concerned, and asked if I was feeling manic. When I said no—perhaps a lie, perhaps not—she just fell quiet again.

It was de rigueur to chat online for a few weeks or so, keeping your real name and address hidden. Then, one person or the other would ask if she or he would like to "meet for coffee." Being in a safe, public place took the fear out of the equation, leaving you to deal only with a healthy dose of nerves over your blind date. If "a coffee" proved successful, you could then proceed to a full-fledged foray to the movies or even dinner.

Gradually I began to sort out the piles of men and their "handles": Luv4U (the dating game romantic), June-September (seeking a very strong maternal figure), etc. For my own handle, I chose something that sounded expensive: July Means Rubies. July was my birth month and perhaps, unconsciously, there was some implication that I wanted the kind of man who could buy me my birthstone. Looking back, it was a stupid choice: what did I care about rubies? I wanted someone who would be compassionate, sensitive, and strong. Someone I could lean on, and who wouldn't be put off when he discovered how truly complicated I was. How would I tell a near stranger of my bipolar disorder and the crippling migraines? How would I describe the legacy? This made me more hesitant about proceeding past the early dates.

But, on the surface at least, one candidate came immediately to the fore: Dan lived only a few miles from me, was divorced, with two teenage daughters my boys' ages. He was a software designer and consultant who had gone to an Ivy League college and graduate school, and with whom I shared some common interests. We liked each other well enough that, a week later, I accepted his invitation to go on a movie date. He was a voracious reader (immediate bonding), loved to eat in really good restaurants (delight!), he had strong and wide experiences and knew a lot about a lot (admiration), and he liked to hang glide (okay, as long as he didn't expect me to accompany him).

After a month and a half we borrowed his brother's vacation house in Tahoe. I had asked for a separate bedroom, and ostensibly we were there for me to learn how to ski, but sex was on his mind in a big way. The morning following our experiment with separate beds, he climbed into mine and we lost our awkwardness in a flurry of lovely sensations. It developed that he even liked to cuddle.

Dan and I dated steadily, and monogamously, for the better part of five months. We had fun together, discovering old movies and new restaurants, and even skiing, of which I had had a childhood fear. Out in the snow, falling down and getting up, making a few tentative forays down the bunny slope—I surprised myself by loving it. For both days of that weekend we skied for five hours: I took lessons as he enjoyed the advanced trails, then we met up for an hour's tandem skiing at the end of the day. When I was with Dan, my depression took a back seat. We were too active to allow me to fall into any dark depths: at last my sense of isolation had been pushed into the background. I could rely on him: he even changed the difficult spotlights at the foot of the drive and repaired Gulliver's dog door. Quite suddenly, I was riding high and I didn't care what was on the other side. Let it be depression: I could conquer that. I kept taking my meds, but I was agitating with Barbara to cut them out. All the manic activity felt rapturous and I didn't want to dampen any of it.

Once again, I felt like someone was taking care of me. I knew such a need was a weakness, but I couldn't help but swathe myself in the attention. Yet I had not really stopped missing Jim, and so I was very wary of any kind of commitment: what if Dan left—I would have to learn how to live alone once again. Even so, I felt jubilant at this score over depression—no matter how temporary—as well as its cronies anxiety, fear, and anguish.

I wasn't "in love" with Dan, though he professed he was with me, but the sex was wonderful in a full-screen sort of way, imperative, not to be denied. However, Dan got petulant if I didn't feel like making love for even one night. Behind his back, Myrna and I called him Once a Day Dan. She began to wonder if he didn't have a sexual addiction, but I waved her off, content to be enjoying myself even if it was a bit more than I could handle. Barbara, however, wondered, too, and that was disconcerting.

Life moved on. I had no desire to write again—it seemed like a dangerous activity, one whose built-in, inevitable rejections could easily lead to another encounter with the wolf who seemed to have given up, at least for a while, gnawing on my gut. Because I was worried about money, and was saving for the future when my monthly marital support checks would cease, I decided— once again in a rather wild, manic state—to get a real estate license. I had an acquaintance who was a realtor, and she loved the business and convinced me I should try it out. There were four months of courses to take and a final rigorous test pass in order to become a practicing agent. My friend assured me that I could go to work for her boss as soon as I got my license. I checked in with her manager, at the most elite realty company in the area, and was assured that "a desk" would be waiting for me as soon as I earned my provisional license.

Throughout that fall, I worked hard to conquer all the course material and to study the tests given in previous years. The work, sometimes mathematical, was very difficult for me—especially after having been out of study mode since my college graduation twenty-five years before. I worried that I would not pass the exam and would be humiliated in front of everyone who knew what I was trying to do. Dan could see how hard I was working, and he encouraged me. In the late winter, I did pass, and I joined the high-profile company of my friend.

I put the idea of writing firmly behind me, looking for something new and exciting to occupy my time. I expected my new job to be lucrative, as I was situated in the middle of a booming market where every house had at least eight to ten competing offers. I could not have known, at such an early stage in the business, that I would have been better off in a small town, where the competition to obtain listings was not so tough.

I began to have anxiety again; it increased as Dan started to pressure me for a commitment and as things at work didn't develop as I had thought they would. When Dan professed his love and his frustration at what he perceived as my reluctance to allow him, deeply, into my heart, I was compelled to answer that I couldn't manufacture a feeling I didn't have, even though I was acutely aware that I must be hurting him. I didn't tell him that I still lived for the occasional call from Jim, for the dinners when we got together to discuss the kids—every little bit of contact we had.

One evening, in the early darkness of a winter day, after we returned home from another ski weekend, I unpacked my suitcase and got into my pajamas while Dan lay on top of my bed watching PBS. I was tired and wanted him to leave so that I could go to sleep. I had the start of a migraine and I worried it might become one of my major multiple-day headaches.

However, he had other ideas. I really wasn't receptive to the idea of sex, but—in the stubborn way rapidly becoming familiar to me—he began trying to cajole me, as if he could coax me to find desire. I said no over and over again, but he didn't give up. He switched his persistence from verbal to nonverbal. Even as I continued to say no, my voice grew weaker and weaker. His persistence wore me down.

I lay motionless on the bed underneath him, swamped under a wave of disbelief. My mind buzzed off onto some gray landscape.

I just lay there; I could not even cry. While he showered, I crept beneath the covers. After he left, I locked the door behind him and set the alarm. I was shaking.

Later, it was a slamdunk to shut Dan out of my life: he had breached some wall of trust and decency and I was absolutely resolved never to see him again, even though I had grown dependent on him. Nevertheless, he pursued me over the next six months, sending flowers and notes, determined emails, using the same line over and over about a "woman's sweet surrender" to a man.

But right then, I was just so numb. Instinctively, I knew that what had just happened was a disastrous repeat of those times from my childhood when my mother had come to my bed and I'd silently let her use me, turning my head to the side and crying, sealing my mouth shut—locking all the anger into the house of my body and then swallowing the key. The ache to hurt myself returned during those first few days after the incident, but I tried to hold myself in check.

My loneliness peaked, and anxiety was pumping adrenaline through my body. I thought miserably of how I had failed yet again: hadn't I done any maturing after all these—thirty—years of therapy? Though at my appointment that week Barbara tried to point out to me that the patterns of a lifetime don't change easily or quickly, I was furious with myself, and when I got home that evening after the appointment, I paced the still and empty house in a state of irritable hypomania. Luckily the children were with Jim for the week.

I set myself up in the bathroom, that site of so much old hurt. Taking out a fresh razor blade, I began. One, two, and then I stopped. Three. I put the blade down, shook my head against the silence. Something curious was happening. Pain. My ankle hurt like hell. I examined the cut: it was deeper than most, longer than any before. But that wasn't the difference. The difference, startling, was that it hurt enough to make me stop. With the blade wrapped in tissue and in the wastebasket, I started to shiver. Ordinarily cutting brought relief and control: today I felt neither.

The phone rang. It was Myrna, the only friend in whom I had confided that I sometimes cut myself. I suppose I felt, in her work as a therapist, that she knew enough about this act so that she wouldn't judge or desert me for something most people would find repulsive.

She could tell right away that something wasn't right. "What's going on? You sound odd."

"I just cut myself," I answered, starting to cry.

"I'm coming over and I'm bringing the dinner I was calling to invite you to."

"Don't," I said. "I'm a mess." As I once had done with my father, when he offered to come to California while I was in the hospital, I tried to talk her out of it. Myrna was more determined than he, and only a car ride away, so she just ignored me; when she arrived she put her arms around me and after a bit she bustled about, setting the food into the oven so it would stay warm. I sat at the kitchen table and sobbed.

She could see that the blood was leaking through the bandages. "Looks like you did a really good job with that gauze," she said dryly. "Why don't we see if we can improve on it?"

I nodded and we sat on the bathroom floor. She unpeeled the layers. When we got down to the cuts, she drew in her breath with a sharp hiss. "Linda, I think this needs stitches."

"It'll be okay if we use these." I handed her a box of butterfly bandages.

"You might get a scar."

I smiled. The thought of a scar was hardly a deterrent. "I'm not going to sit around in some emergency room," I answered stubbornly.

"Well, let's wash it, at least."

I trailed her back to the kitchen, where she took a pot and filled it with soapy water. I sat in a chair while she crouched and began to sluice water gently up over the injuries with her hand. The soap stung.

The pot of water tinged red. She lifted my right foot and set it on a towel, then took a clean towel and wrapped it tightly around the cuts. Elevating my leg on a chair to slow the blood flow, she started tearing open packets of bandages and cutting strips of adhesive tape. Drawing the lips of the wounds closed with the Steri-Strips, she then pressed soft white gauze into place and bandaged it tightly.

"It hurts this time, doesn't it?" Her dark brown eyes held a frank expression and I knew I didn't need to lie.

"Yes. For the first time. Ever."

I sat with my leg up while she cleared away the litter and washed the pot.

"I'm starving," she announced. "Are you hungry after all that?"

She'd brought Chinese food and it was as she made her way around my kitchen, getting plates and glasses, that I at last noticed the smell of garlic and ginger and scallion. My ankle throbbed relentlessly but I ate hungrily. Neither agitation nor depression had killed my appetite.

We cleaned up together, and before she left she tucked me into bed and kissed me on the forehead—an act of mothering made complete.

THROUGHOUT THE SPRING of that year, I worked hard with Barbara, up to three appointments a week, or sometimes four, depending on my mood. I sat in my small cubicle at the realty office, but I repeatedly had to wipe my sweaty hands on tissue after tissue, and try to control my breathing. I kept a paper bag in my desk, in case I had to make a dash to the ladies room to take care of a bout of hyperventilation. I had made no friends there: everyone was a competitor and just as there was no one to whom I could turn with my questions, there was nothing to assuage the fear that was once again threatening to take over.

I began to work in a fever: I burned up the hours crafting ads for other realtor's properties (I was a better writer than anyone in the house), learned how to use the multiple-listing system, and held open houses in the hopes of meeting someone who would want to hire me to sell their home. I was using work as a hammer against my declining mood, but I was less and less able to wield it.

In the midst of this newly dark time, I began to experience a sharp increase of my migraines, if such a thing were even possible. The headaches grew fiercer and longer, sometimes sending me back to bed for five days. Heavier and heavier medication was required to control them, and I became dependent on the drugs again. While I didn't crave the pharmaceuticals for a high, I began to have daily pain that was growing less and less responsive to whatever the doctors chose to administer. I couldn't work on those days, and so found myself scrambling to keep up at the office. Because the industry operated more or less on a "freelance" basis, there was no one to notice how frequently I was not at my desk in the corner.

My online dating responses were still coming in, but I had grown leery after Dan. Most of the men who were responding knew nothing about the literary world or writing or my mother or me. I hesitated to tell them the story of my illness, so our dates stayed removed, with little or no spark, and generally didn't progress beyond more than a dinner or two. I was wary. Barbara said my privacy was important to guard and that I owed no one any explanation of the most personal—and secret—aspects of my life.

And so it was, that as late winter faded into spring, I lost hope again. I kept thinking about the "stash" I'd once again managed to accumulate by pilfering my migraine medications for anything I could spare. After a particularly difficult day, when the rain pounded on the roof as if it would never stop, I sat cross-legged on my bed and began to open bottles. I had enough, just enough. Yet again, the boys were at Jim's for the week.

Urgency overtook me. It was hard to think clearly. I laid out my booty and then took up a piece of paper. A note this time, instead of a telephone call. On Wednesday, two days later, Angelina would come in the morning and could call the police. I taped the note to the bedroom door and then pushed in the button lock.

A glass of water from the bathroom. Under the covers I sank, a handful of stuff beside me. One round white pill at a time, forgetting everything I knew from *Final Exit*, forgetting the glass of wine, the danger of sleep overtaking before the job is complete. Drowsiness began to flower, a slow, white blossoming inside of me, bringing relief. And then, suddenly, there was a small new voice, a tender shoot pushing up in my mind, telling me to stop. I thought I should take another as the rest of the tablets began to disintegrate in my sweaty palm. "Don't," the voice whispered. "Don't."

I awakened two days later, horribly groggy, but not dead, just as Angelina arrived and began her kitchen ritual of clattering around as she did the dishes. I tore the note off the door before she could find it and crawled back into bed to sleep for another twenty-four hours. Within the week, Barbara had shifted my meds again, one mood stabilizer now boosted by another. I was still alive. It was the last time I would try for death.

{gifts of love}

DESPITE MY FEARS of getting involved with another crazy or abusive person, I was ultimately too lonely to resist. By May, my mood had turned upward a little bit and I decided to try again. After sorting through twenty or so possibilities, I answered an email from a man who was as different from either Dan or Jim as an owl is from a hawk.

Brad was a first-rate computer software engineer for a large corporation nearby. On our first meeting, we went to a local coffee-house for what was supposed to be a quick drink. We started talking, each with our own story of work, parenthood, and divorce. He was unusual, unlike anyone I had ever known—having raised two children largely on his own after his wife left him. Following her initial desertion, he and the children did not even know where she was for the first six months: Ellen was eight and Becca was five when their mother suddenly reappeared on Christmas day and swept the kids up with her, ostensibly to compensate for the time she'd been away, still unexplained. Brad was dumbfounded and then just lost. His life had been so inter-twined with the kids that to be without them was terribly lonely.

A pattern established itself: the children spent every two years alternating between their parents. In those years when he saw them only during temporary visitations, he felt adrift. I could relate to this.

But during the time when he had been the parent in charge, Brad had lost advancement opportunities when he had had to place his children ahead of his career. He was the Girl Scout "Cookie Mom" when his daughters came of age, with boxes of peanut butter, mint, and chocolate-covered coconut confections stacked high to the ceiling in the garage. He picked the kids up many days after school. He watched their soccer games—all the while holding down his position at the company. His deep blue eyes crinkled each time he smiled, and merry seemed the best word to describe his face. He laughed a lot, able to turn most ideas and thoughts into jokes that made me smile. I wasn't used to someone who could make me laugh, and there was extraordinary pleasure in that.

The outside patio at the coffee bar became chilly and darkness started to set in: two hours had passed. When he stood up to walk me to my car, I realized how tall he was: six feet three inches and extremely broad shouldered. His brown hair was thinning, but his hands were long fingered and graceful. He had a bit of a tummy, but his butt was adorable. He walked me to my car and before I climbed in, he opened his arms and offered me a big bear hug. It was bliss just to be in a friendly, warm, secure embrace—so unlike those I received from the other guys who felt obliged to stick their tongues halfway down my throat on our first meeting.

I got into the car, soaked with comfort from that hug, which would later become known as a "BH"—a "Brad Hug." As I pulled out of the underground parking garage, I glanced in the direction of his car, wondering if he were still watching me. He was and I smiled back at him. When I turned around to face the parking ramp, I was just in time to see my car plow directly into a massive concrete pillar. Stunned and mortified, I scrambled out to see if there had been any damage. From one corner of my eye I could see Brad walking back in my direction, but I waved him off with a shout of "I'm fine."

Seated once again behind the steering wheel, this time I drove off safely, as fast as I could. Once at home, I promptly wrote him an email about my lousy driving—it was due, I contended, to that fabulous hug that had warmed me so completely. He wrote back the next day, continuing to joke about it, and so it became part of our "courting lore"—that a BH was scrumptious enough to send me into a concrete post in the parking lot. In this way, a new pattern of laughter began in a long, slow roll between us, and then some nights (we lived an hour apart and couldn't get together except for weekends) we would just listen to each other breathe over the phone—warmed by the knowledge that we wished we could be side by side.

Sometime during the next month, he dared to write me a poem in which he referred to me as both vulnerable and courageous. With that poem he was speaking my language, and with his playfulness sought to challenge the darkness of my past, the bright white spotlight of my anxiety. He scolded me for stifling my "inner child" (while we laughed at the clichéd expression), and resolved that he would help me to discover this neglected part of myself. Little by little, I was growing attached to him and his dry sense of humor. Little by little, I found myself trusting him.

I introduced him to Nathaniel and Gabe, who initially appeared wary, probably appropriately so, considering that they were still adjusting to the breakup of our family. Still, I rationalized, they had met Jim's girl, and, over time they began to accept Brad. Nathaniel nicknamed him "the gentle giant." I could also sense their relief that there was another adult around, someone who could help "take care" of me.

That spring, however, we were just getting acquainted. In June, I flew east for my twenty-fifth Harvard College reunion. I bunked in a freshman dorm with my old roommate for that week and held my breath the entire time I was in Cambridge: the pack of fifteen people who had comprised my intimate circle of friends was all in attendance, including, of course, Jim. It was difficult to be thrown together in this group where everyone knew the overwrought details of our divorce, and who, I imagined, pitied me and sided with him. I was so ashamed that he had left me; I tried to renew these old relationships despite my insecurity.

I tried to pull myself out of my dismay at being thus exposed so intensely over that week, and accepted an invitation to speak on a panel of proficient writers about the craft: one did comedy for *Saturday Night Live*; another was a Pulitzer Prize–winning poet; and there was another who wrote for an exclusive television series.

I had thought surely that speaking of my writing would cheer me up. However, when it was my turn to address the audience, I rambled on and on. I felt like a failure sitting among the successful. I admitted to taking a sabbatical from writing to pursue a new living in real estate. When I said this, I was overcome with a deep wash of regret. The others sitting behind the table with me had made important careers out of writing and here I was, talking about being a realtor. Suddenly I blurted out something I hadn't even anticipated: I missed my writing, I said, and real estate was curiously unfulfilling. Maybe I'll quit, I added. For a moment I couldn't believe that I had confessed something so personal to people I had never before met, and said something I didn't even know I felt.

EVEN THOUGH I had sworn I would never depend on another man again, I was soon doing precisely that. Love grew slowly between Brad and me. I found relief in its pace: he demanded nothing and so I was free to find my way a little bit at a time. Silently, he accepted that I was still tied to Jim, and that he could not undo those lines of connection—only I could and only when I was ready. Having been divorced for thirteen years, he was nowhere near as cautious as I, but still, he moved in tandem with me. And gradually I began to tell him the story of my illness. He gave Barbara a nickname and encouraged me to stick with my therapy and with my meds whenever I would rail away about stopping either—or both.

I liked Brad's approach: he assumed nothing except that we would have some fun together. We went to the beach and walked for hours holding hands. We went to a local seaside restaurant and talked about some books that he had read, and then others that I had. He tentatively offered up to me experiences I had never had before, in his endearingly unassuming manner. All of it seemed bountifully its own, without the drag of the usual and inevitable memories of loss.

There were so many things that were different this time around. When we went on our first vacation together, Brad notified his work team that he wouldn't be available for the next two weeks, while Jim would have packed his briefcase and his computer; when I went down with a five-day migraine, Brad brought me Gatorade and cold packs, while Jim held me to his own standards—once, after a surgery of his own, he was up at his desk within six hours.

And simply because of those differences, I began to feel as if I could trust Brad with the realities of my life. I confided in him my history of bipolar disorder, depression, anxiety, and suicide attempts. Though he acknowledged that it frightened him, he appeared to accept it all quietly. He bought me a tube of medicated salve for the scars that were just beginning to fade on my ankles and breast—and, slowly but surely, I stopped hurting myself and began to see once more that the smooth skin of my wrists and ankles could be beautiful. When he pressed his lips against those white lines etched into my skin, as if he could erase them, I knew that I had found someone who could be supportive, for days on end, as well as someone on whom I could lean, for days on end. Serendipity, perhaps, had brought me a partner who was nurturing enough to brave the darkness that drove my depression and self-destructive urges, which then helped me turn toward the light of health.

When I first revealed my bipolar disorder to him, he knew nothing about the disease. I gave him a few respected books on the subject that he read slowly and thoroughly. Over time, he experienced and appreciated the effects of my illnesses more fully: staying in bed all day long; getting up in the middle of the night to wake Gabe and start making pancakes, only to be convinced by Brad that it was two in the morning and that I had to come back to bed; buying ten gallons of milk at a time so that I could make batches of homemade yogurt that wound up rotting in the refrigerator. This manic behavior, coupled with my migraines, surprised—and perhaps even shocked— him. He tried to understand it and to be prepared for both problems. The first time we traveled on a car trip, to meet his daughter (who was stationed in the Navy in Pensacola, Florida), he was taken aback by how many bottles of medication I set up on the bathroom shelf. As we grew to know and love each other more deeply, he began to deal with my illnesses better, and to understand the furious winds that blew on me, first cold and then hot.

By the end of the summer, I was in love. Brad and I were on a rollicking roller coaster ride, wondering if we might burn up like a rocket reentering the atmosphere. For several months, happiness soared in me.

THE HOUSE JIM and I had bought when we first moved to California had become as noxious as if all its rooms were lined with flammable fabric. Everywhere I looked were reminders and mementos, and though he did not say so, I felt certain that Brad felt Jim's overwhelming presence every time he opened his eyes in the morning. Sometimes he made a sharp comment about having to compete with "him," and I knew it stung his pride, having to live in the house another man had chosen.

His own quiet presence was made even quieter, side by side with the endless circle—a vivid parade—of my memories. I spun in the trap of continuing to live in the same, sad place but went house hunting on some weekends with Myrna (because this was one of her hobbies), and on others with Brad. I began to believe that if only I could move from the house, I would get away from all my painful recollections of my marriage. How I envied Jim his small clean abode, stripped bare of all the possessions that bore such weighty history. Continuing to live in the "old" house felt more and more absurd to me—out of sync with the reality of my distance now from Jim, and the growing intimacy between Brad and me. Yet, when I tentatively floated the idea that I would like to sell the house, Jim did everything he could to convince me to stay. It seemed as if he wanted me there, keeping the kids' childhoods afloat, in the comfortable home filled with warm memories, to which they could return whenever they wanted—while he went off to new escapades. With both children grown and away at college on the East Coast, this seemed to me like a perfect time in all our lives.

To move from our large house felt like a way to wash myself clean of all the memories that hounded me so mercilessly. Jim and I and the kids had called it "home," but it had not been a home since the day he walked out, and we had not been a family since, either. Despite Jim's protests, the house went on the market, and then came off again as he decided to buy me out and move in himself. He, too, in his own way, could not let go of the past.

Myrna warned me that it might not work just to move to another place as an escape from my obsession with Jim. For once, I ignored her.

Finding a new house proved to be more difficult than I'd anticipated. With my financial share of the old house, I was cutting in half what I could spend. Real estate prices had risen sharply and then hardened. Spending half meant living on half, or even less.

I also had my own misgivings, of a different sort. Brad and I would now be tied together in a new way. It seemed a pivotal point in the relationship: we were selecting a new place to live together, each taking into account the other's likes and dislikes, making compromises like an old married couple. But we weren't married, and couldn't be, unless I were willing to give up my marital support checks from Jim. Those payments constituted my entire income now that I was not working.

And what if Brad left me? Did I want to depend on him so completely after what I had learned about dependence and desertion? The questions haunted me as up and down stairs, property after property, Brad and I trekked. By the time we had finished our search, we had exhausted the web realty pages for our area, as well as our local realtor, for every town and county except the one from which I was so intent on moving.

Ultimately, we bought our new home in an unfashionable, but affordable, town nearby. The house itself was in need of repair, but the view off the back deck was incredible: at the edge of the property, looking down across the canyon thick with trees and chaparral, you could see the backdrop of the mountain range lying just beyond. Across the mountains, the tops of the deep green conifers cut a jagged line into the expanse of blue blue sky, silhouetted by midday's strong light. This view was of a state park and the next town's pristine and undeveloped watershed. No one would ever be able to build on either place. The ocean was a large platinum platter at the bottom of the other side of those trees, and on some days you could smell the salt of the sea, as it rolled in and out of the beaches at Half Moon Bay.

The reward of the new house dangled in front of us like a lure, a way to escape all the artifacts of my love. Here, Brad and I made our real beginning together: magically, all the furniture and rugs that I took from the other house did indeed somehow look different.

With every room in the house facing the clear sweep from east to west over the canyon, the view followed us from master bedroom through living room and on into the kitchen. The new house was an aerie, its air filled with the swoop of eagles and hawks, the buzz and circle and dip of many hummingbirds at the red bottlebrush trees outside the family room. From virtually any window I could see the stuttering walk of quail and mourning dove, or sometimes even the bravado of a wild turkey, puffing his chest out as he moved through the underbrush. Birdsong died slowly with the onset of dusk, and the glorious purples and pinks and amazing cloud formations of sunset signaled the deer to venture out from the woods, right across our driveway, to devastate my tiny garden. I stopped planting azaleas and tried rhododendrons instead. Gulliver barked, racing from one end of the house to the other, but the deer ignored his racket and glided on.

Every day when I woke, I stood at my bedroom window, looking down upon the native vegetation. There was not a lawn in sight, and most of the other houses were hidden by trees. Without the intensive gardening the other house required, and with the lack of a swimming pool, my upkeep was considerably more reasonable. I drove up and down the winding road, oblivious to its inconvenience, because when I reached home I could go down to my little writing cottage on the edge of the un-landscaped property, sit at my desk and gaze out at the mountains—even if I didn't write a single word.

In summer, the canyon was transformed into a burnt-out yellow from the scorch of the sun, but the mountains were always green because every night they were bathed in the fog from the ocean that unrolled over the ridge like a thick lip of an enormous curling white wave.

As I learned to live in our new spot, I realized that by leaving the old house, I had indeed shrugged off some of Jim's power. He had not wanted me to move, and he had urged me not to sell. I had defied him, and now I stepped across a new line—over the boundaries, into the camp Brad and I were just beginning to settle into and call our own.

{sailing free}

SEVERAL MORE YEARS passed and though depression and manic episodes returned from time to time, beating out their staccato rhythms, I was able to force them away or calm them down as I grew stronger. Gradually their hold on me began to weaken. My medications were in balance, my therapy was stellar, and my moods grew more and more stable. I graduated from napping on the couch to sitting in a chair, reading again. Brad kept working on my computer, telecommuting. He was bolstering my ego silently, just with his presence. Soon I had the self-confidence to venture out into the world one little bit at a time. Increasingly, I tried to put a few emotions and thoughts down on paper. The empty hours were still long, but for the first time I had the urge to fill them.

We watched television in the evenings, especially the history and the cooking channels; often we jotted down recipes for what looked appealing to try for supper the following night, which we then made together.

We went to the theater frequently and the symphony occasionally. Brad also crewed on a sailboat in the regular Saturday races on San Francisco Bay. I loved sailing—it was one of the activities my father and I had enjoyed a few times when I was an adolescent, and I also learned the sport at camp with a regular instructor. My father had always longed to own a boat, but my mother's psychiatric expenses, and our move to a suburb my parents couldn't really afford, took up all the available cash Daddy had earmarked for "the boat." Still, I remembered with fondness those days on the ocean with him and the friends who did own a sailboat: the sea hurled itself up over the bow in a deep green spray and I was transported into a quiet, inner space. In the sharp wind, the snap of the sails sounded like sheets hung on a clothesline. Sailing had been a time of solitude and peace for both of us, providing a retreat from the pressure of my mother's needs.

Now I enviously watched Brad leave on Saturday mornings, and return home smelling of salt and sweat. It didn't take long for me to start agitating to participate, and so Brad asked the owners of his ride if I could come with him as "rail meat." Rail meat is what racers call the people who are just along for the experience, but who also have an easy-to-grasp function: they drape their legs and butts out over the top rail so that the boat can balance itself on a sharp angle, or heel, without tipping over into the water. However, as the "youngest" member of the crew, it wasn't too long before I had graduated to the worst task of all. Being the "sewer rat" meant hauling the spinnaker (a voluminous sail that was deployed on a pole out from the bow of the boat) down through a hatch in the foremost deck. Once I had pulled all of its ballooning folds down around me in the sewer, it was my responsibility to line up the edges, matching them properly, so that the sail could be stuffed into a bag, just so, and then be quickly unraveled into the wind when the guy on the deck needed it again; often spinnakers of different weights and cuts and colors were deployed one after another. Crouched in the bow, which was the rockiest, hottest place to be, I sweated under my

life vest; in the small space, I was battered by the rhythm of the
waves as the bow plunged up and down through each crest, and
it wasn't long before I began to feel nauseated, though I told no
one, because I didn't want to get kicked off the boat by com-
plaining. There was something imperative about all this activity.
In some way it pushed back any negative feelings, or the start of
a headache.

With just the sound of the waves, and the cerulean sky overhead, with the slap and whistle of the canvas as the boom crossed
from side to side—sailing was an exhilarating experience. Soon,
however, Brad and I grew tired of racing, especially on someone
else's boat. We longed to have a home on the water that we could
call our own. We started up a kitty for buying a boat, but it was
slow going.

At the annual boat show that next year, as we boarded one beautiful sailboat after another from the dock where they were moored,
I found myself on an invisible upward swing, spinning giddy and
high. I stretched up into the sky inside my head, and in a burst of
happy mania, convinced Brad that we should buy a boat of our
own right away. Time was passing and soon we might be too old
to take the cruises we envisioned. Brad was startled by the suggestion, and tried to talk me out of it: he had only come to the show
as a way of daydreaming about someday owning a boat.

I'd already been through this kind of reluctance with my
father, and I wasn't about to repeat the experience. Before I even
really let myself know what I was doing, I pushed us further
along in the process. We contacted several boat agents and soon
were off to look at all the different species of sailboats available
at that time. *Mercy Street* is a cruising sloop—bought used, but
still lovely. Brad suggested the name, surprising me with his
intuitive generosity, and so we named her after my mother's
image of searching for a warm protection that could only be
obtained by loving a God she could depend on—rather

than parents, and other people, who were always failing her. Her feelings about having returned to a God she had rejected early in her life formed a deep, personal examination of self, of writing, of bearing witness to the life she found so terribly difficult.

There were some sailing expeditions with other cruisers in our marina, venturing out of San Francisco Bay to the ocean, waves of porpoises jumping beside the bow of the boat with exuberance. We always traveled in a small flotilla for this eight-hour journey down to Half Moon Bay, where we anchored in a picturesque cove at Pillar Point. With nearly twenty other people nearby, we made new friends and visited with old. There we enjoyed the fresh catch, just off the fisherman's boats, in a fish and chips lunch at a dive on the sidewalk. Every Sunday night on this trip we all got together for a barbeque on the beach, just before sunset, grilling halibut and snapper over the fire, with my contribution to the feast always a variety of exotic cheeses and homemade brownies. I hadn't had so many new friendships in years. Brad was bringing people into my life through sailing, and I loved it. I felt as if the tide was reversing for me at last.

Brad and I began to daydream about retiring and sailing off to Mexico, Hawaii, the Panama Canal, and the Galapagos when we were older. For me, all this long-range planning was a novelty; we had been together for two years now, and for the first time in my life I was planning a future, rather than swimming backward in time. The depressive side of the legacy had receded—perhaps only for a week, or a month, but I was willing to take anything I could get.

MY CONTINUING THERAPY with Barbara Ballinger had developed into the strong support I needed as I worked to examine the feelings I had about my mother's suicide and to tear them apart. Although the depression was not as intense, it did sometimes flare up again periodically, often set off by the headaches that still occurred, though less intensely, nearly daily. Both interfered with my tentative, new writing. I would just get a chapter started when darkness or pain descended again and my abilities to create shut down, and I was forced to wait for some upward turn of the cycle to get off and running once more.

When I was moving at a sharp clip during an occasional bout of mania, I found myself getting out of bed in the middle of the night and hammering away at my computer; all the sensations around me poured in as if I were a vessel created just to hold ideas. I couldn't stop the waterfall of thoughts. I didn't want to admit that these exhilarating swings upward were manic episodes that needed more meds. It took me a long time to be willing to work on eradicating them—I knew how important it was to try and defeat them because there was always, inevitably, depression waiting on the other side. Still, even when everything had been brought to heel under the power of my medication, I longed for that upward push that made writing so easy, that made life so much more exciting. All of that continued to make it hard to take my essential meds.

I rested my head on Brad's shoulder, drawing on the substantial, deep comfort he brought, and never once did he judge me for my inability to work. I put my head on the arm of Barbara's couch and tried to absorb her optimism about how far I had come. I organized my medications into two long boxes with daily compartments so that I couldn't make any more errors with something so crucial. There were no longer any excuses for having taken some pill incorrectly, or for leaving something out. No mistakes.

I WAS STILL working hard to put my marriage to Jim behind me, and despite the fact that I was improving at stifling the feelings engendered by the old wound of desertion, there was nevertheless a part of me that occasionally felt as if I were swallowing broken glass; in the early years of the new century there were still times that I wept bitterly, trying to keep all these emotions hidden from Brad, whom I did not want to hurt.

When Jim told me that he was going to remarry, a numb curtain descended between me and the rest of the world, just for a while. It wasn't such a surprise, because they had been together for quite a while, but still it caught me up short and sharp. At a Harvard football game where there were many of our mutual friends, he announced his engagement, and I heard through the grapevine that he had said, "I have never been happier in my life than in the last five years," as a way of introducing his new love. Those words made my brain freeze. I couldn't even swallow, unable to believe that he had said he loved her more than he had ever loved me or more than he had loved, and been happy with, our children.

A week later, I confronted him, furious and tearful all at the same time, in his office. He was quiet for a minute, just coolly watching me lose control, as he had during the therapy sessions we'd had with Rose Kramer so many years before. Then, very quietly, he told me that what I had heard was not exactly what he had said: my source, he went on, had repeated the remark to me incorrectly. And why, he had asked, was I listening to gossip like that anyway? He insisted that what he really had said was that the last five years were some of the happiest he had ever had. I leaned back in the chair, spent with all the emotion, and now embarrassed. I didn't even have a tissue with which to wipe my nose.

"I think you're having trouble with my remarriage," he observed.

I stood up and left the office. What had possessed me to come in and break down in front of him this way? I slunk back home but I didn't tell Brad a word about it. Nevertheless, I did a little more "behind-the-scenes" scavenging and came up with the date of their wedding and arranged it so that I could be out of town on that day, rather than moping about, even though many of our mutual friends would be there for the event; a few had extended invitations to get together, but I explained that I would have to miss them this time around.

On the wedding day, in the last few minutes before everyone headed out the door, Nathaniel's inability to find a pair of socks, and Gabe's inability to press his pants, seemed to me symptoms of their ambivalence though perhaps this was only my wish. All these distractions at the worst possible moment required love and patience from a bride who should have been focused solely on herself. It foreshadowed the future, a predictor of the ways she would treat my children with gentleness and sensitivity. I thought then that I might never like her, but her attention to Nathaniel and Gabe was a powerful response to my family, and for this, I would always be grateful.

In an effort to be able to distract myself sufficiently on the day of Jim's new marriage, I told Brad that I wanted to go out on the boat and anchor for a few days by ourselves in a new spot. Preparing to anchor out was in itself a powerful distraction: getting the boat set for a three-day excursion on the water, provisioning the tiny icebox, making sure all the safety equipment was onboard and current. On the Friday of that weekend we set sail and headed up the San Francisco Bay to China Camp, so named for its roots in the shrimp trade, which was governed at the turn of the century by an outpost of Chinese Americans.

I was feeling good, even a little euphoric. I told myself I didn't care what was going on back home, and focused instead on how lucky I was to have Barbara and Brad, my medications and my boat. I worried just a touch that my mood was getting dysphoric, so I tried to slow down a little. I didn't want to get caught in a nasty cycle of ups and downs.

On Saturday night, at approximately the same time I knew Jim and his new wife would be exchanging their vows, I took my old gold wedding band from my pocket, and hurled it off the rail as far and as hard as I could. It spun, its round outline glowing in the fading light, and then fell into the water silently. I remember feeling surprised at that: I'd imagined it would make a "plunk" or scatter the water upward for a moment, but instead it just sank without fanfare. I had rid myself of the last of the physical remnants from my marriage. Brad hugged me long and hard, understanding the significance of what I had done. Perhaps he, too, considered it progress of a sort.

Brad had always known how attached I still was to Jim, and it seemed to me that both he and I were making peace with these emotions. With this disposal of the ring, Brad could see me moving on. The sun began to set and we went below to cook up a big pot of spaghetti, happily gorging on carbohydrates. Two days later we hauled anchor and sailed back to the marina where we kept the boat. At home once again in our house amidst the hills, I began to feel a new, even more profound sense of liberation. In freeing himself, it appeared that Jim had freed me, as well.

ONE DAY IN February of 2006, I drove up to the house Jim and I had so lovingly purchased seventeen years before, the house Jim and his new wife now called home, four years after I had left. The sun was everywhere, flooding the redwoods with patches of light, bringing into sharp focus the yellow hordes of daffodils I had planted. I had lived there for more than ten years, and so it was no surprise to see the arch of the Akebono cherry trees I had set on either side of the front walk weighted beneath the load of their abundant once-a-year pink and white harvest. I'd always pictured one of the boys getting married under this luxurious bower. The magnolia trees had unfurled their vibrant magenta petals, and the lawn was mowed and green. This was what I had given up when I had moved out, into my much smaller cottage with its beautiful views, up in the county hills. Sometimes I still missed the beauty of this place on the flatlands. Here there were no deer to eat the many roses in the garden I had planted with such love way back then.

Resolutely, I pushed away all my feelings of loss and wondered which end of the house Gabe was in; he was on late winter vacation, and I was taking him out to lunch. I was supposed to steer clear of Jim's new wife if possible, he always said, and so we had still never met after all these years. It was tricky to manage this when I came to pick up the children. From what Jim had said, it sounded as if she was as leery of me as I was of her.

At first, when I had come here just after they'd moved in, I'd roamed through the house, experiencing every change in paint color or new furniture with a jolt. Initially, I couldn't bear the idea that I had been washed off so easily. But as the time wore on, I had stopped feeling the urge even to go inside.

Gabe came out the front door with a big grin on his face, walking fast, because he knew how reluctant I was to encounter his stepmother.

But before he was even halfway to me, I swung my legs out of the car and met him with a hug. I was lucky: both my boys had remained touchingly affectionate with me; despite being twenty-one and twenty-two, they still hugged, kissed, and cuddled—though all in appropriate ways. Gabe was at Harvard for his junior year, bright and intellectual, majoring in History and Literature, one of the most challenging concentrations at the university. Nathaniel was about to graduate cum laude from Connecticut College as a political science major. Despite his academic success, I still found myself worrying some about him. I often thought about what would happen if I had passed on any of the family's emotional difficulties to such an intuitive, creative, emotionally savvy child as Nathaniel, who could perhaps identify with me and my life—just as I had with my mother and hers, albeit on a different scale.

Still, they were both their own men. They would live their own lives and nothing I said or did could alter that.

"Is she home?" I asked.

"Why?" Gabe asked suspiciously.

"Would you go ask her if she would come out?"

"What for?"

"I'd like to meet her."

He took a step backward. "Mom, I don't want you getting all upset. This sounds like a bad idea."

"It's been eight years already. So go ask her."

A minute later, she was walking toward me with a tremulous smile. I noted her hair, perfectly styled, her eyes of bluest blue, her figure an hour-glass shape to envy. Never before had I felt so embarrassed by my expanding menopausal middle.

I didn't know what I could say, not having planned this moment, so impulsively I just put my hand out and we shook.

"I've wanted to meet you for quite a while." I was embarrassed; I didn't know what could stretch across the divide between us.

"Me, too." She smiled and paused, and suddenly it occurred to me that perhaps she was shy.

"I thought while I was stopping by to pick up Gabe, I'd see if you were here." I sighed. "I wanted to say thanks for taking care of them."

"It's nothing, really. I like being here for them."

"Gabe told me you showed him how to iron a shirt, and how to sew a button on his pants. And Nathaniel—he's intense."

"They're no problem," she reassured me, and I thought, once again, that Jim wanted no other children. She would mother only mine.

"Would you like to come in for a cup of tea?"

The idea of having tea at my old breakfast table was a bit beyond me, so I mentioned that Gabe and I were on our way to lunch.

After we shook hands again, I left, with a glow of satisfaction for all I had accomplished in just those few minutes. I no longer needed to be afraid when I drove up the driveway that had once been mine.

{the women of my life}

I DON'T REMEMBER exactly what year it was when Rachael called to tell me that she had lung cancer, but I believe she was then in her early seventies. Though "my other mother" had never smoked a day in her life, the terrible disease had invaded her lungs. She was short of breath and our hour-long conversations were suddenly curtailed. As the weeks passed, and her fragility grew, so did mine: I didn't think I could stand another death of a close friend, one who had given me the adult friendship that my mother had been so unable to provide, one who had helped me push back the veil of depression and, even now, to laugh at myself.

The cancer was localized to her lungs, and the prognosis was somewhat hopeful because the lymph nodes were not involved. Though I had dealt with death so many times before, I was nevertheless caught totally unawares, as if this were the first time I had ever lost a special member of my family. I had expected more of myself, but the news caused a terrible dip in my mood. Little by little, it set me back from the progress I had made, and I teetered on the edge of depression once again.

The day after she told me her news, I was so distressed that I could not call her back for a little while, until I got my emotions under control. I knew that I wouldn't help her by crying, which might require her to deal with my grief, instead of her own fear. I wanted to be the best friend I could be, as strong as I could be, but it felt too much as though I were losing my mother all over again. And so I waited, until I were certain: she would be able to depend on me for anything.

Once more, death was sniping at my back, ready to take one of my beloved. Rachael's treatment progressed to repeated biopsies and painful procedures to drain her lungs of the excess fluid that made it so hard for her to breathe. After the standard radiation and chemotherapy—which didn't seem to help—my ex-father-in-law and Rachael's husband (both doctors) managed to get her into a new drug trial. She went into remission once the experimental drug took hold. Once again, we could talk on the phone without a shadow hanging over us.

In a superstitious act of faith—to keep her safe and to guard her—I sent her my good luck gold chain and its lucky medallions, some of which had originally belonged to my mother. I had lent it out to several troubled friends more than once. Hanging from it were: a gold disk that my mother had given me before she died, inscribed with "Don't Let The Bastards Win"; a lithium crystal given to me by a good friend that was reputed to keep your body in psychological balance; a large ostentatious diamond ring of my mother's that I couldn't think to wear any other way; and my Elsa Peretti Jewish star that Jim had given me the day of our joint b'nei mitzvah. The chain represented what I wanted to be able to do and could not, no matter how hard I wished and prayed: to protect her. She wore it for the year of her remission, just as I had hoped. Terrified of being in pain at the possible end of the course of the illness, she began hoarding sleeping pills. If needed, a member of the family could help her to die comfortably, accompanied by the dignity with which she had always lived.

She had just turned the corner of one year with no new tumors, and we were talking at least once a week, sometimes more. I had learned my lesson well: you never knew when someone was going to die; the regret you would feel over not taking advantage of last days, or of not having said goodbye, would last your lifetime. Even though she was in remission, I worried incessantly.

After she went for her checkup in the spring, Jim called me to tell me that her cancer had spread to her liver, her kidneys, and her brain. The experimental drug had not saved her life, nor had my lucky medallions. She had bought herself an extra year with her family and friends, but that was all. When I spoke to her on the phone after hearing the bad news that day, she was already growing confused, a symptom of the disease invading her brain. At one moment, she appeared to recognize the severity of her condition, and then, at another, to be confused over what was happening to her. Later, I discovered that her daughters and husband had chosen not to tell her too much about the aggressive progress of the tumors. I disapproved of keeping her in the dark, but it was not my decision. If anything, it emphasized that I was not really a part of the family—except in Rachael's eyes.

Quickly, I realized that if I wanted to see her again, I would have to fly to New York before her condition deteriorated any further. I swallowed my fears about traveling alone, which had persisted since my first breakdown, and suggested that I come quite soon, but she put me off, saying she was too tired for visitors. I believed she was telling me not to come because she was denying that there would be any immediate need; I would be there to say goodbye, and that, above all, was what she did not want to do.

In the end I chose to lie to her: I said that I was coming to town for a sudden business meeting with my agent and that I'd like to see her over the weekend for a very short visit. She obviously did not remember that we had talked a day before and that I had made no mention of coming to Manhattan. She invited me to have lunch with her, at her apartment, on Saturday of that week. On Friday I flew in and settled myself at the Harvard Club with Brad, who, fortuitously, had been in New York on business that particular week. I awaited my visit with her eagerly, but with fear. Would she look any different? Would she remember who I was? How far had the cancer progressed inside her brain? Brad and I decided not to mention the fact that he was in Manhattan, as well. His presence might confuse her, and I wanted to see her by myself.

AT HER DINING room table, we ate lightly of the sushi her daughter had brought from Rachael's favorite Japanese restaurant and made desultory small talk about their grandchildren and my kids. But during the meal she seemed more and more confused: she thought Nathaniel and Gabe were still in summer camp even though they had long since grown past that; she thought Jim and I were still married. I felt glad that Brad had not come with me to see her. She insisted, almost angrily, on telling me that she was dying, perhaps wanting to see that recognition, and acceptance, on my face. When her husband got up to clear the plates, she dropped her voice to a whisper. "I'm afraid of the pain," she said. "I have enough sleeping pills saved up. If my family can't do it, will you come?"

I had thought of this eventuality before, and so I was not shocked by her question; it was without hesitation that I promised to be there if she needed me.

After lunch, we went to sit in her blue and gold living room. I had never been in that particular room. It felt stiff, with its brocade sofas and careful artwork. Was there some unfathomable reason she didn't want to sit in the den, a cozy haven where we had always curled up before for intimate talks? I didn't understand, but I said nothing. Perhaps the formality of the room, so contradictory to chatting, was one way of keeping taxing visits with friends to a minimum.

Her husband took a few pictures of us, but I could see that she had begun to look even more tired and fragile. It was time to go. She turned her body away, just slightly, from my hug. I could not see, one last time, her beautiful face. Instead, she just squeezed my hand. Her skin was very soft. I could feel her thin bones pressing against my palm.

"Goodbye," I said in a choked whisper, unable, at the end, to contain the emotion I had been so diligently trying to repress.

"Never say goodbye." Her voice was husky now, as she fought for the air her lungs could not provide. She needed to get back to her oxygen tank. "Just say, 'So long, see you tomorrow.'"

The promise of another tomorrow were the last words I ever heard her speak, though she would live a little while longer in a terribly confused state.

Her husband walked me to the door. There was an anticlimactic feel to my sudden departure. No marker. No real long hug. No words to acknowledge what was happening to all three of us.

In the foyer of the building, I fell apart, sorrow pounding me down. Out the door I went, tears in a steady stream down my face. My gait uneven, I wanted to lie down on the sidewalk and press myself into the cracks. My loss was purely selfish: I did not grieve for her family or for her other friends; I grieved for myself. Another mother gone. This time, however, there was an important difference: this time I had had the chance to say goodbye.

When I returned to the Harvard Club after walking many, many blocks in an effort to calm myself, Brad put his arms around me and I just stood in the circle of his warmth and cried yet again. He held me until I was totally wrung out. And then he held me some more.

Back at home again, I tried to call Rachael several times, but her husband was guarding the phone, giving reports about her condition to friends, but allowing no one in. As her dementia grew stronger, they increased her morphine so that she was comfortable, with no pain, still in her own bed at home. She lapsed into a coma, and then, one day, death.

Jim was the one who came to tell me. I asked about the funeral, ready to rush and make a plane reservation, but he shook his head. The funeral was closed, solely for family members. The pain had been too much for all of them, something I could well understand. Nevertheless, it left those of us who had also adored Rachael no way to grieve, no ritual with which to let her go. I felt angry at being shut out. I, too, had been part of her family, even though no one would recognize it now. I felt a strong need for some kind of ceremony with which to mourn her.

Two weeks after her death, Brad and I sailed *Mercy Street* out onto San Francisco Bay, and I strewed purple and white orchids over the water just under the Golden Gate Bridge. I recited Kaddish (the Jewish prayer for the dead), and told her how much she had meant to me and how much I would miss her. And then there was only the vigil of watching the lift and tug of the tide as it pulled her flowers out to sea.

The weeks passed, rolling me under with the loss. When I went outside for my nocturnal cigarette, I studied the night sky and saw a bright new star I had never noticed before. From that moment on, I would always pretend that Rachael and my mother lived on in that luminous pinprick. I talked to them both and told them how I was doing in their absence. That star made me feel connected to all those women I had lost: my mother's mother before I was six; my Nana, after her stroke when Nathaniel was about two years old; my aunt Joanie, who had died at thirty-six during her honeymoon. Since first discovering the star, I have had to add another close friend to the community of women living there: my good friend Pat, who, in her sixties, died a painful and unnecessary death of colon cancer.

All of these women were amazing, all of them provided me with different, and yet crucial, perspectives on life. My grandmother brought me stability and a taste of childhood. Joanie showed me the fun that could be part of my life when everything else was so bleak. Rachael taught me to laugh and guided me, for a long time, toward health. Pat showed me how wonderful a true companion could be. And last, but not least, my mother encouraged me to be the most generous person I was capable of being, while still remaining true to myself—and, too, that reconciliation is always possible, even in a life we often find to be both mercurial and dark. I believe she knew that there is no harm in forgiveness: perhaps this is how we heal even ourselves.

I always feel like crying, standing alone there in the dark, looking heavenward—at this point without the red ember of the cigarettes I have given up. Perhaps articulating my loss with the symbol of a star is childish, or foolish, or even preposterously romantic. However, it comforts me, and will continue to do so for a long time to come. I still pray to that star, and every time I do, all the women of my life watch over me.

{lucky loves}

IT WAS 2005, and my father and I were preparing the roast tenderloin and the garlic string beans for Christmas dinner. Cooking in my new kitchen, a spacious, inviting space, several of us lingered over glasses of wine or vodka or soda, while the different aspects of the meal gradually came to fruition. Conversation wove through the aroma of cherry tomatoes sautéing in butter and basil.

Brad was playing Barbie with his granddaughter, as she and his daughter had come out from the East Coast for the holidays. I still couldn't get used to the idea of being a step-grandmother. My father couldn't reconcile himself to playing the role of a great-grandfather, but still, he and Brad got along very well. He was forever grateful to Brad for the ways in which he had helped me to heal. My stepmother was taking eggnog cake from its tube pan for dessert. It seemed natural and pleasurable that I was cooking alongside my father, because he was the one who taught me how, just after I had graduated from college in 1975.

"Are you working again?" he asked. This was the fourth day of his visit and the first time he had brought it up.

I simply nodded, stalling for time, almost hoping he would not delve any further, because I specifically dreaded telling him about the subject of this book.

"What's this one about?"

I drew in a quick breath and then paused for an answer to occur to me. "It's about the family legacy of suicide."

He stood at the sink, his shoulders tense. He obviously did not want to pursue the conversation that delved into a subject that had touched all of us so deeply. Even Marty, his third wife, had had a son who killed himself. My father had called me immediately following the suicide, and, interestingly enough, had cried—even though he had never met Sam, who lived in the Midwest and ended his life a few months before my father and Marty were even married. It seemed to me that perhaps, through Sam and then through me, my father had been living through my mother's suicide again. Yet, his reaction to the death of Marty's son was to provide his new wife with comfort and warmth.

I felt sad. Some part of me—perhaps a selfish one—wished he had been as able to cry over my attempts—despite their failures—as he had Marty's son. In some strange manner, I was jealous. But then I reminded myself: first, I could not know that he had not cried, I only knew that he had not cried with me; and second, I needed to look at our past in a different light—it was not only his fault that communication had failed, it was also mine, a painful result of my illness.

Thinking back on it, I saw that, in part, it was once again the family legacy that had distanced us for those long eight years. My father had desperately wanted me to be well and he had expressed that desire with the gruff exhortation: "Straighten up and fly right." He still shrinks to hear of any depression I may be experiencing, no matter how minor—perhaps especially because he remains very angry with my doctors, who had, he believes, managed my medications so poorly. He continues to be upset about those times I sat at the dinner table with my mouth open, when whatever I had been ready to say had deserted my brain midstream, or when I fell asleep sitting up on the couch in the middle of a sentence. Looking back, though, I see now that his anger did, in fact, prove useful in helping me; it was his urging, in part, that brought me back to Barbara and my neurologist for better medication control. And, despite his despair when I do fall into a slump, he now at least asks how I am doing: how my mood is and how my headaches are.

At eighty-two years old, he has aged remarkably, feeling lonely and lost as, one by one, all his friends have died. At this point, I am loathe to push any questions at my father about either my mother's, or my own, attempts, largely because I sense such queries might disturb him and I don't want to upset the fragile balance we have regained, so similar to that with my sister.

After the trauma of her brother's death, Marty's daughter established a nonprofit organization that would rapidly achieve national repute. Families for Depression Awareness provides education, outreach, and advocacy for families whose family members experience depressive disorders. It comforts those who have lost a loved one to suicide, or who helplessly watch a family member or friend suffer from debilitating depression. Enlightened emotional support such as this would have helped my own family immeasurably, particularly my father. With the new medical treatments and medications available to us now, my mother might have survived her illness and gone on to write more books of poetry, as well as having had the support of a nurturing, rather than bewildered, husband and daughters. In 2003, I was asked to join and I accepted.

Initially, phone calls between my father and me were difficult due to the strictures of my depression; he grew angry at how infrequently I called during the early days of the new decade. But now, I am at last finally able to reach out once more. I have developed new habits: I call him once or twice a week and from time to time send him silly little cards out of which he gets a kick and he sets them up at his place at the breakfast table. I try to get to Boston a couple of times each year.

For at least five years or so, the immediate family has felt that my father might be depressed, but when both Joy and I suggest to him, in a mild manner, that there are specific medications designed to treat the physical pain that sometimes accompanies depression, and which therefore might help him with his arthritis and his chronic obstructive pulminary disease, he growls that he is not depressed. For him, depression remains a taboo topic. This, I believe, is his legacy from my mother's suicide. He cannot admit to his own emotional pain and thus he remains untreated, soldiering on, growing sadder and sadder day after day. He, too, has been touched in very personal ways. We are not so different after all.

Many things about his life have changed for the better: his old tendency toward physical violence has vanished and his twenty-year union with Marty, who is a very accommodating person, suits him well. When she does things he doesn't like, he simply prowls the house, muttering. The days of the clenched fist are long gone.

At some point, I had thought what a terrible, terrible experience it would be were I not to say all I have to say, or do all I have to do, to bring about a reconciliation between us, no matter how incomplete it might be, before my father dies. I had to know that I tried. I can now see how difficult his life has been in so many respects I never fathomed before: his alcoholic father, whom he adored, killed by a drunk driver when my father was in his early thirties; his strong-willed mother with whom he struggled for control all her life; his sister, a source of sibling rivalry despite her precipitous early death on her honeymoon. And, of course, his early marriage to an immensely talented woman, who overwhelmed him with her mental illness when they were both very young, a wife who then went on to try to commit suicide many, many times before she finally succeeded, leaving him with two daughters still in need of a mother. That terrible shock.

Yet now, little by little, I am able to talk with my father about my mother. Once a year, we share our mutual loss by visiting my mother's gravesite in the Forest Hills Cemetery in Boston, where we always go for a short time—whatever the weather—when I visit. We cry just a little and hug each other and remember quietly all those who are buried there: my mother, my father's sister, and, of course, my father's parents, uncles, and aunts. This hour never fails to draw us together in a shared loss: loss of love and dreams—and yet it also feels good and fulfilling because it is of a proper proportion.

Going to the gravesite and seeing the many piles of small stones crammed on top of my mother's footmarker always gives me a frisson. Strangers have journeyed here to rest, or to pray, mourners and celebrants both, those who find peace and relief just as my father and I do, under the big oak tree that shelters the granite monument marked *Sexton*. I have never gone there with my sister since the time we interred my mother's ashes, and I have never taken my sons either.

There was so much I could not share with my father right after my breakdown. Yet now I have begun to feel empathetic with him, just as I had learned to be empathetic with my mother. And this is a start.

THE RELATIONSHIP WITH Joy is more difficult to mend. Seven years after my breakdown, she still seemed distant, unwilling to talk about my health, my depression, or my former suicide attempts, even when I broached the topics in a desperate attempt to heal the breach. It did not occur to me that she was simply not ready, and that this kind of emotional response could never be forced.

Yet, despite my attempts to clear the trouble between us, I was probably not really ready to bear the force of the anger she felt about the time when I was so troubled, or my own anger at her reaction. And so, both uncertain and both wounded, we spoke on the phone rarely, and then only briefly. The shutdown of our affections made itself felt in all the facets of our lives, from minor to major—we had grown far apart indeed.

Sometime after that Christmas in 2005, following my father's visit, Joy called to say she was taking a vacation during her children's spring break in April, and that she would like to come to California. This would be the first time in ten years—since Nathaniel's bar mitzvah; she had not attended Gabe's—that she had made the trek to the West Coast. On the other hand, it had been several years since I had visited her for any length of time, apart from her very busy wedding weekend a few months the previous autumn. Over the years, who would visit whom had turned into a silent tug-of-war.

I stopped and thought: wouldn't this visit be the perfect opportunity for us to sit down and talk about the years of estrangement? The idea made my stomach clench, but I was resolved: at the least I would ask her. A week before she came out, I did, and she agreed that along with traveling to see Big Sur, the redwoods at Muir Woods, and taking the ferry to Alcatraz, we would make time to talk about "the family legacy of suicide." It would be one way of giving her a voice.

But when she arrived, our time together seemed a precious gift and we resisted the possibility of ruining it. Though initially tentative, we soon were relaxed with one another again. We spent the four days laughing and remembering the odd details of our childhood:

"Do you remember the Christmas you got that red wooden rocking horse I really wanted?"

"And how about when Mom made up Anne's Blizzard the night of that humungous snowstorm?"

"And that gross slumgullion with the leftovers of Halloween spaghetti?"

Still, we avoided talking about the past ten years of our relationship. Gradually, I began to wonder if we had the guts to discuss that lost time. Could Joy speak with candor? Was I strong enough to hear her various truths? Would we be able to arrive at that elusive condition that was so difficult and yet so imperative: could we begin to heal?

On the last day of her visit, we sat in front of a fire in my living room, and I made small talk, nervously sipping my coffee, after I had turned on a tape recorder so that I could be accurate when I began writing. I knew that if I attempted to protest any of her perceptions or to rationalize what I had said or done back then, she would withdraw and there would be no chance of reconciliation. I resolved simply to be quiet and let her talk, hoping that I would be able to maintain my equanimity throughout the revelation of emotions that might be traumatic for both of us.

After some desultory conversation, we finally came around to the topic of the family's legacy. She explained that she had never been depressed enough to consider ending her life, and she wasn't sure she believed that there even was that kind of inherited tendency.

Already I felt that there was a fence between us: if she didn't feel that there was such a legacy in our family, how then did she view my suicide attempts?

It took her a minute to continue. "It was manipulative," she replied, "an indulgence." The sort of indulgence that our mother's attempts had been. Several years later, on a program for the BBC, she echoed that sentiment by remarking that she wondered "how much of [our mother's] madness was a choice."

Hiding my hurt, I mulled over what she had just said. Joy excels at her job in the sizeable hospice of which she is the clinical nursing director, and she comes into contact with people who are depressed and/or dying frequently. Not surprisingly, having come from a home where it was requisite that all of us learned how to care for my mother during her wide variety of moods, needs, and illnesses, Joy sought out a career in which she could devote herself to the care of others, and she has done an admirable job of it, rising through the ranks of nursing to the higher administrative levels.

In her role as a nurse, she explained, she sees those who have mental illness and depression, or suicide issues, and is able to keep it at a distance from her inner life. But she can't seem to reach out and help during this kind of medical emergency when it concerns her family. She understands there are the effects of biology and the efficacy of medical intervention, but, still, she cannot overcome her reaction. She is helpless before it.

That day she finally elaborated on her feelings at the time of our mother's death, emotions that persist to this day because they run underground: "I felt like the minute Mother died you began to slide into her shoes."

It was still difficult for me to hear this particular comparison. As the years had turned into decades, I had spent much time determined to outrun the image of "Anne Sexton's daughter," especially professionally, though often I failed. Even at fifty years old, I had been still on the same voyage of establishing a voice for myself, both in writing and in life. I believed I had a right to my own history, even if that history touched down on my mother's at certain points. As she was growing up, Joy had not continually compared herself with our mother as I had. To her, *my* psychological identification was a behavior in which I should simply stop indulging. She wished, for me, that I could be something other than a writer, something less involved with my mother and something more rewarding. She felt certain that I could have defeated my mental illness and risen above it all with a sustained effort.

And what of that day back on the bed right after our mother had died? Why couldn't she talk about her feelings right then? Perhaps she sensed my intense need. Maybe she knew that I would cry and maybe she didn't feel like dealing with all that. And what, after all, was it that I was so desperately seeking?

She related the story, then, of what had happened to her on that day when Jim had called to tell her that I was hospitalized for the first time. She was in the middle of moving to a new home, and was single-handedly trying to unpack all the boxes while her toddler romped around the house creating havoc. She called her husband, who was unable to come home and help, and so she just sat on a box and cried. As she told me this, I was not surprised, but distressed once again that I had caused her this kind of pain.

Part of her, she confessed now, was still angry with me. Believing that depression and suicidal tendencies in our family should and could have been controlled through "willpower," Joy remembered that the two of us felt continually threatened while we were growing up. Thus, she was stunned that I would make a similar attempt and allow myself to hurt the people who loved me. To some extent, she had picked up my father's old query: "Why can't you just get past all this?" I wondered if perhaps she didn't have the energy to deal with me and my problems because she had her own very active life with a family of two pre-adolescent kids.

I then asked what was, for me, the most important question of all. "If I get deeply depressed again, no matter how vigilant I am with my therapy and my medications, will you support me this time?"

Her reply made me want to cry but I stifled my response: her memories were "too twisted and torn," and they made it impossible for her to change her reaction. She couldn't separate my drop into mental illness from our mother's: the way that our mother had held the whole family dancing on marionette wires. My breakdown did not seem to her to be involuntary or ignited by severe emotional pain. If I succumbed to a disease like breast cancer, one that was "life threatening," then she would be out to help me "in a heartbeat." Silently, I wondered why she didn't perceive suicide as a life threatening disease.

I appreciated the courage it took for Joy to tell me the truth about how she had felt so long ago. I realized then, sadly, that she did indeed experience a legacy from my mother's suicide, but that, like my father's, it was a different legacy than mine: hers was that she had been too poisoned by our mutual past to grasp either the severity of our mother's situation so long ago, or my situation over the last few years—that of being in the grip of an intense clinical depression. And I recognized that hers was a reaction common to many families. So few are able to stop themselves from blaming their affected member—be it mother or child or sister. Even someone who had the benefit of a medical education couldn't seem to handle the hurdle my illness had set up right in the middle of our relationship.

At last I had my answers, even if they were unsurprising ones that hurt. I saw clearly how the issue for Joy was so complex: dominated by her own history of pain, she could neither give, nor forgive, in this particular situation. She hadn't forgiven our mother yet—how could she forgive me? At least I finally knew how little and how much I could ask for—and how far I could go without threatening her.

When we said goodbye at the airport the next morning, we hugged each other hard. Once again, I had a connection to one of the most important people in my life—as did she. After she left,

I set on my bedside table her birthday present to me from the previous year: a small photograph of us as little girls, in a frame with a border that reads "Sisters Forever."

HOW DID I summon the gumption and the strength to get up from the couch, shake off both my depression and the strong impulse toward suicide that I believed had so changed my life, without the help of my father or Joy or Jim? How did I eventually manage to forgive my mother for all her desertions, and, finally, her own self-orchestrated death?

In order to accomplish those steps, I recognized that I had needed a special person with whom, in tandem with Barbara and Brad, I could forge a strong and nearly magical connection. And so it was in 2005, luck smiling on me at last, that I found him.

"Come to visit, come to visit," Gabe cajoled during the autumn of his sophomore year at Harvard. And so I summoned up a wavering sense of fortitude despite my travel anxiety, and went east to Boston. It was the first time I traveled alone since I had met Brad in New York to visit Rachael, and I didn't know how well I would tolerate being away from him and the sleepy cave of my house for the first time in many months. Yet, despite my worries, Gabe and I had a wonderful time, topped off by his request that I help him edit a paper he had to turn in the following day. Though I wanted to talk to him frankly about everything we had gone through as a family over recent years, I couldn't figure out how to begin. I was frightened of alienating him. The boys knew I was writing a memoir about depression— but nothing more than that. I hadn't even brought up the idea of a legacy of suicide within the family.

During this visit, I also attended my first board meeting for Families for Depression Awareness. I was seated next to Dr. Howard King, a very active pediatrician in his seventies, who was ferociously lobbying the medical establishment to provide better care by focusing not only on the physical health of the child, but also on the psychological and emotional aspects of the total family as well. His work—where good parenting was as essential as an immunization—intrigued me.

Though Howard was a stranger, we began talking at that meeting and never stopped. He was remarkably open and an easy listener. After the meeting—which had focused largely on depression, bipolar disorder, and suicide—came to a close, he and I simply sat for a while and discussed my situation, including my fervent fear that Nathaniel and Gabe would never truly forgive me for the trauma of my suicide attempts. I confided how they now seemed to be so guarded with me—but I had no one else to blame but myself.

Howard disagreed that they would never be able to forgive— and it was his confidence that the boys' trust could be regenerated that eventually enabled me to approach them with my myriad questions about their experiences within the family during those precarious years following my breakdown.

When I returned home, I found an email message from him waiting for me. And so began a correspondence that produced a communiqué nearly every day, several pages long, as we grew to rely on each other in the many different realms of our lives. Howard had a hand for skilled insight, and also the rare ability to articulate his ideas in a thought-provoking manner. Frequently, I was able to take some new and previously unanticipated action to the dilemmas my life presented because of his comments—and the reverse was also true.

What I couldn't see during those first days of corresponding with Howard was that there were three more questions running under the surface, and which were for me, too, another kind of legacy. Was I willing to relinquish the pain I felt over my mother's suicide, and thus be able to complete the process of forgiving her? And then, perhaps even more importantly, there remained the questions that were not, really, so different. In fact, the three of them were all tightly intertwined. Would I ever be able to forgive myself for what I had done to Nathaniel and Gabe? And lastly, would my boys inherit the legacy?

Like Brad, Howard rapidly became a champion for me, someone who was not alarmed by my difficulties. He knew the ups and downs of bipolar disorder; he understood the dark depths of depression. I turned to him increasingly—at that time, it seemed the fragile bridge between my father and me could not bear the weight of so many difficult truths. When I had mourned my psychological distance from my father initially, Howard pointed out that all we can do is to nurture ourselves, and hope that our parents may conclude that perhaps they hadn't been such bad parents after all. I took Howard's observation one step further. The remark could be interpreted in two different ways, both of which could be applied to so many of the difficulties I was experiencing with my own living parent: my father was the one looking back at the ways he had raised me, hoping that he had been a better parent than he knew. Now, simultaneously, I am the parent, looking back as a mother at the way I raised my sons, and hoping for exactly the same thing.

Howard was the one to point out that it was time to talk to Nathaniel and Gabe. And so I asked them: "Would you sit with me and a tape recorder and talk about my suicide attempts? About a legacy of suicide that I believe runs in our family?"

"Yes," they both said.

IT WAS IN the autumn of 2006, six months after Joy had come to visit, that I sought out and pinned down both my sons in the hope that I could bring about the same kind of healing and resolution I had experienced with my sister. For each of these long talks, we sat in the alcove off my living room, a nest sheltered by big easy chairs, a fireplace, and bookshelves whose contents spilled down onto the floor in high piles. Once again, I chose to listen to them silently, one at a time, on different days. It had worked well in coming to terms with Joy and her concerns, and I hoped it might work as well with the boys. Still, I was frightened to learn about their feelings. Once again the question dominated my thoughts: had they been able to forgive me? If not, would they someday be able?

As we sat there, Nathaniel stunned me by characterizing that time of his life, after my second attempt, with a single image: "I used to come home every day after school not knowing if I was going to find you dead in your bed." While I had been a woman whom he characterized as a "fantastic mother," life spiraled downhill for him at the time of my first suicide attempt. When I came home from the hospital, both he and Gabe (then fifteen and thirteen) had wondered who would take care of them, and then—most importantly—who would make certain that I didn't try to kill myself again. I remembered my own worry as a child about who would manage my mother's care after she returned home from the mental hospital. Thus—though I cringed—I had to acknowledge that another frightening emotion had been passed down through my family.

Blame, I asked, what about blame? I had laid in place one more section of the bridge that spanned the generations of my family, connecting the legacy of suicide just a little bit further. However, now the recipients were my own children.

Nathaniel answered that in some ways he had found it difficult to blame me entirely. He understood that I had experienced a lot of depression when I was young, probably inheriting those negative emotions from my mother—but he'd felt that I'd always kept it in control. I had done a "great job" of raising him and his brother—and then suddenly I was a mother who had abruptly tried to remove herself forever from her own life, and therefore his life. He claimed not to have been angry with me, but rather that he was simply a boy who wanted his mother back. He remembered me getting better "slowly and bravely" over the year following my first suicide attempt. He couldn't understand what had happened to make me spiral out of control so rapidly.

As Nathaniel spoke, reliving the part of his experience when he worried about coming home to an overwhelmingly depressed parent, I came to see how well he understood my illness. He saw that I had lost the ability to control my life, and my love for them had not been sufficient to prevent me from trying to kill myself. Nathaniel also told me that he understood how he had the same genetics as I did, and thus perhaps the same demons; nevertheless, he felt he and his brother were provided with the stability and the strong sense of love and family, despite the fracture of the divorce, that I had never had when I was a child, and so his future would be different than mine had been.

Nathaniel's empathy enabled him to recognize how much I loved both of them, and how hard I had tried to stay in control; how grateful I was to hear that he chalked my depression up to pain rather than self-indulgence. When he told me that he didn't hate me for that phone call I had made to him and Gabe from the car on the night of my second suicide attempt, I was astonished. I still loathed myself for having done it. Calling them on the phone for a protracted goodbye was brutal—perhaps worse than anything my mother had ever done. And so, in addition to the second suicide attempt, there was this for which to atone.

Yet it appeared that neither Nathaniel nor Gabe felt this way. Nathaniel claimed that the "lucky love" which provoked my phone call was something he did not revile, but instead cherished. He didn't find the act cruel.

And so Nathaniel made me see that ultimately, it was this lucky love for my children that had led to my accidental rescue from a suicide attempt that was a serious bid for death. I nearly made the jump into oblivion; save for the phone falling from its cradle to the floor, my boys would have been motherless. And so, perhaps indirectly, my love for my children had ultimately saved my life.

Though I still remembered the longing for death, by 2006, I no longer wanted to die: I was fervently committed, once again, to being a mother on an even keel and on her meds, a mother who was neither depressed nor agitated. Right then, I had everything I needed to defeat the brain chemistry that might—or might not—predict my future: love, medications, work, therapy, insight, and support.

Nevertheless, I continued to worry that I had passed down the inclination to suicide in some inevitable and final sense, despite his bravado. And so it was that I put the question again, this time to Gabe, several weeks after my conversation with Nathaniel, once again in the chairs in front of the fireplace with the tape recorder between us, whether *he* felt a legacy?

"Do you even believe in one?"

Gabe only shook his head.

He explained that he and his brother had made a pact that my illness and the suicide attempts would cease with me. Between the two of them, they would stop the flow of our family's history—and never put a child through the trauma of a parent's attempted or successful suicide. He believed, somehow, that he was immune, protected, having had so many "benefits" that his mother and grandmother hadn't. He didn't worry about my suicide attempts predisposing him to the same disintegration of mind and soul—even armed with the knowledge that such a propensity was in the role model my life had set for them. It was probably a confluence of personality and life circumstance that pushed you over the line, he said, a line that he and Nathaniel had resolved never to cross. His theory was that if you are depressed it's hard to get yourself out of that rut and back into a healthy cycle.

He felt that their "previously great childhood" had given him the tools, and the desire, to go out and do something with his life, to refuse to slip into depression. I wondered if I had been a strong enough mother despite it all to help him become his own self, an individual not shadowed by me. He had a right to his own future. And he was well on his way to becoming an adult, he insisted, a happy one, and hoped to have a contented family of his own some day.

I remembered my own teenage boldness about halting my mother's repeated suicide attempts, about keeping the legacy from becoming part of my life, so like my children's ironclad promises to themselves now. About the pact my sister and I had made. I found their naiveté and innocence about this more worrisome, really, than any other aspect of their explanations.

There is no answer to the question of how they will be affected. My mother had brought the possibility of suicide to me, now I had brought it to them. Will they carry this struggle to their children? Only the passage of time will reveal the answer.

Finally, I expressed aloud my most important fear: "Will you forgive me?"

"I've begun to trust you once again," Gabe insisted that day. "I don't ever come home anymore thinking I might find you dead. It is as if you have become the same old Mom once again."

It appears as if Gabe and Nathaniel are indeed in the process of pardoning me. They will always know that even in the best of times, acute depression can swamp anyone's life, even that of someone they love, and drive them to attempt suicide. But dealing with the idea that you may lose someone you love, says Gabe, is something everyone has to deal with anyway.

I think to myself how lucky I am: my mood has been superbly balanced for the last three years—no depression, no mania, no cutting, no attempts to end my life. And, in the main, no negative inner voice to taunt me. Only the headaches have continued unabated daily, and for these there is medication that works some of the time, and so I have also learned to cope with chronic pain.

"I'll always be there for you," Gabe said. Love, he went on, is what brought all of us through the difficult times. Love has been the cure for the intense upheaval we survived, each and every one of us, in the last eight years. Love might not ensure that I would stay well, but love could help me through the darkness.

ULTIMATELY, JIM'S REACTIONS to my suicide attempts were worse for me than anyone else's, as he left me at the very bottom of my deep dark tunnel. Yet, to be fair, perhaps he could think of no other way to terminate our inextricably entwined relationship except in an action so violent that it would sever the grip I had upon it. Or perhaps he felt he had given as much as was possible for him to give.

He continues to be exceptionally generous to me financially, enabling me to move onward in fighting the depression. Among other things, his monthly support check helps me pay for my health insurance and my medications and my therapy, surely all protections I can never imagine being without. And so, it is with his help that I have recovered a more normal life wherein I can, once again, try my hand at love and at work.

Miraculously, he and I have begun to be tentative friends; nothing pleases us more than having lunch together every so often to talk about the boys' progress and our own. Nathaniel is now twenty-six and has co-founded a sports journalism website that is beginning to take off. At twenty-three, having just graduated from college, Gabe took a year off to study photography—that old interest of his aunt Joy's—and is now working as the senior financial analyst at a high-tech company. He loves his work, despite the long hours he must put in.

Jim and his wife and Brad and I have become friends as well, through our repeated exposures to the children's activities, like graduations, birthdays, and the parties that celebrate their new ventures. We even went together to the funeral of my mother's biographer, Diane Middlebrook, and Jim took my hand in support during the service, because only he really knew how much she had meant to me. I accompanied them to a golden retriever breeder and helped them pick out a pup. I sometimes drop in when Jim's father, now ninety-six years old, comes to our old house for a visit and asks to see me. It no longer bothers me to be in the place that once was the stage for our marriage.

Having gotten to know Jim's wife better, I see and feel her strengths; and discover her to be a genuinely warm person to whom I am always grateful for the love she gives both my boys. As the children have matured into young adults, the bonds between Jim and them have strengthened. As I was once their primary caregiver, now it is Jim to whom they turn, in the main, for answers about certain aspects of their lives, like graduate schools and careers, areas which grow in importance as the years pass. Jim is well-connected in many fields, and is able to facilitate a wealth of choices in the chaotic new world they now face. Still, both children do seek emotional support from me, and it appears that you never leave behind your love for your mother's cooking. When they come up to visit me—"Hey, Mom, what's for supper?"—overflowing with the tales of their very full days, I listen joyfully, and set out every dish with anticipation and pleasure, accepting that my role as a mother now rests somewhat in the background of their young lives, as if I am an old and sturdy tree upon which they can lean. I offer up as much as they want from me, even if that is nothing beyond the simple love of meatloaf and mashed potatoes.

{hope}

I HOPE I have put my mother's legacy behind me, that old dance partnered with a death wish. I hope my life never again becomes as filled with despair as it did when Jim left me. I hope I will always be able to put hard work into my therapy, no matter how difficult. I hope I will always be able to depend on the love of Barbara. I hope I will always be able to discipline myself to take my medications—despite their side effects, until there are other, better ones that don't make me chubby, or my hands so shaky. I hope I will never again lose my friends (many of whom I have regained), or, more importantly, my family. I hope my children will continue to forgive me. I hope I will never again become as frightened as I was when I told Brad about my desire to die. I hope depression will never again eat me alive. And I hope none of these wishes are only magical thinking.

In September of 2009, Brad and I married, having decided to commit ourselves in a public ritual that was significant to us. We took each other's hands in a magnificent redwood grove that was quintessentially Californian, in a ceremony that we wrote ourselves. The service was accompanied by a poem from *The*

Prophet, which was read by Joy; and a special set of chairs were marked with roses to signify our love for both our absent mothers. The entire day was absolutely unique, brimming with the love that had buoyed us through the many difficult times we had endured together.

Brad sometimes traces the scars of my cutting with his finger, and we both know that they will always remain: silvery white lines—not unlike the stretch marks that follow pregnancy—but created, this time, not from health and celebration, but rather from sadness and sickness. I pray that I will never again feel the terrible pull of suicide calling to me; I pray that I have succeeded in burying the legacy somewhere here, among the mountains which I love. For despite it all—despite my own history and my mother's black magic—I am once again at my desk, this time beneath a wide window, where a scrap of melody from a wind chime somewhere in the distance rides the slipstream of clear air to encourage me. I remember what a friend once said: sometimes you cannot know which is harder—when you feel you can't possibly go on anymore, or when you start to realize that you will.

Each day turns now in the ever-strengthening hours of daylight saving time, and a fragile green spring toughens into the gold sere of our summer. Led by my scribbling hand, mind, and soul—conscious and unconscious—everything moves forward in an attempt to find some kind of conclusion, however elusive or ephemeral. I stand in the immediate present under a high noon sun: I cannot see how much shadow falls behind me, or what its shape may be. The shadow is the story I tell.

Many evenings after dark, Brad and I sit on the back deck, our hands linked. The dog lies down in front of us, and, in a comfortable rhythm, I scruff the fur of his back with the sole of my bare foot. He is nearly thirteen years old now, and there is no day that he fails to accompany me down to my cottage, curling into a tight ball in the old blue armchair. As I see his joints begin to stiffen with arthritis and watch the graying of his muzzle, I confront once again the specter of loss. When it comes, I will remember the way he gives me a Dalmatian "smile" as he waits for me at the head of the stairs; the way he scampers to his crate, knowing he is about to be fed his dish of kibble first thing in the morning; the way, when it is raining, he hesitates at the back door, no matter how badly he needs to go out; the way he loves how I rub his face, over and around his eyes just before he finds sleep in the crook of my arm. The way he guarded my life.

The moon climbs the night sky, and we wait patiently for the nocturnal howling of our resident coyote pack to begin. The first wail and Gulliver raises his head, ears lifted, alert for the cousins that call him. The second voice joins in and then the third, until there is a chorus of many, and we all listen, transfixed by the clamor of life that rises from the great silver bowl of the canyon.

ACKNOWLEDGMENTS

MY DEEPEST THANKS go to: Nathaniel, Gabe, and Jim, who allowed me to tell the story; Joy, who tries hard to forgive; Erica Jong, who was the first to see that the story was worth telling; Susan Cheever, who was always there to cheer me even on the darkest days; Joyce Maynard, who never failed me with her generosity and savvy; Dr. Barbara Ballinger, who took my hand in hers four times a week; Dr. Howard King, who urged me on; Dawn Mauel, Myrna Robinson, Julie Kaufman, Pat Maciejewski, Alan Tenney, and Tor Shwayder, all of whom remained determined friends; The folks at Counterpoint, especially Charlie Winton and Jack Shoemaker, who took such good care of me; my agent, Gail Hochman, who never failed to believe; and my editor, Dan Smetanka, who guided me step by step with insight and inspiration.

NOTABLE STATISTICS

In the United States someone commits suicide every seventeen minutes.

Nearly one million people worldwide take their own lives annually.

There is twice as much suicide in America as there is homicide.

Ninety percent of the people who commit suicide suffer from a mental illness, such as major depression or bipolar disorder.

Mood disorders are medical conditions, just like diabetes or heart disease.

Fourteen million Americans suffer from a major depressive disorder each year, and 730,000 of them make a suicide attempt.

Suicide is the third-highest cause of death among teenagers, following by a small margin accidental death and homicide.

Fifty percent of wives caring for a depressed husband will develop depression themselves.

Adult children of depressed parents have five times the rate of cardiovascular disease.

Among the adult children of depressed parents, the rates of anxiety disorders and depression are three times higher than those of the general population.

The tendency to commit suicide is now considered to be partially heritable.

AUTHOR'S NOTE

THE NAMES OF individuals who did not wish to be identifiable have been changed to provide them anonymity, and those who did not wish their stories to be included here have been accommodated.

JOIN LINDA AND her readers in a discussion of *Half in Love* at www. lindagraysexton.com.

ABOUT THE AUTHOR

LINDA GRAY SEXTON was born in Newton, Massachusetts, and is the daughter of the Pulitzer Prize–winning poet Anne Sexton. She graduated from Harvard in 1975 with a degree in literature, and then continued to live in the Boston area. After the death of her mother, Linda became the literary executor of the estate at twenty-one and edited several posthumous books of her mother's poetry, as well as *Anne Sexton: A Self-Portrait in Letters*.

Linda's first novel, *Rituals*, was published in 1981, and then *Mirror Images*, *Points of Light*, and *Private Acts* followed over a ten-year period. *Points of Light* was made into a Hallmark Hall of Fame Special for television and was translated into thirteen languages. Linda made a very brief foray into writing soap operas, though throughout she stayed devoted to her love of fiction; however, her most important work was raising her two sons, who were born in 1983 and 1984.

In the spring of 1989, Linda left her lifelong home of the East Coast to move her family to Northern California. There, while working in a soup kitchen, becoming a bat mitzvah, and running a Meals on Wheels program for her temple, she finished her first memoir, *Searching for Mercy Street: My Journey Back to My Mother, Anne Sexton*, which was named a *New York Times* Notable Book of the Year and was optioned by Miramax Films.

On the West Coast, with a big enough backyard at last, Linda added three Dalmatians to her family—the type of pet she had when she was a child. She developed a passion for showing them in the breed and obedience rings, and she bred and then whelped two litters of puppies on her own. She and her new husband are avid sailors on the San Francisco Bay and own a sloop named *Mercy Street*.

Half in Love: Surviving The Legacy of Suicide is her second memoir. *Searching for Mercy Street* will be reissued by Counterpoint in April 2011. Linda is now at work on a third memoir and lives in California with her husband and their dog, Breeze.

Please visit www.lindagraysexton.com to learn more about Linda and her books, connect with other readers, and join in the conversation about the issues present in her work.